Jewish
Musical
Traditions

Jewish Folklore and Anthropology Series

General Editor

Raphael Patai

Advisory Editors

Dan Ben-Amos
UNIVERSITY OF PENNSYLVANIA

Jane Gerber
CITY UNIVERSITY OF NEW YORK

Barbara Kirshenblatt-Gimblett
YIVO INSTITUTE FOR JEWISH RESEARCH

Gedalya Nigal
BAR ILAN UNIVERSITY

Aliza Shenhar
UNIVERSITY OF HAIFA

Amnon Shiloah
HEBREW UNIVERSITY

Books in this series

The Myth of the Jewish Race, revised edition, by Raphael Patai and Jennifer Patai, 1989
The Hebrew Goddess, third enlarged edition, by Raphael Patai, 1990
Robert Graves and the Hebrew Myths: A Collaboration, by Raphael Patai, 1992
Jewish Musical Traditions, by Amnon Shiloah, 1992

Jewish Musical Traditions

AMNON SHILOAH

WAYNE STATE UNIVERSITY PRESS   DETROIT

Publication of this book is made possible through the generosity of the Bertha M. and Hyman Herman Memorial Fund.

99 98 97 96 95 94 93 92 5 4 3 2 1

Library of Congress Cataloging-in-Publication Data

Shiloah, Amnon.
Jewish musical traditions / Amnon Shiloah.
p. cm.—(Jewish folklore and anthropology series)
Includes bibliographical references and index.
ISBN 0-8143-2234-4 (alk. paper)
1. Jews—Music—History and criticism. I. Title. II. Series.
ML3195.S4 1992
781.62′924—dc20 91-39456

Designer: Joanne Kinney
Cover art: prepared by Joanne Kinney

Silence is Better than Speech
But Song is Better than Silence

HASIDIC SAYING

Contents

Preface

My keen interest in the multiple and variegated musical traditions in Israel is directly connected with the intensive field work I conducted in the 1960s. It was also at that time that I made a first attempt to divulge facets that characterize the wonderful world of sounds and the inherent socio-cultural message of those traditions in the framework of a regular radio program called *Morashah* (heritage). Seeking to penetrate the spirit and roots of those musical traditions I later proceeded at the Department of Musicology of the Hebrew University and the Jewish Music Research Center to study selected historical and morphological aspects. It was only after a long period of contemplating the matter that I dared to spell out a broad view of the subject and endeavoured to combine the disparate elements into a cohesive methodological entity. Subsequently, in the form of a general course offered to my students at the Hebrew University, I suggested what was essentially a personal statement of the diachronic and synchronic characteristics of the bulk of Jewish musical traditions. The impetus to give a more crystallized form to my sketchy plans came from the Open University, which invited me to prepare a course on the subject. This occurred at a crucial moment in the recent history of Israeli culture. It was a time of ethnic protest, with the Oriental communities demanding wider recognition of their particular heritages. The resulting course of study, therefore, may have fulfilled a socio-cultural mission in addition to its major purpose which was to establish a new field of inquiry.

I owe deep gratitude to the Open University for being instrumental in initiating and supporting the huge project and its beautiful publication. In accepting the challenge it was my good fortune to benefit from the competent and devoted editorial assistance of Bat-Hen Fuerst who accompanied the project from its inception until, after four years of hard labor, the Hebrew text appeared. I wish to express special gratitude to her. I am grateful to E. Gerson-Kiwi, Ph. Bohlman, A. Amzalag and Y. Kadari for their valuable contributions in the writing of certain parts of the eight hundred Hebrew pages. I also wish to thank G. Baron, Y. Daliot and Y. Saporta for their considerable help in the production of the text.

While remaining faithful to the spirit and scope of the massive original Hebrew text, *Ha-moreshet ha-musiqalit shel qehillot Yisrael* (The Musical Heritage of the Jewish Communities), the present book obviously constitutes a revised, improved, and considerably abridged version, more appropriate to the new purpose. The eloquence of the present text is primarily due to the perspicacious and inspired editing of Shirley Shapira to whom I express my special gratitude. It is my pleasure to express my indebtedness to the Jewish Music Research Center for granting me assistance toward the preparation of this book.

Introduction

Let us begin our journey through the winding paths of Jewish traditions by discussing some of the landmarks we will meet on the way. Our point of departure is the concept "heritage." Heritage implies a measure of continuity and permanence, of commitment to a cherished cultural tradition that is transmitted from one generation to the next, each contributing to its survival by protecting and enhancing it. Has this been the case in the history of the Jewish people? If so, what has been the nature of the heritage thus transmitted? Can we speak of a single tradition shared by all the constituent communities of the Jewish people, and, if we can, for how long has this process of transmission from been going on—in other words, how old is this tradition? These and other questions derive from the special circumstances that have surrounded Jewish life for two thousand years.

In dealing with Jewish musical traditions our approach can be systematic, geographic, or historical. The systematic approach focuses on exploring the basic components of the music itself: scale, melody, rhythm, compositional structure, and stylistic aspects specific to a given repertoire. The geographic approach focuses on the attributes that characterize the music of a particular region. In our case this would mean examination of the musical traditions according to the locations in which the various Jewish groups have lived, their ties to the region, and the relation of each specific Jewish tradition to all other Jewish traditions. The historical approach attempts to present the music in an orderly, chronological sequence, from the time of the Patriarchs to the present.

No matter which of the three methods we decide to use, due to the unique historical situation and complex nature of the tradition we are considering, the study and presentation of the material will be subject to certain imperatives and limitations.

Were we to choose the systematic form of presentation, the picture evoked would depend entirely upon the time and place in which the study is carried out since the basis of discussion would be the music as actually heard. We are dealing with living, dynamic traditions transmitted orally from generation to generation. A version derived from the systematic approach, therefore, would reflect only the specific time at which the research has been carried out and the particular renditions of the informants selected.

Should we prefer the geographic approach, each specific tradition would necessarily have to be studied against a broad background of its cultured matrix. This would confront us with two problems. The first is the great number of primary and secondary Jewish musical traditions with which the Jewish people has been blessed. Even were we to choose only major traditions and their ramifications and discuss them in accordance with their relationship to local musical forms and other types of Jewish music, they could hardly be contained within the limited scope of the present study. The second is that their interrelationships, so important for our discussion, would remain obscure, and the total historical picture would elude us.

Recourse to the historical method is also fraught with problems. The music we are dealing with has been transmitted from lip to ear, and whatever literary sources exist are too scattered to permit a systematic presentation of progressive development—which in itself is a concept almost incompatible with oral traditions.

In Western art, changes are described as a succession of events; as each event evolves, either it improves and enhances or reacts to the one that preceded it. But in a general overview of the history of music one finds a cumulative process: the new is added to the old, thereby enriching it, while the old, to some extent, at least, remains a part of the tradition. As a result, with the help of available documents we can trace, for example, the development from monody to the various polyphonic forms or the progress of musical notation from the neumes all the way to the novel, sophisticated notations in use today. In contrast, oral traditions appear as a series of separate units, independent in time and place, each existing in its own right. Hence it is almost impossible to construe them as any sort of continuum. This does not mean, however, that oral traditions stagnate. In chapter 10 we shall discuss the different approaches by which changes in our oral traditions can be described.

Meanwhile, it should be borne in mind that when studying Jewish musical traditions we face a situation in which, essentially, we rely on what we can actually hear in the course of our research. This means that the further back we go, the more difficult it is to determine with reasonable certainty the character of the tradition and the way the music sounded. We can, of course, refer to verbal sources that provide information about the past, but no matter how much knowledge we derive from them they cannot help us reproduce lost sounds. In such circumstances, is it possible to propose a solution to the problems raised earlier? Can we assume, for example, that the melodies we hear today are more or less faithful reflections of past tradition?

Faced with this situation it seemed necessary to seek a special method of coping with the problems presented by the musical traditions of the various Jewish communities. We have chosen a method that presents the material in the form of central themes determined in accordance with four principal objectives.

We have tried to choose comprehensive themes of broad interest in order to encompass the greatest possible number of traditions, with a view to making it easier to trace shared problems or common denominators. Through our exemplification of common elements the reader can learn to identify a variety of traditions, even if only on a superficial level. Conceptual and methodological problems are addressed, among them the relation between music and religion, cantillation in general and biblical accents (*ṭaʿamei ha-miqra*) in particular, the influence of the world of kabbalah, hymnody (*piyyuṭ*) as a factor in the development of singing practices in the synagogue, music in communal and individual life, the confrontation of the musical traditions with an emerging Israeli culture, etc.

The approach we have adopted to develop these themes views the music in its cultural context, i.e., as part of the values and basic concepts of the particular culture within which it exists.

This approach, an accepted one in modern ethnomusicological research, will be expanded to combine the synchronic concept (analysis of current data) and the diachronic one (analysis of the data with reference to the past). These two concepts, borrowed from contemporary linguistics and applied to music research, imply the systematic and historical approaches. As we have indicated, neither one on its own can help us to acquire a comprehensive view of the subject. Therefore we must analyze the present with the help of the past and the past with reference to the present. Since musical documentation from the past is sparse, problems of textual interpretation will sometimes have to be approached through an understanding of what is happening to the music at present. Thus we may clarify musical examples with the help of historical sources, and simultaneously attempt to understand the sources in the light of the living music.

1

Identity and Character of Jewish Music

A Musical Tower of Babel

A person arriving at a given place for the first time often seeks a tower or hilltop for a panoramic view of the unfamiliar surroundings. Is there perhaps something similar in the impressions gathered by the ear, i.e., is there an angle from which one can experience a simultaneous panorama of sound? Happily, there is indeed such a possibility with regard to the Jewish musical tradition. The vantage-point—or, in this case, the listening point—is physically low but spiritually, emotionally, and historically raised to great heights. It is the Western Wall, a remnant of Jerusalem's Temple. Passing there at midnight one can hear mournful voices weeping over the destruction of the ancient Temple; multitudes gather there on holy days in joyful commotion; on Mondays and Thursdays families come for Bar mitsvah celebrations. At sundown on Fridays groups of worshippers gather before the massive, moss-covered stones, all singing the same Sabbath prayer texts, but using many different melodies. All are simultaneously performing the same fundamental ritual: welcoming the Sabbath at exactly the same hour, expressing the same feelings, experiencing the same emotions. Only the melodies differ. The listener, even one with an untrained ear, can distinguish a wide spectrum of musical styles.

The aural impact is a sort of musical Tower of Babel. Is this only a momentary impression, or can one find hidden ties that bind this mélange into a unified whole? In view of the specific circumstances of Jewish history can we perhaps discern a common core uniting all these separate elements? Indeed, this variety of styles is not fortuitous, as is known by all who participate. In fact, the respective adherents of each style and each tradition pray in a specific, prescribed way. General names such as Sephardi and Ashkenazi are used to distinguish the customs;

more specific appellations indicate the source and location, e.g., Persian, Yemenite, Baghdadi, Moroccan, Cochinian, Lithuanian, Alsacian, etc. The multiplicity of names, which often designate different local subtraditions as well, reflects actual or alleged stylistic variations that are due to time and place. The names and distinctions are not arbitrarily imposed by the scholar, but are rooted in the history of those who adhere to each particular tradition.

Although it is evident that the traditions heard today in Israel crystallized in many lands spread over the four corners of the earth, this does not necessarily rule out the possibility that far beneath the surface we may find an ancient, common core. This will be discussed below; here it is sufficient to point out that in the search for that hypothetical core, antiquity is not the only problem that confronts us. Both the practitioners and students of the traditions are troubled by another theoretical issue as well—that of their specific Jewish identity: how are they distinguished from the non-Jewish traditions surrounding them, and what marks them as Jewish? Regarding this question we find disparities between the position taken by the practitioners of the traditions and that taken by the external observer—be he an ordinary listener or a scholar. Among the various communities there are also disparate views as to the definition of Jewish characteristics. Moreover, in most cases the Jewish community will claim that its music differs from that of the non-Jewish society around it, while the objective listener will hardly notice any difference.

Jewish Identity

We will attempt to clarify important aspects of the question of Jewish identity by citing examples taken from actual reality. Instrumental music might seem least suitable for the explication of this question because, as we shall see in chapter 3, it was forbidden to use instruments in the synagogue service; their use was sometimes prohibited even outside the synagogue (at family celebrations, for example). Nevertheless, for reasons indicated below, we shall begin our discussion with instrumental music, despite the tenuous foothold it affords.

Let us use the *qānūn* (a Near Eastern zither)[1] as an example. This instrument has an important place in the sophisticated urban style of Near Eastern art music. It represents the "Great Tradition"[2] that crystallized in the wake of the emergence and expansion of Islam. Jewish and Christian musicians, and those of other religions as well, were influential in shaping this Great Tradition. The *qānūn* as we know it today, is mentioned in Arabic sources from the tenth century onward. Several scholars, among them the illustrious student of Arab music Henry G. Farmer (1957, p. 445), subscribe to the view that the *psanterin,* which is referred to in the Book of Daniel,[3] is the *santūr*[4] of oriental instrumental ensembles: the *santūr* resembles the *qānūn*.

Improvisation based on certain set principles is a most important characteristic of Near Eastern art music and ability to improvise is one of the measures of a player's talent. Such improvisation demands a high degree of proficiency, accomplished technique, lively imagination, creative ability, and respect for the artistic standards of the performer's social milieu and its musical traditions.

One of the outstanding instrumentalists in Israel in recent decades is a Baghdad-born Jew, Abraham David Cohen. He had been a renowned *qānūn* player before he migrated to Israel in the 1950s and had often performed not only for his community but also for his Arab neighbors. In Israel his playing has continued to delight both Asian and African Jewish audiences, as well as the Arab community. In the course of time the change in his environment and situation have expanded his activities, and he has enriched and variegated his musical work. He participated in the instrumental ensemble that accompanied the Inbal Dance Troupe,[5] has accompanied individual singers from different communities, has belonged to a jazz group, and has even performed special works for *qānūn* and symphony orchestra.

With respect to this *qānūn* player, the question inevitably arises: Is there anything specifically Jewish in his work? Does he not represent an unquestionably Arabic musical sytle, and is his Jewishness not irrelevant? An apt analogy might be a Jewish pianist performing works of Bach or Brahms. Does the pianist's Jewishness color his performance of the works of those composers in any special way? In fact, though, the two instances are not entirely analogous, since in the case of Cohen we deal with traditional music which demands creative talent of a special nature and also requires an ability to adapt quickly to different styles. Therefore what we have to concentrate on is not the actual music, but rather the ways of making music and the creative processes involved. To clarify the basic question of Jewish content and identity, let us venture from the East to the West and use the Jewish *klezmer*[6] as our second example. The term *klezmer* (derived from the Hebrew *klezemer,* meaning "musical instruments") is the Yiddish designation of a small popular ochestra.

As far back as the fifteenth century there were organized Jewish musical ensembles that wandered from place to place; they performed at Christian as well as Jewish celebrations and events. Members of these klezmers had no formal musical education or knowledge of theory but were blessed with a fertile musical imagination and a fine, discriminating ear. For them music was a craft. Impinged upon by many varied influences, they played typical Jewish-style music and popular gentile tunes as well. Depending upon what their listeners wanted, they could perform a rich and diverse repertory ranging from sad airs to gay dances, all part of an oral tradition acquired by ear. Characteristically, the klezmers were talented, imaginative musicians, quick at picking up music, capable of creating and improvising and of incorporating newly adapted styles into their existing repertory.

At the end of the nineteenth century several klezmers, some of them from Romania, others influenced by the Romanian musical style, left Eastern Europe for the New World. There they continued their musical activities within the Jewish community.

In the 1960s, in America, a movement emerged among musicians in their twenties who called themselves Revivalists—a term usually associated with religion and faith. These young people used the word in its broadest sense—they were reviving the melodic and instrumental music of their immigrant or American fathers. Groups of young musicians, who might be described as a new generation of bards, returned to Ireland's folk music and the fiddle, to the music of the Appalachian mountains and the banjo.

One young Jewish student, a member of a primarily Irish-oriented Revivalist group, though totally accepted by his non-Jewish friends, admitted to a feeling of discomfort and tension. This led him to search for a comparable Jewish form of music. With the help of friends he discovered the music of the klezmers and at once identified with it, initiating a parallel movement of Jewish Revivalists. They took as their model the orchestra and repertory of the klezmers, learning it primarily by listening to old, worn records. They adopted as their mentor Dave Tarras, the last of the old klezmers, by then retired.[7]

These young musicians soon came to view themselves as the successors of the klezmers, and believed this to be the most authentic kind of Jewish music. One of the fascinations this music held for them was the possibility it offered of adapting and absorbing different styles; they pointed out that their teacher, Dave Tarras, had learned to incorporate swing and jazz into his clarinet playing. Some of them even claimed that klezmer music was a more authentic Jewish style than the Hasidic *niggun* and the Yiddish songs, which in their view simply represented folk music derived from the surrounding gentile environment. Choosing the klezmer style enabled them to identify with a type of music that had a Jewish label, lent itself to a mingling of old and new styles, and could be performed for young and old and for non-Jews as well as Jews.[8]

On the level of natural creativity, inventiveness, ability to absorb and recreate different styles in their playing, the old and new klezmers have much in common with the Baghdadi *qānūn*ist; both embody a special type of musician, a product of the Jewish milieu in the diaspora. Interestingly, the young Jewish Revivalists rejected the Yiddish songs and Hasidic *niggun*s that had represented Jewish identity for their parents, and presented klezmer music as *the* authentic Jewish music. It may be assumed that were they—or their parents—to hear our *qānūn* player, they would describe his music as Arab, certainly not Jewish. What, then, is Jewish music?

So we find the question of Jewish identity a rather disturbing, uncomfortable one, with no easy answer. We must remember that virtually none of the types of music mentioned thus far are related to liturgy, the musical repertory of the synagogue. It is therefore very difficult to reach a definite conclusion; were we to judge by instrumental music alone, we would find ourselves very wide of the mark, since it is precisely the noninstrumental tradition that characterizes Jewish music. And yet, the same problem seems to exist with regard to the vocal synagogue music. Even in the case of the melodies to which the prayers are sung the number of vocal variations is considerable. This not only exacerbates the question of Jewish identity: the sensation of a musical Tower of Babel described above becomes even more powerful. Is there a solution to this predicament? We shall return to a detailed discussion of this question in the coming sections.

Has All Jewish Music a Common Source?

The question of the multiplicity of traditions—which we have called a musical Tower of Babel—and the problem of what binds such extremely diverse music together, was of great concern to Abraham Zvi Idelsohn, the pioneer of Jewish ethnomusicological research.[9]

Upon arriving in Jerusalem in 1906, Idelsohn found three-hundred synagogues serving a Jewish population of forty thousand. Excited by the great abundance of musical traditions crowded into such a relatively small area, he decided that although he had been trained as a composer and performer, he would become an investigative observer. His observations and field work led him to pinpoint some of the fundamental questions we have posed above, and to seek the answers to them. Among the theories he constructed and bequeathed to future scholars are his contentions that Jewish identity in music can be traced to a common source and that the traditions of Oriental Jewry are of ancient origin.

Born in 1882 in Felixburg, a small Lithuanian town, Idelsohn received a traditional education and was trained as a cantor. In those years German culture had a strong hold on the Baltic countries, and like many other young musicians in that part of the world, before he was twenty years old Idelsohn left home for Germany where he studied theory and composition. He kept in touch with Jewish music by serving as the cantor in a synagogue. In 1906 he moved to Palestine, settling in Jerusalem. It was there that he first encountered the diverse musical traditions of the East.

Working along lines established by German scholars then studying non-European music, and aided by their material and moral support, Idelsohn devoted the next fifteen years of his life to researching the history of Jewish music.[10] His equipment for this tremendous project consisted of a phonograph—a cumbersome recording instrument newly invented by Edison—endless patience, and of course his own knowledge of music. Using wax cylinders, he began the systematic recording of the traditional music that was still extant within the various ethnic groups living in Jerusalem. In the course of time, at the request of the Vienna Record Archives, he amassed an extensive collection containing hundreds of recordings. While engaged in this vast enterprise, Idelsohn taught music and composed Palestinian songs as well as an opera *Yiftah*.

Idelsohn's most important contribution to Jewish music is his monumental *Thesaurus of Hebrew Oriental Melodies* (1914–32), published in Hebrew, German, and English. The volumes include more than a thousand musical examples transcribed in Western notation. When transcribing the notes for his *Thesaurus* he introduced an

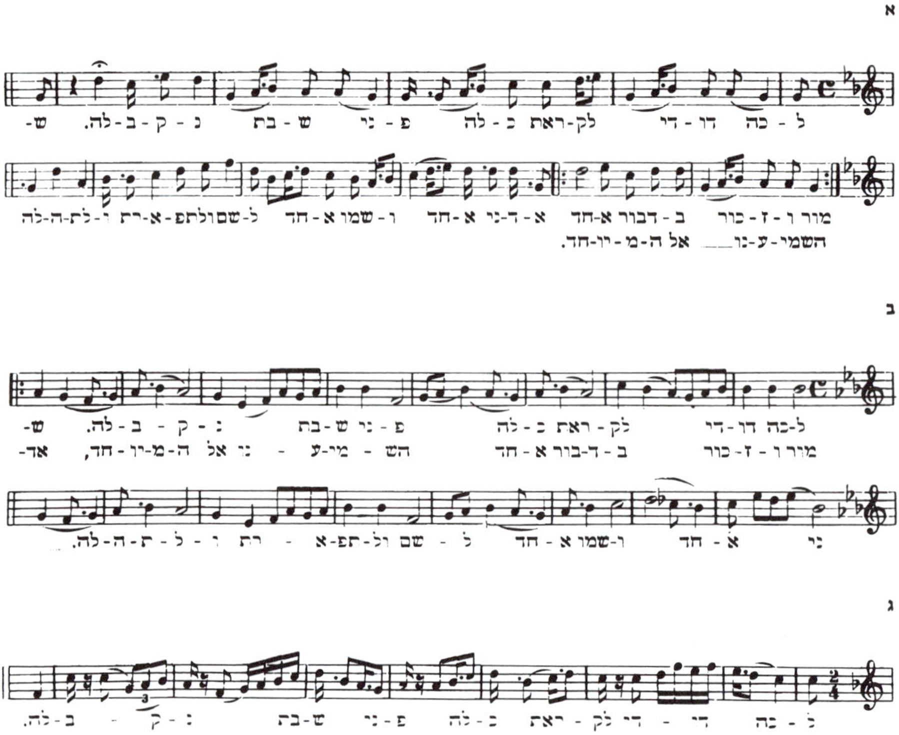

Fig. 1. Three versions of the Sabbatical hymn Lekhah dodi.

interesting innovation: the notes, like Hebrew writing, were to be read from right to left. Fig. 1, taken from page 110 of volume 4, demonstrates three different versions of the *piyyuṭ* (liturgical song) "Lekhah dodi." The first was widespread in Turkey, Syria, Palestine, and Egypt; the second is the version sung by the Portuguese community in London; and the third is that of the Sephardi community of Northern Italy.

The ten volumes of the *Thesaurus* are devoted to ten major Jewish musical traditions discussed in the following order: 1. Yemen 2. Babylon 3. Persia, Bokhara, and Dagestan (Mountain Jews) 4. Eastern-Sephardi Jews (Turkey, Syria, Egypt, and Palestine) 5. Morocco 6. German Jews in the eighteenth century 7. Jews of southern Germany 8. East European synagogue music (Poland and Lithuania) 9. East European Yiddish folk songs; 10. Hasidic melodies.

Each volume of the *Thesaurus,* with the exception of volumes 9 and 10, includes transcriptions of biblical cantillations, prayer tunes, *piyyuṭim* for the Sabbath and holidays, etc. Volumes 9 and 10 are organized in accordance with musical characteristics.[11] In addition, the introductions cover history, language, dialect and accents, ethnography, and musical analysis. Some of these introductions are important contributions in themselves.

Thus, for example, in introducing volume 4, Idelsohn discusses at length the Arab *maqām* system,[12] which had a profound influence on the music of the Sephardi Jews of the eastern Mediterranean basin, the Balkans, and Turkey. This introduction first appeared as a separate study published in German (1913a), and became a cornerstone for all later musicological work in this field. The introduction to volume 7 is a discussion of the *steiger,* a Yiddish term meaning modus or manner. It deals with the special traditional styles of chanting that characterized the Ashkenazi synagogue. According to Idelsohn (introduction to vol. 6), the Viennese Cantor Josef Singer (1840–1911) was the first to try to bring the *steigers* into a system. There are four *steigers* named in accordance with the first word of the prayer each melody accompanied: *Ahava Rabba, Adonay Malakh, Magen Avot, Yishtabbaḥ.* The introduction to the last volume contains a historical analysis of the Hasidic songs and melodies.[13]

We find, then, that Idelsohn was not satisfied with merely recording, transcribing, analyzing, and classifying the traditions, but tried to find ways of presenting Jewish traditions against a wider background in a manner that would facilitate their comprehension. One of the many fundamental issues that concerned him was the one in which we are primarily interested at this point: he tried to determine whether these variegated Jewish traditions stemmed from a common source, whether they possessed a common denominator. While as a musician with a discriminating ear, he perceived the miscellaneous assortment of styles, as an indefatigable researcher, a contemporary of the founding fathers of comparative musicology, he sought to develop a scientific comparative system for the study of ethnic styles. Beneath the countless layers of accumulated tradition he tried to discover a melodic archetype that had ancient Jewish roots. This he found in the basic musical motifs of the biblical cantillation.

Idelsohn first summarized his findings on this subject in his volume introduction to 2, in which he deals with the musical heritage of Babylonian Jewry. He included his theory about the existence of common sources in this particular introduction for technical reasons, which, however, were much less important than his contention that the oldest form of traditional reading was that practiced by Babylonian, Jewry the descendents of the biblical Babylonian exiles. He established initially that the reading of the different biblical books is done in basic musical modes characterized by a system of scales and specific melodic patterns. With this assumption as his point of departure, he conducted a comparative study of the Bible-reading traditions of the various Jewish ethnic groups. His conclusion was that all the melodies still in use were related to ancient reading modes which in themselves were derived from folk songs (the subject of another chapter) that were popular in ancient Israel before the destruction of the Second Temple. Idelsohn's theory is best expressed in the following brief excerpt from his introduction to the second volume: "We shall prove the antiquity of these versions by the fact that they can be found in all Jewish communities regardless of how isolated they have been from one another since the destruction of the Temple. This is apparent from the following examples taken from those various communities." He summarized his findings in a comparative table, part of which appears in fig. 2. This table compares the biblical cantillation of various Jewish ethnic groups. Each column contains the versions used by the different traditions for a given accent (for example, the first column to the left shows *sof-pasuq*) in the version used by each, and it demonstrates their overall similarity.

The nature and history of biblical cantillations will be discussed in chapter 4 below, but even before enlarging on the subject, we feel it necessary to take issue here with some aspects of Idelsohn's tempting theory. Our first reservation involves the assumption that the texts were sung to music associated with the folk songs of the period before the destruction of the Temple. First of all, we know nothing about those folk songs and their musical nature. Second, it is not at all certain that folk songs of the Jews in those remote times were distinct from those of the surrounding peoples. Third, we possess no proofs of the musical connection between a folk song, which is usually metrical, and a chanted text, which is rhythmically free. Our second reservation derives from the possibility that the melodies Jews used for reading were part of a general cantorial style that was, and perhaps still is, widespread throughout the Orient.

There is reason to believe that Idelsohn himself took these reservations into account when, at a later date, he returned to a discussion of the subject in his English-language book *Jewish Music* in which we find the following passage:

> The public reading of the Bible as performed in ancient times, and as still done in the Orthodox Synagogue, was not according to the manner now employed in the Reform Synagogue (since 1815). In the latter it is simply spoken or declaimed without any musical flavor, whereas the manner of reading, according to tradition, is a cantillation, a chanting of the text, a recitation in which music plays a great part. This way of reading the Bible is mentioned in ancient times—at least as far back as the first century. It was not the general manner of public reading, for in the Orient the usual public reading is done in declamation as in the Occident. There may be more flavor in the voice, but it is without musical tone. This usage is true of the Arabs to the present day, whereas the reading of the Koran is done in the same manner as the traditional reading of the Bible. There is, therefore, no foundation for the current notion that the cantillation of the Bible is derived from the Oriental manner of reading in public. (1929, p. 35)

Idelsohn goes on to stress the importance of the basic musical element and its function in enhancing comprehension of the text. It is very difficult to dispute this theory; no melodic evidence from those ancient times has been preserved as there were no means then of documenting music either through written notation or recording.

Fig. 2. Idelsohn's table of comparative Torah readings.

Briefly, the above theory consists of two parts: one deals with the fundamental reading modes that according to Idelsohn were basically shared by all Jewish traditional reading; the other relates those modes to folk songs that were unique to the Jewish people its dispersion after the destruction of the Second Temple. What he is saying, then, is that the common denominator, which, despite two thousand years of exile, can be found in the readings characteristic of the various traditions, bears witness to antiquity and continuity. On the other hand, if the source of reading modes can indeed be traced back to the typical Jewish folk song of antiquity, it may be claimed that a Jewish identity pervades the reading traditions of our own time.

The Antiquity of Oriental Jewry's Musical Traditions

An important tier of Idelsohn's theory pertaining to Jewish identity was a fundamental hypothesis derived from his thorough acquaintance with the traditions of Oriental Jewry. Buttressed by opinions prevalent in his day, he assumed that these traditions were very old. He proposed three points:

1. Traditional music by its very nature tends to preserve and perpetuate early forms and ancient stylistic elements. Despite some inner changes that attest to the vitality of the tradition, it nevertheless tends to maintain basic patterns.

2. People who possess a musical tradition revere their ancestral heritage and take pains to preserve its essential nature.

3. In the particular case we are concerned with, the musical legacy of the Oriental Jewish communities has constantly remained associated with the same geographical area and may even have perpetuated fundamental concepts and behavioral patterns similar to those of the past. Hence there is reason to hope that beneath the surface—which may appear to have changed in the course of time—the scholar will be able to discover the delicate thread that continues to link the present with the past.

This line of thought was fairly widespread, and long before Idelsohn published his theories certain Christian researchers reached similar conclusions. Searching for the roots of ancient Christian music, they viewed these matters from their own perspective, as can be seen in the work of two French scholars, both Catholic priests.

The first was the French musicologist, Guillaume André Villoteau (1759–1839), who was a member of the scientific delegation Napoleon sent to Egypt after his conquest of the country. Villoteau stayed in Egypt from 1798 to 1800, studying Egyptian music. He published the findings of his ground-breaking research in two volumes, which marked the first comprehensive study of non-European music by a European scholar. The first volume (1823) deals with musical instruments of Egypt, the second (1826) with art and folk music. Although the subject matter of both books is mainly Arab music, Villoteau devoted short sections in each to ethnic minorities then living in Egypt: the Copts, Ethiopians, Syrians, and, of course, the Jews. The book on musical instruments includes a brief description of Jewish women drumming, dancing, and singing in choirs, and Villoteau compares them with the women described in the Bible. The entire fifth chapter of volume two is devoted to Jewish music, with particular emphasis on the biblical cantillations, which he transcribed in musical notation. Marshaling quite convincing arguments, he maintained that what he was hearing was an ancient tradition.

Villoteau's concern, however, was not Jewish music and its sources; he considered his major task the study of Arab music in Egypt. Wisely, he decided to round out the picture with short descriptions of the minority traditions that he felt were important and seemed to deviate from the mainstream. Villoteau recorded some of the melodies of the Egyptian-Jewish tradition in Western musical notation, showing the biblical cantillation above the Hebrew words that are the names of the cantillation signs or punctuation marks (see fig. 3).

While Villoteau was not particularly concerned with the question of the relationship between Jewish and Christian music, that relationship figures prominently in the research done by Father Dom Jean Parisot (1861–1923).[14]

Parisot was sent by the French government as a member of an official scientific mission to study the ancient sources of Christian music. Upon his return he published a book (1901) in which he reported on his work in Turkey and Syria. In his introduction he wrote: "Striving to fulfil my mission, in the search for ancient songs, I first collected melodies from the Syrian Church. The latter is a generalized term denoting the vocal music of the Christian churches in the East; their musical tradition was rooted in the earliest years of Christianity. Then, to acquire other music of an ancient character, I began to collect Jewish melodies." Parisot was assisted by the director of the Alliance Israelite School, who acted as a go-between and consultant, attending Parisot's sessions with Jewish informants.

In the third section of his book Parisot develops his thesis about the antiquity of the Jewish music he collected in Damascus, and the relationship of those melodies to the Gregorian chants.

> In connection with the Oriental church chants, I have mentioned that I collected Jewish melodies in Damascus. In approaching the local Jews to supply me with the melodies I wanted, I was aware that it was my privilege to turn to a community that had never ceased to exist, one whose musical and ritualistic tradition was undoubtedly extremely ancient. Thanks to the fruitful cooperation of the director of the Alliance Israelite school, I managed to transcribe eighteen melodies—nine *piyyuṭim,* four melismatic recitatives for certain specific holidays, and five readings in accordance with biblical cantillation. All these tunes have unusual melodic purity and rhythmic freedom. For the first time the melodies of the biblical cantillation can serve as proof of a contention that has been making the rounds for a long time but has not yet found adequate substantiation. I refer to determination of the extent of the Jewish influence in moulding the form of liturgical songs of the West.
>
> It can be established with certainty that when the Christians received the texts of the Psalmody they also took over the manner in which those texts were chanted.[15]

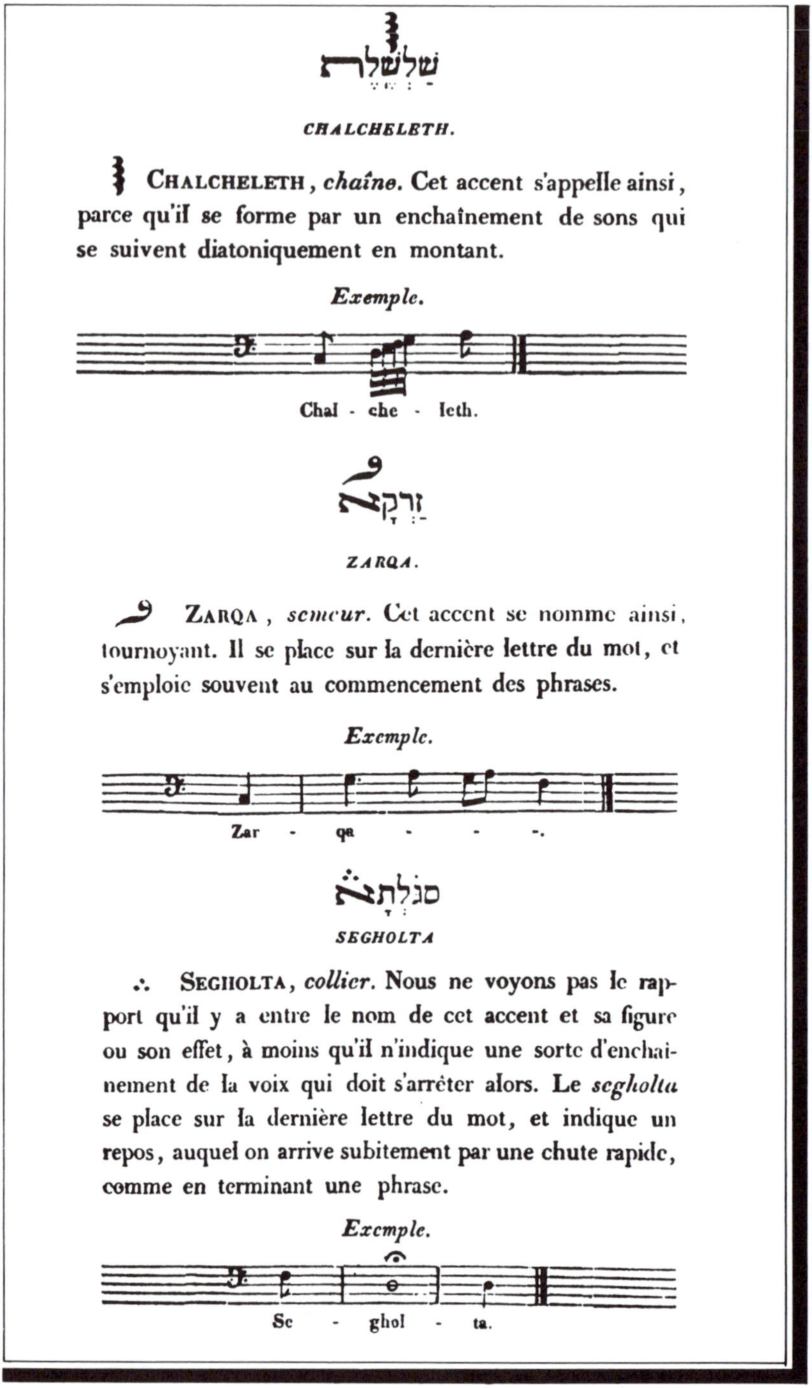

שַׁלְשֶׁלֶת

CHALCHELETH.

CHALCHELETH, *chaîne.* Cet accent s'appelle ainsi, parce qu'il se forme par un enchaînement de sons qui se suivent diatoniquement en montant.

Exemple.

זַרְקָא

ZARQA.

ZARQA, *semeur.* Cet accent se nomme ainsi, tournoyant. Il se place sur la dernière lettre du mot, et s'emploie souvent au commencement des phrases.

Exemple.

סְגֹלְתָּא

SEGHOLTA

SEGHOLTA, *collier.* Nous ne voyons pas le rapport qu'il y a entre le nom de cet accent et sa figure ou son effet, à moins qu'il n'indique une sorte d'enchaînement de la voix qui doit s'arrêter alors. Le *segholta* se place sur la dernière lettre du mot, et indique un repos, auquel on arrive subitement par une chute rapide, comme en terminant une phrase.

Exemple.

Fig. 3. Villoteau's Egyptian biblical cantillation.

> Of course, there may have been contradictory theories that maintained that the Greco-Roman modes played an important part in the composition of the Christian tunes.[16] The patterns of melodic reading I cite here, however, confirm the former assumption without entirely ruling out the latter. The cantillation heard in the synagogue is more similar to the patterns of our Medieval chants than are the Syrian and Greek songs, in that the scales are identical, there are similar intervalic combinations and the integration of the melodic pattern is the same. One of those passages, "The Song of Songs," incorporates characteristics of the ancient recitative type that has been preserved in the songs of the Mozarabic tradition.[17] The reading of Lamentations is another example; it was transmitted to me as unique to the Jewish community of Damascus, but it is read with the same tonality and musical formulae as the Lamentations that accompany the Holy Week religious texts.[18] On the other hand, the highly ornate and melismatic tunes of the Jewish High Holy days with the rich, protracted development of the notes of the final syllables, afford practical analogies with the neumes of the Alleluia and the Gregorian Responsorium.[19] Moreover, many of the melodic lines are so alike that if we were to give Latin words to some of these Jewish recitatives we would create the impression that these are ancient Ambrosian tunes or similar liturgical songs.[20]
>
> Thus this documentation can help us to prove that the musical legacy received from the East by the Christian church included, if not whole songs, at least clearly defined melodic patterns rather than extremely simple types of psalmody. In the course of time, the chants of the present Gregorian repertoire were spun from the threads of those patterns.
>
> I have considered it useful to underscore these similarities as they are so numerous that they cannot be fortuitous. . . . They prove that the Latin chant rests on the music of the synagogue, and this also enables us to determine the antiquity of both traditions. (Pp. 174–75)

Thus Parisot maintains that one can find versions of given melodic patterns that are common to both synagogue and Catholic church chants, versions that were borrowed originally from the Oriental synagogue. Performing practices were also borrowed: either a soloist with the audience responding or two choral groups singing antiphonally. The church adopted the ancient Jewish practice of using melodic formulae that essentially retained the same structure even when the text changed.

The example of notation in fig. 4 is the first of a series of recitatives and Jewish *piyyuṭim* that Parisot included in his book. It is his transcription of an excerpt from the Song of Songs, under which appears a parallel Mozarabic chant quoted in one of the ancient codexes. The first two notes of the syllable *per* are C and D and they serve as guides for reading the following notes. The range of the recitative is from A*1* to A*2* and according to Parisot, it is organized around the D axis which serves as finalis. In other words, the D becomes the central note on which the melody concludes, the tones above it reaching high A and those below it descending to low A. It is Parisot's contention that this structure is identical with the first two church modes, the Authentic and the Plagal, with the D serving as the recitative note common to both.

Fig. 4. Parisot's Song of Songs and parallel Mozarabic chant.

The two major church modes can be distinguished in accordance with the finalis and the range, the octave being the official range of church melodies. The Authentic mode is recognizable in the coincidence of the finalis with the extremes of the range (that is, it is both the lowest and the highest tone); in the Plagal mode the finalis is in approximately the middle of the octave. Thus the first Authentic mode is bounded by D to D, with D as the finalis; the first Plagal mode is from A to A, with the finalis again D.

The relation between ancient Jewish and ancient church songs discussed by Parisot also concerned Idelsohn, and his theories in this connection had much more extensive repercussions among later musicologists. However, whereas Parisot happened to choose the tradition of Damascus, which historically and geographically was close to Palestine and had steady contact with it from ancient times onward, Idelsohn turned mainly to the musical tradition of the Jews of Yemen. He became thoroughly acquainted with this tradition in Jerusalem and devoted several studies (1908–9; 1918–19; 1924–25) as well as the first volume of his *Thesaurus* to it. The basic support for Idelsohn's theory in this context was historic evidence attesting to the antiquity of the Jewish community in Yemen, which some believe preceded the destruction of the Second Temple. This would mean that the most ancient Jewish musical tradition had been preserved there, as Idelsohn maintained that the Yemenite Jews had completely isolated themselves from all non-Jewish environmental influences.

The similarity Idelsohn found when analysing the music of the Yemenite tradition and the Gregorian chant, despite the great geographical distance separating them, points to the possibility that they emanate from a common source, that is, the music of ancient, pre-exilic Israel. This theory, which has many interesting and attractive aspects, has been widely accepted by Christian scholars and it earned Idelsohn international recognition. It opened an additional road that concerned scholars hoped would lead to new discoveries about the sources of Christian church songs. Dozens of studies have been devoted to this problem, some of which deserve mention here since they discuss it from a broad historical perspective. From the standpoint of Jewish tradition, the question of interrelation between church and synagogue in the realm of liturgy, words, and melodies has been extensively explored in Werner's two-volume *The Sacred Bridge* 1955; 1984). In her book *L'église à la conquête de sa musique* (1960), Solange Corbin devoted several highly informative chapters to synagogue singing and its relationship to early church music. Three eminent scholars, H. Avenary (1982), Dom Jean Claire (1982), and K. G. Fellerer (1982), discussed points of contact between church and synagogue in the framework of the World Congress on Jewish Music held in Jerusalem in 1978.

The point of view of the eminent ethnomusicologist Robert Lachmann differed from those we have described above. Born in Germany in 1892, Lachmann arrived at Jewish music through Arab music. Because he knew Arabic, he became a translator at a prisoner-of-war camp during the First World War, and it was there that he was first exposed to Arab music. He wrote his doctoral thesis on Tunisian music, visiting Tunis three times between 1925 and 1929 to make recordings and do fieldwork.

During this period Lachmann discovered the ancient tradition of the Jewish community living on the Isle of Djerba, near the Tunisian coast. He later wrote an important study based on the material he collected there, but in the meantime he concentrated on the study of Arab music. At the first International Congress of Arab Music in Cairo in 1932, Lachmann was chosen to head the Phonogramme Commission. As a result of the vital pioneering work of this commission we now possess a long series of the time's highest quality musical documents, representing the musical traditions of this entire region. Between 1933 and 1935 Lachmann was employed as a librarian in the Berlin State Library and edited the most important pre-WWII ethnomusicological journal, the *German Journal of the Science of Comparative Music* (*Zeitschrift für vergleichende Musikwissenschaft*). In 1935 he was invited by the Hebrew University to found a record archive of Oriental music in Palestine. Edith Gerson-Kiwi, who worked with him, tells about that period in an article commemorating the 80th anniversary of his birth.

> Lachmann's activities during his last four years in Jerusalem (1935–39) as head of the Archive, marked the beginning of modern ethnomusicology in Israel. . . . Lachmann brought along with him his earlier collections as well as his most up-to-date recording equipment. [He] was able to salvage some 500 items of his own recordings, and in addition some fifty cylinder recordings of Jewish music which A. Z. Idelsohn had made during his stay in Jerusalem.
>
> . . . Lachmann was able during these last few years to record about a thousand new items—now mainly centered around the subject of Oriental liturgies: Jewish (of many communities), Samaritan, Islamic, and Eastern Christian ones. . . ." One of the musical questions Lachman tried to explore is . . . the relation between the Jewish cantorial tradition and Arab art song. . . . From being a recognized expert on Arab music . . . Lachmann worked his way slowly toward Jewish music. . . . His *Study of Jewish Music in the Isle of Djerba* (1940) demonstrates quite new possibilities through the analysis of traditional song within the boundaries of one small community.[21] Thus the almost limitless space in which Idelsohn moved is, in Lachmann's treatment, reduced to a small and controllable unit. . . . With the help of further comparative analysis, the single phonogram begins to reveal a deeper, richer life and many hidden points of contact with neighbouring or parallel civilizations. (Gerson-Kiwi 1774a, pp. 102–3)

Gerson-Kiwi concludes her article with an inventory of the Lachmann Documentary and Recorded Archives, text notes, transcriptions and many unpublished articles that can be found today in the National Sound Archives in the music department of the Jewish National and University Library in Jerusalem. Gerson-Kiwi herself later published some of Lachmann's posthumous texts (1974b; 1978).

Lachmann's work indicates a different approach to the question of the antiquity of Jewish musical traditions, and focuses on different perspectives. He refrained from treating the connection between church music and Jewish music and, by using precise analytical methods, chose to examine painstakingly the Oriental Jewish traditions he was familiar with, against the background of the Muslim musical culture within which those Jewish traditions throve for hundreds of years. He could work in this way because of the extensive knowledge he acquired through his study of theoretical texts and his exhaustive research into the living music of the region. He tied in the question of the antiquity of Jewish traditions with the total complex of Near Eastern musical culture. In other words, unlike other scholars, he recognized the importance of attempting to trace the influences of Islamic culture on Jewish musical traditions. There can be no doubt that during the four years he worked in Israel until his untimely death in 1939, he established new norms for ethnomusicological research in this country.

2

Problems of Methodology in the Study of Jewish Music

The student of Jewish music who wishes to pursue research in the most comprehensive manner, taking into account both the diachronic and synchronic dimensions, finds himself caught in a complex web of musical styles rooted in many and diverse cultures. In the pictures that emerge of past and present, different musical traditions from East and West sometimes appear in juxtaposition and sometimes seem to be in conflict with one another. Many of these traditions have been kept alive in memory through oral transmission from generation to generation; others, primarily those associated with later Western traditions, have been preserved in writing. Then there is a category that includes works unquestionably belonging to the world of Western art music, among them some created for the Reform synagogue[1] by well-known composers (the sacred services of Ernest Bloch, Darius Milhaud, Arnold Schönberg and others).[2] In addition, several unique characteristics are inherent in the major musical traditions discussed in these pages, and they too must be taken into account.

From the musical standpoint, the multiplicity of idioms necessitates, among other things, reference to the interaction of non-Jewish musical cultures with Jewish traditions through the long years of dispersion. Furthermore, each of the traditions has numerous forms of expression: they include both simple and solemn readings of the holy Scriptures, prayer tunes, metric hymns that are folkloristic in character and invite the participation of the whole congregation, solo hymns which in their most developed form draw upon the sophisticated art music of the surrounding environment. Non-Jewish art music from the surrounding culture insinuates itself into the Oriental synagogues[3] in special ways, through the use of certain attributes of the Great Tradition that crystallized after the rise of Islam and spread through most areas under Islamic control. Indeed, despite the considerable sophistication attained by the Great Tradition, it was based on oral transmission, which enables those who use it to exercise a large measure of creative freedom. This freedom may be expressed by way of improvisation, by imbuing a performance with a distinctly individual interpretation, or by introducing significant deviations from existing models. Cantors in Oriental synagogues working within these parameters—and others as well—were able to chart their course more or less successfully through vaguely defined territory, as we shall see in the next chapter.

The fragile fence guarding the unique Jewish quality of synagogue songs was breached when music from the outside world made successful inroads into non-synagogal music. It introduced much more varied types of expression, including dance forms and instrumental music—until then absolutely forbidden in the orthodox synagogue.[4]

Another characteristic that sets Jewish musical traditions and their study apart from other musical traditions, is the use of Hebrew as a common language and the recourse to the same corpus of sacred classical texts for readings from biblical books and the liturgy. This has created a special blend of highly varied musical lore transmitted orally from generation to generation and written textual lore that operates as a unifying and stabilizing factor. Moreover, research into Jewish musical traditions can take advantage of a large body of relevant archeological, literary, and iconographic evidence that has appeared in different contexts from biblical times almost until today.

In view of the foregoing, it is quite obvious that the researcher attempting to unravel this complex picture cannot be content to study it in accordance with any single method. For a deeper, more comprehensive understanding of the material under consideration, several different methods must be combined, all of them informed by an interdisciplinary approach.

Eric Werner, doyen of Jewish music scholars, whose important contributions for over fifty years particularly stressed historical aspects of the subject, delivered a programmatic lecture at the fourth World Congress of Jewish Studies in which he said that as of the mid-nineteenth century, the study of Jewish music had been based on historical and morphological approaches, to which the last generation had added another one: "The systematic research of the substance, the significance and the relations of Jewish music to other civilizations" (1968, p. 157). Ten years later, when discussing Jewish music's identity and character at the World Congress on Jewish Music, he introduced a variation on the same theme: "Taking as axiomatic the existence of Jewish music, we have not said anything about its identity. Indeed, the identity of our subject allows ontological, historical and anthropological as well as musicological approaches. The last-named includes both the ethnological and the strictly musicological methods, the former stressing the morphology, the second rather the historical aspect." And as he concluded the lecture he alluded to the third aspect as follows: "To judge from its programme, this Congress is much more concerned with the identity and morphology of Jewish music than with its history. This is as it should be. However, let me, to conclude, say a few explanatory words on my personal attitude to the history of Jewish music. It shows constant interdependence with the main cultures with which we have come in long-lasting contact during three and a half millennia of our recorded history" (1982, pp. 1–14). The implication is clear: the problem of the identity of Jewish music cannot be studied only morphologically; the intrusion of historical aspects and the ways in which, since time immemorial, it has interacted with other cultures must be studied as well.

The investigator must therefore seek out events and literary records that are of musical interest. The nature and import of such records will be clarified by the following discussion of sources and the examples selected to illustrate each major type.

The Sources

Many and varied types of evidence relevant to music can be found in sources thousands of years apart, extending from the biblical period until almost our own times. The references are widely dispersed among sources too numerous to count: the Bible, the Talmud, the *halakhah* (traditional laws and customs), homiletic discourses, religious philosophy and kabbalah, the *piyyuṭ* (liturgic poetry), masoretic literature, linguistics and other sciences, journals of travelers—to mention only a few. On the whole the material consists of small items that cannot stand alone but are woven into collections dealing with a variety of subjects. They can be found in biblical passages, talmudic sayings, the rabbinical responsa; music is used metaphorically in the science of esoterics and is described by travelers visiting strange lands, as well as in numerous other contexts. This rather fragmentary kind of information, though sometimes marginal, can be of great importance, as it can reflect various aspects of musical life.

During the Middle Ages, alongside information thus transmitted, specialized professional studies began to emerge that became known as "the science of music." Its literature rested largely on views borrowed from other nations. Unlike the earlier sources referred to, the science of music deliberately set out to discuss music as a separate, distinct discipline, a branch of knowledge that—pursuant to tenets generally accepted at that time—differentiated between the theoretical study of music and daily musical activity. This conception has its roots in the classical world, which ranked the theoretician who can analyze, define, and solve musical problems as infinitely superior to the singer or instrumentalist who "makes music." The theoretician was considered analogous to the architect, while the performing musician was compared with the builder who merely follows the architect's blueprint. Some even went so far as to claim that the theoretician need not necessarily have a musical ear. Theoretical writings of Jews, Christians, and Muslims during the Middle Ages echo this conception.

The science of music was expounded either in treatises written as totally independent texts or as separate sections within a comprehensive work (encyclopedic, mathematical, philosophical, etc.). It concerned itself, among other things, with the definition of music and its place among the intellectual disciplines, with pure or speculative theory that proposes definitions and concepts belonging to the world of ideas rather than that of practice, and with applied theory stemming directly from musical activity, for which it acts as a theoretical framework. Other dissertations focused on the study of acoustics, the definition of scales and modes, the study of melody, rhythm, instruments, etc. There were philosophical discussions about the importance of music in the life of the individual and society, its influence on the spirit, how music as the element introducing order and balance to the universe and man is inherent in the concept of cosmic harmony, its place in magic, religion, and medicine, its importance in ancient Israel. Extensive studies were also made of the relationship of word and sound.

During the Middle Ages the science of music was considered one of the basic secular disciplines, looked upon as essential in preparing the enlightened individual for the study of philosophy and the contemplation of ideas. Most Jewish writers of the time followed conventional, ubiquitous models; they created almost no original works on music, concentrating mainly on Hebrew translations or adaptations of texts originally written in other languages. The original language of some Arabic and Italian works was even preserved, but the texts were transcribed in Hebrew letters. These works were nonetheless very important as in many cases both the original and its copies were lost; only the Hebrew renditions remain to perpetuate the fruits of important intellectual labors.[5]

To summarize, painstaking exploitation of these sources can to some extent fill the historical vacuum resulting from the absence of musical documents. They offer the researcher a wealth of information about philosophical and cosmological speculations associated with music, about musical thought and the production and organization of sounds. Performance practice with respect to musical genres, instruments in use at a given period, the musical concepts and approaches that are so important for a true understanding of music and its role in any given group, the perpetuation or disappearance of musical customs, changes that have occurred and what caused them, can all be gleaned from the major types of sources discussed below.

Ancient Hebrew Sources

The Bible is the principal and indeed the richest source for knowledge about Israel's music in ancient times. The information distributed throughout its pages offers the scholar a picture of music's role in religious as well as mundane life. One can discern the place of music in ritualistic, magical, ecstatic, therapeutic, official, military, and folk events; the forms and types of songs, performance practices, performers and their status are revealed, and reference can be found to the components and functions of some sixteen instruments. All these references, of course, must be subjected to the same analytic investigation required to solve other complicated aspects of biblical research.

In describing instruments and interpreting various musical terms and events, one must turn to relevant comparative linguistic and musical material from neighboring cultures, to postbiblical sources such as the Mishnah and Talmud that refer to ancient musical customs, to the writings of Josephus Flavius and of the Judean Wilderness Sect—as well as to archeological findings. The latter are undoubtedly the most dependable source, at least with respect to certain musical instruments referred to in the Bible. Archeology has opened a new era for research in ancient music by unearthing well-preserved ancient instruments. There are lyres and pipes from the royal cemetery in Ur (Mesopotamia), trumpets from the tomb of Tutankhamen (Egypt), the aulos from Greece, and also many drawings and sculptures depicting musical instruments.

Despite the geographical proximity of these countries to Palestine, the musical instruments of their cultures were not always considered representative of instruments described in the biblical texts. On the face of it, one could hardly expect to find any ancient drawings of biblical musical instruments because of the prohibition in Jewry against making images. But a list of findings compiled recently by Bathja Bayer (1963) includes no fewer than 280 archeological items, some 130 of them actual musical instruments—primarily concussion idiophones such as castanets, bells, and bone horns, as well as horns of ivory or shell. Excavations in Israel contributed a large number of items such as the Bar-Kokhba coins bearing lyres and trumpets from the years 132–35. These findings make it possible to reconstruct the musical instruments in use along the eastern shores of the Mediterranean Basin during ancient times, and to compare them with those referred to in the Bible.

Another conceivable source—one that, as we shall see below, must be used very carefully—traces the vestiges of ancient customs that can be identified in traditions still alive today in the Near East. A number of contemporary ethnomusicologists have used this method.

The first mention of music in the Bible appears in the stories of the Creation. Gen. 4:21 states that Jubal was the "father of all such as handle the *kinnor* and *ʿuggav*" (translated as the "harp and the organ" or "pipe"). Taken literally, the passage tells of the first musician or the inventor and player of these two instruments. But early biblical commentators already extended the meaning, maintaining that the reference is to the invention of music in general. And this is the way Jubal is perceived in the medieval literature of both Jews and Christians; they considered him the biblical inventor, the counterpart to Pythagoras, the pagan world's inventor.[6] This story of the invention of music was the subject of midrashic commentary stressing music's negative aspects, as will be seen in the next chapter. Then again, some modern scholars have interpreted the "*kinnor* and *ʿuggav*" as metaphors for the two families of instruments: the chordophones and aerophones.

While Israel was emerging as a nation, during the wanderings in the wilderness when worship was in tabernacles, then when the people settled in the land of Israel and the First Temple was begun, music played a minor role in the ritual. It was important, however, on occasions of a folk character. The element of rhythm was conspicuously present in song and dance, during processions and ceremonies when the accompanying rhythmic beat was associated with the drum either as solo or as part of an ensemble. In a few passages the presence of the drum even acquires symbolic significance of life, joy, and hope.

The drum is mentioned seventeen times in the Bible, each time in connection with different ensembles including singing, dancing, and a variety of instruments. The largest ensemble described is connected with the depiction of the joyful religious folk event—the jubilant procession in which the people accompanied by King David bring the ark of the Lord up to Jerusalem. The description appears in two places: in the first, in 2 Sam. 6:5, it includes "all manner of instruments made of cypress wood, and with *kinnorot* (harps), and with *nevalim* (psalteries), and with *tuppim* (timbrels-drums), and with *mena'ne'im* (sistra), and with *tsiltselim* (cymbals)."[7] In the second description of the same event (1 Chron. 13:8) we are told that David and all of Israel "played before God with all their might, and with singing, and with harps, and with psalteries, and with timbrels, and with cymbals, and with trumpets." Both descriptions tell us that King David expressed his joy by dancing, as a result of which Saul's daughter Michal, who was watching through a window, despised him. This may indicate that according to the prevailing ideas of the day, such behavior was beneath the dignity of a king.

The drums were also important during folk celebrations at which women fill the main role. After the Egyptians drowned in the story of the Exodus from Egypt, Miriam, sister of Moses, followed by all the other women, "went out with timbrels and with dances" (Exod. 15:20); Jephtah's daughter came out to meet her father upon his victorious return from battle "with timbrels and with dances" (Judg. 11:34); the women of all of Israel's cities went to meet King Saul accompanied by drums to celebrate his victory over the Philistines, singing a type of song based on a short responsorial formula repeated by the choir: "And the women answered one another as they played and said, Saul hath slain his thousands and David his ten thousands" (1 Sam. 18:7). It was customary in ancient Israel as well as in neighboring societies for the women to be the main participants in victory celebrations. Vestiges of the custom can still be found among Arab women of both the desert and the village. Moreover, throughout the Mediterranean area, there is still a pervasive connection between the drum and female musicians and dancers. Indeed, women accompanying their singing and dancing with drums are a familiar sight in many ethnic groups in Israel today.

"Drumming" is the appellation used to characterize professional female singers in at least two communities: the Spanish Tañaderas and the Iraqi Daqqāqāt. *Daqqāqāt,* which means players or drummers, was the name of a troupe of four or five Jewish women who beat on different drums. The troupe's leader was the soloist by virtue of her particularly pleasant voice and outstanding talent. She beat small kettle drums and sang while the rest of the group, using other drums, accompanied her responsorially. Both Jews and Muslims invited these women to appear at celebrations. Women's drumming and singing groups are also popular among the Bedouin in the Persian Gulf region.[8]

The term for drum in the Bible serves as a generic name for a large variety of drums popular in the ancient and modern orient. The women seem to have used frame drums while the words of the prophet Jeremiah (31:4) suggest another type: "Again thou shalt be adorned with thy tabrets." In other words, adorn yourself with drums, hang them on your body like ornaments. It may be assumed that the reference is to something like the large double-headed drum that hangs from the performer's neck and is used for processions and other outdoor occasions.

The Wonderful Power of Music

There are many indications of the remarkable power of musical sounds. Some of them are associated with the *shofar* (ram's horn), the only ancient instrument that did not disappear after the destruction of the Temple. The shofar was even awarded the distinction of participating in the most sublime moments of synagogue ritual: on Rosh Hashana (the New Year) it marks the outgoing of the old year and advent of the new and on Yom Kippur (Day of Atonement) it announces the end of the fast.

The Bible mentions the shofar seventy-two times in varying contexts; on religious or festive occasions it sometimes appears together with trumpets. One example is the description in 1 Chron. 15:28, of David bringing the holy ark up to Jerusalem: "Thus all Israel brought up the ark of the covenant of the Lord with shouting, and with sound of the shofar, and with trumpets and with cymbals." The psalmist also juxtaposes the two instruments: "With trumpets and sound of the shofar shout ye before the King, the Lord" (Ps. 98:6). The affinity between trumpet and shofar is also expressed in the words used to describe the sounds that issue from each, as well as the method used to create the sound: *teqiʿah* (blow), *teruʿah* (blast), and *teqiʿah gedolah* (fanfare), are used interchangeably for both instruments.

At the time of the Mishnah and Talmud terminological confusion begins to creep in, that is, the distinction between the trumpet and shofar is blurred and as a result passages are introduced into the Rosh Hashana prayer that refer only to the trumpet. One example is the blessing of the wine on Rosh Hashana: instead of "and you shall blow the shofar" the words are "and you shall blow the trumpet" as appears in the all-inclusive biblical injunction: "Also in the day of your gladness and in your appointed seasons and in your new moons, ye shall blow with the trumpets over your burnt offerings, and over the sacrifices of your peace offering; and they shall be to you for a memorial before your God: I am the Lord your God" (Num. 10:10). On Mt. Sinai, "the voice of the shofar exceeding loud" is heard from out of the thunder and lightening on the mount and frightens the people so that "all . . . trembled" (Exod. 19:16). This is the strongest expression of the miraculous quality inherent in the shofar, a quality attributed to it by all succeeding generations. The sound of the shofar is associated with awe and fear, an association that was reinforced by the story of the "long blast" that felled the wall of Jericho (Josh. 6:6–20). Indeed, until today the sounding of the shofar on Rosh Hashana is accompanied by the same religious-magical awe, the same faith in the shofar's power to subdue the mightiest forces of nature and overcome the greatest evil.

The Bible invests the shofar with other functions: for one, it sounds the alarm, as we see in Ehud and Nehemia, who use it to rally their people around them (Judg. 3:27; Neh. 4:12–19). The shofar also serves as the definitive weapon, so to speak, with which to frighten the enemy (Judg. 7:8, 22); it announces victory (1 Sam. 13:3); sounds the signal to revolt (2 Sam. 20:1), and so forth. In the days of the Talmud the shofar fills other magical roles such as causing rain to relieve a drought, arresting an epidemic, counteracting evil spirits in time of war, or challenging other adversity. In such cases it was customary to declare a public fast and accompany prayers with the blowing of the shofar. All these attributes and activities associated with it evoked amplification in the Zohar and kabbalistic literature, and these added new symbols and meanings that strongly influenced the use of the shofar and the beliefs surrounding it.

But the most telling biblical evidence of the power of music, evidence that has been quoted time and again in Jewish and non-Jewish literature, is connected with King Saul. "After that thou shalt come to the hill of God, where is the garrison of the Philistines: and it shall come to pass, when thou art come thither to the city, that thou shalt meet a band of prophets coming down from the high place with a *nevel,* and a *tof* (timbrel), and a *ḥalil* (pipe), and a *kinnor,* before them; and they will be prophesying. And the spirit of the Lord will come mightily upon thee, and thou shalt prophesy with them, and shalt be turned into another man" (1 Sam. 10:5–6). These two verses describe the role of music in inspiring ecstasy and prophetic vision. Something contagious in the urge to prophesy is stimulated by the playing of four musicians. The music causes the spirit of the Lord to rest on Saul too; the text tells us that it will draw him out of his normal spiritual condition and turn him into "another man." Inspiration resulting from listening to music is further affirmed in the story of Elisha: "But now bring me a minstrel. And it came to pass, when the minstrel played, that the hand of the Lord came upon him" (2 Kings 3:15). Although these two examples have much in common, they are different in several important respects. The passage from Samuel refers to a group prophesying while in motion, accompanied by several instruments. There is no mention of dancing, which typically accompanies ecstatic practices, but the movement that is an inherent part of the situation described may well allude to its ritual nature. Two of the instruments that accompany the prophesying are of particular importance in any ecstatic awakening: the drum—which usually has pride of place when it comes to rousing emotional excitement—and the pipe or flute (*ḥalil*). The biblical *ḥalil,* like the many reed instruments known to us from neighboring cultures, was apparently double-piped each pipe having a mouthpiece with either one reed (as in the clarinet) or two (as in the oboe). Various findings substantiate this assumption, such as, for example, the stand of an oil lamp from Megido (found in the fourth level excavated, presumably from the ninth century B.C.E.), which is a figure playing a pipe with a double reed (Gressman 1927). It can be assumed that the pipe referred to in the band of prophets was of the oboe type, with a nasal tone appropriate for creating a strong aural stimulus to abet the provocative rhythmic stimulus of the drumbeats. By contrast, the passage in 2 Kings describes one player and one listener. We do not know what instrument is being played; it may have been the *kinnor* such as was played by David and was shown to have had a therapeutic effect on Saul, who has been afflicted with the "evil spirit" (1 Sam. 16:16–18). David's intimate, meditative playing seems almost to have cast a hypnotic spell and exorcised the evil spirit. The same kind of playing probably had a refining, uplifting influence on Elisha. From antiquity until this very day, when many members of the medical profession believe in the efficacy of music therapy, music has been widely recognized as a medium possessing curative powers as well as one capable of inducing ecstasy.

Jewish students of music during the Middle Ages, above all the kabbalists who belonged to Abraham Abulafia's school,[9] frequently quoted the above passages to affirm the connection between music and prophecy. One of the main uses of music in Abulafia's kabbalistic prophetic system is its exploitation as an organic part of the techniques used to achieve prophetic vision. The musical ensemble accompanying the band of prophets includes two instruments more characteristic of folk festivities: a percussion instrument—the drum—and a wind instrument—the pipe or flute. The two string instruments—the *kinnor* and *nevel*—are usually mentioned together in the Bible. In most cases they were used by the Levites who held the official position of Temple musicians. These instruments, which as stated above appear on coins from the time of Bar-Kokhba, belonged to the lyre family; they were used not only in the Temple, but also at secular celebrations and feasts (Isa. 5:11,12; Job 21:12). Each had a pair of arms fixed to a sound board, with a crossbow or yoke passing between the arms from which the strings are stretched down to the sound board. The *nevel* had a stronger sound than the *kinnor,* its arms resembling horns and its body something like a pear-shaped sack.

Symbolic Significance of the *Ḥalil*

In an enlightening article based on ancient Hebrew sources, Hanoch Avenary (1971) acquaints his readers with some of the symbolic aspects of musical instruments used in the ancient Orient and Israel. His point of departure is a passage in the Mishnah *Baba Metsiʿa* 86:41: "And the flutes (are for) the bride and the deceased," meaning that flutes are used at weddings and at burials. Avenary initially notes: "The strange connection of that instrument with both sorrow and joy is associated with the pseudo-Aristotelian Problemata: 'Why do those who are grieving and those who are enjoying themselves alike have the flute played to them?' "

This twofold usage, Avenary explains, already appears in the words of the prophets. Isa. (30:29) associates the sound of the *ḥalil* with joy, whereas Jeremiah (48:36) uses it in a sorrowful context. On the other hand, the musical heritage of the ancient East gives prominence to the flute as a symbol of fertility, life, and revival. According to Avenary, the combination of the myth of the revival—the resurrection—with the symbol of fertility enables one "to understand the role of this instrument at two cardinal points in the life of the individual—mating and death." These roles, clearly expressed in various places in the Mishnah—and particularly in the passage from the *Baba Meziʿa*—are confirmed by Greek parallels and others that Avenary cites. He believes, however, that these views, widespread until the Second Temple period when they were directly associated with neighboring cultures, disappeared soon after the destruction of the Second Temple and are not referred to again in the Jerusalem or Babylonian Talmud. Avenary explains why in his concluding sentences.

> After the destruction of the Temple and the state in 70 C.E. and during the general devastation that followed it, the world changed for the Jewish people, and also the Pharisees of old have changed their ideas. The spirit of Yavne where the rabbinical architects of reconstruction settled, drew a sharp dividing-line between Hellenism with all its ancient-eastern ingredients at the one hand, and Judaism on the other. They became intolerant of mystical and orgiastic cults, theatre, and music that catered tor the taste of the masses, as did also the early Fathers of the Church. The "flute" and its extra-Biblical symbolism of fertility came to stand outside the four cubits of religious law. Its representing the idea of life and revival faded not long afterwards.

Writings of the Judean Wilderness Sect

A wealth of material relevant to the study of sacred music at the end of the Second Temple period can also be found in sources other than the Mishnah and Josephus. Scrolls of the Judean Wilderness sect indicate special interest in music, and just as the members of the sect fostered unique ways of thinking, so they developed unique approaches to music. Living and working in the Dead Sea area, in 134 B.C.E. they established their center at Qumran. They believed in austerity, lived collectively, and rigorously observed the laws of purification and of the Sabbath. The original doctrines they promulgated included elements of messianic-apocalyptic thought; they advocated worship without a temple, created a special liturgy, and replaced sacrificial offerings with prayer. Communal meals where hymns were sung and other ceremonial rites were performed was considered a religious act of prime importance.

Their writings began to come to light some forty years ago and became known throughout the world as the Dead Sea Scrolls or the Judean Desert Scrolls. They included a set order for prayer, for the singing of hymns and chanting of psalms; condification and emendation of songs and liturgy; descriptions of choral performances; dance and responsorial singing that coincide with existing theories about the way Israel as a whole performed the psalmody in those days. The story of the war of the sons of Light against the sons of Darkness depicts a fierce battle accompanied by an involved series of trumpet and shofar signals, very much like those we are familiar with from stories about the Roman army's battle procedures.[10] The remains of other texts contain descriptions of the angels singing before the throne of the Lord and the entire universe singing at the End of Days—an eschatological motif that was later developed in the mystical literature. Thus the writings of the sect evoke the picture of a rich, highly developed musical practice. It also becomes apparent that studying the place of music in the life of this sect is important not only for its own sake: it can supply a missing link in the history of Israel's music, particularly its liturgical music, as the nation's independence came to an end and its dispersion began. It also helps fill a gap in the study of sources of Christian music.[11]

Literary Evidence

Until now we have presented a few examples of how the information found in many diverse sources can be exploited for the purpose of eliciting as comprehensive a picture as possible of music's place in the life of the people of Israel before they were dispersed among the nations of the world. The period we are now about to discuss introduces us to sources relating to a different, but no less complex, musical reality. The splendor of the Temple ritual gives way to intimate synagogue worship; musical events associated with the nation's life in its homeland are replaced by many and varied traditions that drew upon the cultures within which dispersed Jewry lives. Musical conceptions change and henceforth are viewed through the prism of theological and procedural-methodological doctrines.

Two literary sources have been selected from among the great variety available, to demonstrate the use of music in the synagogue and at wedding celebrations; they also indicate the extensive flowering of theoretical literature as of the beginning of the tenth century.

In a chronicle written in the tenth century, the scribe Rabbi Natan ha-Cohen, son of Yishaq ha-Bavli, vividly describes the inaugural ceremony of ʿOukba, newly appointed head of the Babylonian Jewish community. Babylonian Jewry is known to have enjoyed internal autonomy for many generations before that time and the man who was the head of the community could always trace his ancestry back to the Kingdom of David. The non-Jews looked upon him as the Persian king's representative; in fact, he ranked fourth in the Persian ruling hierarchy, which entitled him to all appropriate pomp and circumstance. The announcement of the candidate chosen was accompanied by the blowing of shofars, singing, and magnificent ceremonies and parades. R. Natan ha-Bavli's description of the inauguration attests to the perpetuation of ancient rites and customs, while the rabbi adds that Oukba was a poet and musician "who every day, throughout the year composed and performed his own paeans of praise to the King." Further on, there is a description of the festive Sabbath prayer held in honor of the community's new head:[12]

> And when he rises early on the Sabbath to go to the synagogue, many of the prominent members of the community gather around to walk to the synagogue with him. In good time the faithful had prepared a wooden tower for him seven cubits high and three cubits wide and had draped it in pleasing cloth of silk woven of blue and purple and crimson threads until it is altogether covered and nothing can be seen of it. And beneath it gather young men chosen from among the leaders and notables of the community and elders endowed with musicianship and with beautiful voices who are well versed [in the prayers] and all about them. . . . And the cantor opens with: "Blessed art Thou" and the men respond after each verse "Blessed art Thou, blessed be He." And when he chants the Sabbath psalm they respond after him: "It is good to give thanks to the Lord" and the congregation chants verses of the psalms in unison until they come to the end and then the cantor stands up and begins "and the soul of all that lives and breathes" and the men respond: "Blessed be thy name." He [the cantor] chants the words and the men answer until they reach the Trisagion and all the congregation murmurs softly and the men out loud and then they immediately become silent and the cantor continues alone until "Israel shall be redeemed" and all the congregation rises to pray. And when he passes before the ark and comes to the Trisagion the men respond with "The Almighty, blessed be He" in loud voice and the cantor finishes the prayer and the congregation sits. After prayers all the people go out before him and after him extolling him with words of homage until he reaches his house.

From this description it becomes evident that a cantor and choir performed those prayers that were sung. The choir's role was mainly responsorial, the most usual form being antiphonal, the parts divided between the cantor and the choir. For example: the cantor sings, "A psalm for the Sabbath day," and the choir responds "It is a good thing to give thanks unto the Lord"; the choir sings aloud while the worshippers all murmur the prayer. We also learn that the choir was an established, trained group and included men "endowed with musicianship and with beautiful voices who are well-versed [in the prayers] and all about them." Furthermore, they were chosen from among "the leaders and notables of the community," that is, from elite families. There were also other songs and liturgies, less sophisticated than those sung by the cantor and choir. They were apparently of a more popular folk character and were sung by all those who took part in the processions.[13]

The fixed Sabbath and holiday prayer "The sound of all things that live and breathe" is part of the ritual of all traditions in Jewry. Joseph Heinemann (1966, p. 152), renowned expert on the history and development of the prayers, has written: "Of all the fixed, ordinary prayers, this is the greatest, most glorious hymnal work, outstanding for the many styles it employs." Indeed, many elements within it beg, as it were, to be sung. With respect to beautifying embellishment, "The soul of all things" was the source of special inspiration for the liturgic poets. According to Ezra Fleischer (1975, pp. 396–97), following the original verses added to it by the first of the great Spanish liturgical poets, Yosef Avitur, this prayer made an outstanding mark among Spanish poets. Essentially, the prayer was poetically enhanced in separate categories, following its key words such as: "The soul of," "were our mouths full of song as the sea," "all my bones," etc.

None of the foregoing, however, indicates whether or not the embellishments added by the Spanish liturgical poets found a place in the fixed prayers of Israel's Oriental communities. Judging from the customs followed today, most of the Sephardic communities stress the verbal poetic aspect, singing only passages of "The soul of . . ." itself, and occasionally adding one of the accepted introductory verses. The Portuguese community of Amsterdam is exceptional in that they added a new dimension as well as further embellishments: they combined vocal compositions with a Western cantata-like style created by eighteenth-century composers. One example is C. G. Lidarti's "He who maketh the mute to speak."[14]

Finally, the musical importance of the prayer "The soul of all things that live and breathe" finds further confirmation in an interesting eleventh-century document from the city of Ashkelon. Found in the Cairo Genizah, S. D. Goitein presents and reproduces it:

> A controversy ensued in the city between an aggressive community leader and fifty men, "the Ashkelon people who were joined by Hebronites and others," and the Egyptian *nagid* [prince] who had authority over the Ashkelon community [in Eretz Israel] sent a learned scholar to restore peace to the city. The side that rebelled against the community leader accepted the mediator, but set a condition: that he [the mediator] no longer recognize the leader's special privileges such as that only his son would always be the one to chant "The soul of . . ." [the special morning prayer recited on the Sabbath and holy days that preceded the reading of "Hear, O Israel"]. The rebellious ones had refrained from coming—or, in their words—from going down to the synagogue but now they agreed. Here the letter to the *nagid* goes on:
>
> "We said to him [to the mediator]: We will not go down with you [to the synagogue] except on condition that the son of the leader will not chant over our heads [that is, from the *bimah*-pulpit] 'The soul of . . .' because we had conceded this issue only because we were united and peace reigned amongst us and we were as one. But now, after you have banded together against us and connived against us under oath, we have all sworn that he will not again chant 'The soul of . . .' over our heads, but that there shall also stand up a youth from our side and one will have a Sabbath and then the other will have a Sabbath. Then the judge, may the Almighty give him strength mediated between us; after much argument that would require lengthy clarification, [the judge ruled] that the one would have a Sabbath and the other would have a Sabbath. On this condition the next Sabbath the entire public entered the synagogue and it was decided among the public figures that all the youth would go up to chant 'The soul of . . .' so that peace would prevail. But the community leader and his son said to the boys: Get down! or . . . [out of respect, the coarse

imprecation was not written in full], it cannot be that this prayer will be chanted by any but the cantor alone. And when they said this thing and sent our youth down from the *bimah,* and the one was an orphan, and they wounded his heart, and we, the fifty people mentioned above swore that 'The soul . . .' shall never be chanted above our heads by a youth, not ours and not theirs but only the cantor shall chant it." [Goitein adds an editorial note to the effect that apparently only one boy sang the prayer, the others singing an accompaniment.] (Goitein 1962, pp. 39–40)

Travelers Describe a Jewish Wedding in Tangier, Morocco

Travelers who record their impressions usually display exceptional intellectual curiosity, but they often lack the specific training necessary to transmit a well-informed picture of the music indigenous to the strange parts they visit; nor are they always thoroughly acquainted with the culture they describe. Nevertheless, their observations can be helpful, even when garnered with the help of local guides and interpreters. After careful screening, these first-hand accounts can supply important evidence. They can transmit information on the place of music in a given culture and on the local population's approach to it. They can evoke a picture of music's various functions, of instruments used for various occasions, differences between urban and rural, secular and religious music, the role of dance, types of instrumental ensembles, the relationship of vocal to instrumental music, the kinds of songs and melodies performed.

The traveler's reaction and attitude to the music can be quite influential as his countrymen read his account and it colors their vicarious experience of alien cultures. For the present day scholar, the recorded impressions of visitors can also facilitate a study of degrees of stability and change in musical cultures; travel books can help show how the contemporary musical scene compares with that of the past as they indicate what has disappeared, what has remained stable, and where changes have occurred.

From the Jewish standpoint, to a certain extent these accounts help to pinpoint Jewish music's affinity with the music of the surrounding communities: they note the differences and similarities, the mutual relationships, and the metamorphoses brought about by migration to Israel (as compared with the musical milieu in the country of origin).

By an interesting coincidence, three different travelers who lived and worked decades apart from one another recorded their impressions of three different wedding ceremonies held in the same Jewish community of Tangier, Morocco. Some of the scenes and events they recorded are reproduced below; needless to say, these descriptions are of particular value to ethnomusicologists.

Romanelli Visits Tangier

The first travel book of particular interest in the present context was written by the Jewish author and poet Samuel Aaron Romanelli. Romanelli was born in 1757 in

Mantua, then an important center of Jewish writers, philosophers, and poets. His broad general education included knowledge of some ten languages. For many years he wandered from place to place and in 1787 arrived in Morocco. He recounted his experiences during his four-year sojourn there in a fascinating book in Hebrew called *Massa be-ʿarab* (Essay on travels in Morocco),[15] which is the source of the following description of a Jewish wedding in Tangier. It is interesting to note that Romanelli weaves many biblical terms and expressions into his descriptions of musical and other performances. In the first passage (p. 29) he interprets the phrase from the prophet Amos "*bimot yisḥaq*" literally, as a stage on which laughter occurs—in other words a "comedy"—rather than as ordinarily rendered: "And the high places of Isaac" (Amos 7:9).

In other passages (p. 55) he calls the musical instruments by their biblical names: "*nevel*" for *ʿūd* (Arabian short-neck lute) and "*mashroquita*" (an orchestral instrument referred to in Dan. 3:10) for oboe.

At one point he describes a dancer:

> . . . and a dancing girl, her head tilted sideways, holds an edge of a kerchief in each hand, one high above her head, the other pointing below her waist at her stomach, and then slowly, lithely, she reverses the position of her arms. I thought she was made, but they told me that was how they dance in their city. This was accompanied by young girls beating quietly on goblet drums which have tops shaped like open bottles and skin stretched over the bottom, or like the drums seen on "bimot yisḥak" in the comedy Axor [the reference is to A. Salieri's opera *Axur Re D'ormus*]. However, the drumming was entirely at random, conforming to no known rules of composition. How could anyone present at this performance refrain from laughing? (P. 29)

Romanelli modifies his critical reaction with philosophic comments: "Humankind is nothing but vanity; all people on the face of the earth beguile. The deeds of people from the Magreb [Morocco] seem strange in our eyes and our deeds seem strange in their eyes, but in truth, all is vanity. We mock the child who weeps for we know how vain is the reason for his weeping and the heavenly hosts on high mock us, for even unto ripe old age we are like young children."

In another passage Romanelli describes a custom widespread in the East—in times of joy the women voice special sounds called *yelulah* or "*yuyu.*"

> An old woman will emit sounds like a horse neighing loudly that set the ears of all within earshot a-tingle, and this bodes well for the members of the household. . . . And this whooping bird will be found in all houses of celebration. God forbid that her warble not be heard at every joyous occasion! This would turn the festivity into mourning.
>
> In the evening they will lead the bride to the home of her groom accompanied by the warbling woman and drums, and she is as if deaf, mute, and blind until she comes to her house; and she will stand still on Friday from the time they dress her;

she is like unto a monument of stone until she comes out from under her bridal canopy and has been placed upon her bedding. (P. 54)

Then there is a section with a detailed description of dressing the bride, arranging her coiffure and making up her face, as well as of the ḥenna ceremony. At this ceremony, which is widely practiced in the Islamic countries—although a variety of different meanings are attributed to it—a special paste (*ḥinne*) is spread over certain parts of the body of the bride, groom, and close relatives.

"On each of the seven days of the festivities someone comes to play the *nevel* [apparently either the violin or the *ʿūd*—A.S.] and when the musician sang in Hebrew or Arabic the guests would all place coins as a gratuity on his instrument. Perhaps this is an interpretation of the passage . . . That drum on the psaltery, That devise for themselves instruments of music. . . .' (Amos 6:5)." By modifying the original sense of the verb *paroṭ* (to pluck) into placing a *peruṭah* (a coin), Romanelli tries to give an ironical twist to the description of the custom of paying the musician by placing a copper upon the opening of the *nevel*. In the same chapter he describes the instruments generally used by the native non-Jewish population, first declaring that by Western criteria the Moroccans do not have the faintest notion of the art and theory of music.

The science of music is entirely and altogether unknown to them; even our instrumental music and singing as performed on stage [that is, Western theater/opera] are terms unknown to them. Their only instruments for song are the drums I have mentioned, the *mashrokita* with a shape that calls to mind the hautbois [oboe] and has a sound like that of the piper summoning his flock, and the flute contrariwise brings the plague upon you ". . . and he that smootheth with the hammer him that smiteth the anvil" (Isa. 41:7) [a metaphoric description of the flute's grotesque tones (ed.)]. Those two [the oboe and flute], rejoice "in the joy of the *ḥudjādj*"—the celebrants or the pilgrims—the people who have returned from the holy of holies in Mecca, as Jews go [on pilgrimage] to Jerusalem and Christians to Rome. And they are as if hallowed and in their business transactions they will pay only a half tax to the king. The trumpets, that looked and sounded like those of the postmen of Mecklenburg [who in Romanelli's time traveled in special coaches from one independent Duchy of Mecklenburg to the other, trumpeting aloud to announce their arrival], would play fanfares in the month of Ramadan . . . the month during which they fasted for thirty days from sunrise until the moon appeared. They would blow the trumpet from the tower of the mosque three times a night (many travelers of the nineteenth and early twentieth century have mentioned the nocturnal trumpet blasts during the month of Ramadan),[16] to wake the people to eat, saying to them: "Rise to eat and drink what the Lord has provided for you." And [they have] the metal concussion instruments [referred to as bowls in Ezra 1:10—sort of metallic castanets called *krakeb* that also accompany the dancing]. Two are wound around their palms and beaten against each other. This instrument is special for the blacks [Negroes are mentioned in many other

> sources, both modern and ancient, as well as in the painting by Delacroix described below], who dance as spryly as new-born colts. The Jews use more than just the *nevel*.
>
> In singing songs all are equal, each group using its own language. They add meaningless syllables between letters, interspersing na, na, ah, ah, to prolong the syllable. This is a most fundamental characteristic of Moroccan singing: the vocalists add nonsense syllables that often become an integral part of the text; their singing, therefore, is not syllabic. (Pp. 55–56)

As can be seen, Romanelli's description includes important details about instruments, performance practice, dance, and distinctive ethnic characteristics.

Delacroix Visits Tangier

In 1832, that is, forty-five years after Romanelli's visit, the famous French artist Eugène Delacroix was a guest of the same community. In one of his paintings he depicted a Jewish wedding that took place on the twenty-first of February, 1821. He also wrote a description of the wedding in his journal (1983, 154–58). Of particular interest are his comments about the participation of Muslim neighbors in the festivities of the Jews, his description of the trio consisting of the fiddle, *ʿūd* and tambourine (or, in his words, the violon, guitar, *tambour de Basque*), and the dancing. The dance he describes is performed only by women, each woman rising in turn and dancing alone. The sole male dancer participating is a Negro. According to everything we know, the musicians were all undoubtedly Jews. This assumption is strengthened by Delacroix himself who points out elsewhere (p.. 215) in the same journal that the Jewish musicians in Mogador are the best in all of Morocco. It may be assumed that in other parts of the country too they were outstanding.

Alexandre Dumas in Tangier

In 1845, thirteen years later, another famous Frenchman arrived in Tangier—the writer, Alexandre Dumas, père. In the book he wrote (1849) about his travels he devotes a fascinating chapter (pp. 79–93) to the colorful description of a Jewish wedding he witnessed in the city. The author's guide was a merchant, a member of the Jewish community who brought him to the wedding and apparently supplied him with basic information about the customs and activities he observed. Other travelers also probably took advantage of the services of members of the community who knew foreign languages and could fairly easily fill the role of cultural intermediary.

The picturesque description covers some fifteen pages crowded with details noted by the talented writer. Dumas describes in words, as Delacroix does on canvas, the musicians who accompany the singing and dancing: three players sit cross-legged, one holding a violin upright on his knee as if it were a cello (in that part of the world they were still using the stringed instrument called *kamanje;* it was not replaced by the Western violin until the nineteenth century) and the others were beating tambourine-like drums.[17] Their playing was audible from quite a distance away, as Dumas informs his readers:

"At a distance of a hundred steps from the house we already heard the din from inside caused by drum-beats, the squeaking of violins and the tinkle of bells—that did not lack a certain savage, original harmony."

Dumas returns to the music-makers further on in the chapter: "From time to time the elder of the two drummers put his drum aside and clapped his dry palms together. They sounded like pieces of wood beating against one another, as if all the flesh had disappeared from the hands and the skeletal bones were producing this special noise."

As stated, the musicians accompanied the women's singing as well as their dancing. Ten or twelve women danced, one after another, and even the most careful observer would have been unable to discern choreographic talent in any of them. The dancing was spontaneous with all the female relatives taking part as an active expression of their participation in the festivities—something that is quite normal in other communities as well. But Dumas, who was accustomed to more sophisticated dancing, in all seriousness explains the simplicity of the dance:

"They all danced to an endlessly repeated tune accompanied by the same words. The music was not actually melodic, but a kind of monotonal declamation with a range hardly covering an octave. And as for the words, I would offer a prize to anyone guessing what they were about." Indeed, the song told about the French bombardment of Tangier when they stormed the city. Amazed, Dumas asked why this theme was celebrated in song at a Jewish wedding—the bombardment of the city did not seem a particularly appropriate subject for a wedding. In his attempt to explain the contradiction, he arrives at the conclusion that the horrendous event commemorated by the song was, so to speak, "the beginning of the redemption" for the local Jewish community that had been suffering under Muslim tyranny. Certain traditions still practiced today can go far to allay the kind of amazement Dumas felt almost a century and a half ago. Until this very day it is not unusual at folk celebration to sing about events of overall national import, or even to repeat personal dirges. Countless songs have been written in Israel about coming to the country, about the Six Day War, about the rescue of the hostages at Entebbe. Once they have been accepted as part of the repertoire, these songs are considered timeless and are used as fill-ins on all occasions. Thus at a Druze wedding in the north of Israel one can hear a song about the murder of the Syrian prime minister, or at a wedding in Moshav Bareqet near the Judean foothills one can hear the people who originally came from Ḥabban (Ḥadramaut) in South Yemen lamenting the death of a son.

Dumas returns to a description of the festivities: "The dances were always the same and the song was always the one about the bombardment." He then adds that he placed some coins in the peaked headpiece of one of the dancers. "This is a form of tribute paid by foreigners who come to watch the dancing, and we complied with the greatest pleasure. The entire spectacle was so curious that we had no regrets over the money spent."[18] This comment touches on a very important subject—how professional folk-artists are paid. A professional artist is one who earns his livelihood from his art, but this is not the only applicable criterion. There are semiprofessionals, and one can also be a highly accomplished artist without being called a professional. Certain other details become apparent from Dumas's description, among them two aspects previously noted: the participation of the Muslim neighbors in the Jewish wedding celebration and the behavior of the bride who, in Dumas's words, "remains as immobile as a Japanese statue."

These descriptions by three different travelers have much in common. Supplementing one another, they evoke a reliable picture not only of the wedding but of broader aspects of Jewish musical culture and its affinity with its surroundings over a period of some hundred years. They also afford a background against which to compare today's situation, and thereby enhance our understanding of changes that have occurred in this sphere.

The Science of Music—Texts from Islamic Countries

The oldest known text about the science of music from Islamic countries is from the tenth century. It appears in the concluding section of the *Book of Beliefs and Opinions* by Rabbi Saʿadia Gaon (882–942), the major figure in Jewish thought during the Gaonic period. His book on the philosophy of religion was written in 933. The rabbi wrote in Arabic, but used Hebrew letters. The musical doctrine he expounds is borrowed from the writings of the Arab theoretician and philosopher Abū Yūsuf ibn Isḥāq al-Kindī (796–873) who was one of the first to deal with the theoretical aspects of Arabic music.[19]

The earliest texts in Arabic that discuss musical principles are from the ninth century. They owe a significant debt to the systematic translations of Greek and Syrian texts rendered by the Baghdad Academy of Sciences. Among the important writers known to us from that period are al-Kindī and Thābit ibn Qurrah (836–901). In the following century the famous philosopher al-Fārābī (see below) introduced a speculative-mathematical approach to music that dealt with basic questions of theory such as the intervals and scales. Al-Kindī represents a broader, cosmological approach; he discusses the basic harmony of the universe and the balanced order inherent in human beings. Others who followed in al-Kindī's footsteps were members of the "Brotherhood of Purity" (see below).

To return to Saʿadia Gaon: The end of the tenth chapter of his book discusses the proper behavior of a person in this world, and deals with the eight rhythmic modes as they influence the soul of the individual.[20] He opens this section with the statement: "Indeed, the sound alone and the separate note and melody will move only one of the soul's virtues, and can sometimes even be harmful, but in combination they will lead to a harmonious balance between the different virtues and powers." This sentence obviously requires explication, not only because of the involved thought it expresses or the problem of rendering the extremely concise style, but also because the terms used are abstruse.

The terms "sound" (*qol* in Hebrew), "separate note" (*neʿimah nifredet* in Hebrew), and "melody" (*neginah* in Hebrew) represent ibn Tibbon's translation for the Arabic terms *al-ṣawt al-mufrad* (the separate sound); *al-tanghīm* (a verbal noun meaning something like the organization or putting together of notes—naghamāt, plural of—*naghmah*) and *luḥūn*, a special plural of *laḥn*—melody—that may signify melodical or rhythmical patterns. Thus in the Arabic original we obtain a gradual logical sequence. Saʿadia's key term *naghmah*, rendered by ibn Tibbon also as *neʿimah*, is used in the context of this treatise as analogous with the word "beat." It follows that *tanghīm* means dividing the rhythm into groups of beats or rhythmical patterns; the term *luḥūn* does not refer to tunes, but to rhythmic modes, and the "sound" that appears at the beginning of the sentence refers to the sound or group of sounds produced by the beats. Thus three innocuous terms manage to create great confusion; even after their meaning has presumably been deciphered, it is not at all certain that the idea of the sentence as a whole has become comprehensible. The difficulty now is subject matter as well as manner of expression.

In language more accessible to today's reader the sentence might be written as follows: Single groups of sounds or given rhythmic patterns each affect spiritual powers in a specific manner, an effect that can be harmful as well as beneficial. When sounds and rhythms combine harmoniously, they have the power of bringing desirable balance to the spiritual-intellectual qualities (referred to by Saʿadia Gaon as "virtues"). In other words, Saʿadia does not recommend affecting the spirit by means of a single drastic measure, but prefers the "golden mean" advocated by the philosophers of antiquity. As stated, the theory of the eight modes and rhythms and their influence on the soul is borrowed from the writings of al-Kindī.

The manifold intricacies involved in deciphering a sentence such as this indicate the three hurdles the scholar must overcome in fathoming the theoretical literature: the linguistic, the thematic, and the web of parallel and comparable opinions set forth. The examples discussed below will make this clearer. Rabbi Saʿadia Gaon's work, however—the first essay by a Jew on a subject involving the science of music—was a model for many of his successors who derived most of their theoretical material from Arabic sources.

In the vast majority of cases theoretical Arabic literature was consulted for the purpose of clarifying the meaning of obscure passages in a Hebrew source. This is well illustrated by a section—also originally written in Arabic—translated by Yehuda ben Shaul ibn Tibbon.[21] The subject is taken from paragraphs 69–70 of Rabbi Judah Halevi's *Book of the Khazari*.[22] Halevi was one of the greatest poets of Israel and an important Jewish philosopher who lived in Spain from about 1075–1141. His book about the king of the Khazars deals with the uniqueness of the religious history of the people of Israel and their special connection with God.

In discussing the qualities of the Hebrew language with his interlocutor, a rabbi, the king of the Khazars says:

> Thou wilt only succeed in placing it thus on an equality with other languages. But where is its pre-eminence? Other languages surpass it in songs metrically constructed and set to music.
>
> The rabbi said: It is obvious that a tune is independent of the meter, or of the lesser or greater numbers of syllables. . . . Rhymed poems, however, which are recited, and possess good meter, are neglected for something higher and more useful. . . ."
>
> The Khazari said: It is but proper that mere beauty of sound should yield to lucidity of speech. Harmony pleases the ear, but exactness makes the meaning clear. I see, however, that you Jews long for a prosody, in imitation of other people, in order to force the Hebrew language into their meters."
>
> The rabbi: It has already been clarified that the melodies do not require the meter of speech, and that both the empty and the full [notes of][23] "O give thanks unto the Lord, for He is good" can be sung to the tune of "To Him who alone doeth great wonders." (Pp. 69–70)

The subject is sufficiently clear: As opposed to the rabbi, the Khazari claims that the Hebrew language is inadequate in comparison with Arabic, which has metered poetry that facilitates its adaptation to melodies. The rabbi develops a theory to the effect that the tunes merely follow the meter of the poem. When he says it has "already been clarified" he is referring to the lengthy debate in the Khazari book on the *teʿamim*—the biblical accents and their musical meaning that will be discussed in chapter 4. Less clear and comprehensible, however, is the manner in which Halevi illustrates his thought. The two examples quoted in paragraph 70 are from the 136th Psalm. Although the sentences are of unequal length, both are sung to exactly the same tune. To explain how two sentences of different length can be sung to the same musical motif, Halevi adduces the special technique that he called "empty" and "full." These terms have confounded all commentators, and kept them busy trying to unravel the puzzle. In actual fact, the terms were simply taken from one of the most famous Arabic books on musical theory, *The Grand Book of Music* (*Kitāb al-mūsīqī al-Kabīr*) written by the renowned philosopher (and outstanding *ʿūd* player) Abū Naṣr al-Fārābī (known in Europe by his Latin name: Alfarabius—873–951).[24] His fame in the musical world derives primarily from his monumental book, which establishes the basic groundwork for Arab theoretical literature in this sphere. Some of his works, among them a book of scientific classifications that also contains a chapter on musical theory, were translated into Latin.[25]

In the chapter of his *Grand Book of Music* that deals with the study of composition, al-Fārābī explains the different ways of adapting the syllables of a given poem to the notes of the tune associated with it. In this connection he mentions, among others, three types of songs: "those with empty sounds," "those with full sounds," and those with "mixed sounds." An empty sound results if a given syllable is sung to a note that is prolonged uninterruptedly or may even have other notes added to it, without a consonant to interrupt the vocal modalization. By a full sound al-Fārābī meant that each note has its own consonant that stops the flow of air; from start to finish the note remains at the same pitch, until stopped by enunciation of a consonant. This is a graphic description of the recitative sounds typical of cantillation (see chapter 4). Because an empty sound is uninterrupted, it lends itself to the development of vocalization. If the number of syllables of a given text exceeds the number of notes in the melody to which one wants to adapt it—that is, if there are more consonants than notes, the song will necessarily be composed either partially or totally of full sounds. By the same token, if there are more notes than textual syllables, the song will be composed either totally or partially of empty notes. Al-Fārābī writes that when the song is based on full sounds, its text emerges clearly and comprehensibly, but the tune is not pleasing to the ear. The song with "empty sounds" has a pleasing melody but its words are very hard to understand. Hence an intermediate system is best.

In light of al-Fārābī's explanation of full and empty sounds, Halevi's meaning becomes clear. Indeed, in "O give thanks . . ." the melody is longer than the text. Hence the use of empty sounds is essential—that is, each syllable or at least a certain number of syllables, must be sung to more than one note. On the other hand, in "To him who alone doeth . . ." a number of syllables have to be sung on one note. This technique is familiar to anyone who has tried to adapt a melody to a text that was not originally written for it.

The Seeker by Shem-Tov ben Yosef ibn Falaqera

This third source from the Islamic world was again rooted in Spanish soil and also emerged from the milieu influenced by Arabic theoretical literature. The Spanish poet and philosopher Shem-Tov ben Yosef ibn Falaqera (1225–95) found a very attractive form in which to review the various scientific disciplines. He wrote *The Seeker* (Sefer Ha-mavaqqesh) in the form of a dialogue between a young man pursuing truth—the Seeker—and various experts to whom he turns. The thirteenth dialogue, which discusses music, follows immediately after the science of astronomy-astrology, which had been preceded, as was customary in medieval literature, by the other disciplines included in the *quadrivium*. (The *quadrivium* was the group of studies—arithmetic, geometry, astronomy-astrology, and music—required in the Middle Ages to prepare the candidate for the study of philosophy and theology.)

The section dealing with music begins and ends with passages taken from biblical books that in one way or another are associated with music—the only connection with Judaism in the entire work. In this chapter, six questions are put to the expert; they deal with the principles and purposes of music, its influence, the elements that it comprises, etc.

Careful analysis leaves no doubt at all that the fundamental ideas in *The Seeker,* as well as the form in which they are presented, are based on "The Epistle on Music" of the secret cult known as the Brotherhood of Purity (Ikhwān al-Ṣafā')—a secret brotherhood that was active in the second half of the tenth century. "The Epistle on Music" is the fourth part of a comprehensive encyclopedia containing fifty-two epistles and a summary that covers all fields of knowledge and research then known.[26] The three passages below from *The Seeker,* if juxtaposed with their counterparts in "The Epistle on Music" demonstrate the similarity with which the central ideas common to both essays are worked out, as well as some of the themes that were the concern of the Science of Music in those days. Such a juxtaposition was made in Shiloah (1978a) from which we quote the following examples.

> The first seeker's question: How can it be that some animals emit sounds and they have neither lungs nor throat? Answer: The bee or the wasp and other animals like them without lungs, make sounds—for they set the air in motion with rapid [and] light wing movements. And they will thus create different sounds as will setting the string of the *kinnor* [*'ūd* or lute] to vibrate. And the variety of kinds of these sounds is in accordance with the thinness or thickness of their wings and their length or shortness, as well as the rapidity with which they move them.
>
> The Second Question—What is the instrument closest to perfection in the eyes of people who practice this art? The Answer:—It is the *kinnor* [*'ūd*]. And they say that its length should be as its breadth and its depth about half its breadth and its neck should equal one quarter [of its length].
>
> The Third Question—And why have they said that one needs four strings, each thicker than the other, so that there will be a noble proportion between them? The Answer: They have done thus so that the sound of each one will be stronger than the humors (mood) of the other four.[27] And one of them called *al-bamm*[28] is of sixty-four silk threads and its mood and crudeness will strengthen the black bile and the second, called *al-mathlath* is composed of forty-three strings and its sonority corresponds to the phlegm. The third is of thirty-six threads and it is called *al-mathna* and its sound will reinforce the blood. And the fourth is of twenty-seven threads and is called *al-zīr* and strengthens and refines the yellow bile.

In the "Epistle" of the Brotherhood of Purity we find the same subjects treated in almost the same language:

> As for the sounds emitted by animals deprived of lungs, such as wasps, locusts, and crickets and others of the kind, these animals set the air in motion by means of two wings that vibrate rapidly and lightly, producing varied sounds like those produced as a result of setting the strings of the lute vibrating. The modalities and the variety of kinds of these sounds depend on the fineness or thickness, the length or shortness of their wings, as well as the rapidity with which they move them.
>
> Know, my brother—that the philosophers have invented several instruments and apparatuses suitable for producing musical sounds and melodies [this is followed by a

long list of instruments] . . . but the instrument closest to perfection to have been invented by the philosophers and the best that they have made is that called the *ʿūd* . . . the people of this art have said [that the *ʿūd* should be made of wood and that its length, breadth, and depth should stand in a noble relation to each other, that is] that its length should be in the proportion of (3:2) with its breadth; its depth should be equivalent to half its breadth and its neck should equal one quarter of the total length of the instrument. Then one chooses four strings, each thicker than the one before. Their respective thickness should be in a noble proportion to each other, that is, the thickness of the fourth string [*bamm*] should be in the proportion of 4:3 with the third string [*mathlath*]; the thickness of the third string in the proportion of 4:3 with the second string [*mathna*]; the thickness of the second string in the proportion of 4:3 with the first string [*zīr*]. . . . Thus the fourth string should be composed of sixty-four silk threads, the third of forty-eight, the second of thirty-six, and the first of twenty-seven.

They [the musician philosophers] limited themselves to four strings for the *ʿūd,* no more, no less, so that their productions would be comparable to the natural things that are under the lunary sphere and in the image of the science of the Creator, may He be exalted [a comparison with the four elements transferred to the effect of the sound of the four strings on the state of mind of those who hear them]. . . . In effect, the sonority of the first string [*zīr*] reinforces the humor of yellow bile, augments its vigor and its effect; it possesses a nature opposed to that of the humor of phlegm, and softens it. The sonority of the second string reinforces the humor of the blood, augments its vigor and its effect; it possesses a nature opposed to that of the humor of black bile, it refines it and makes it more tender.

The Second Period in the History of Texts and Jewish Music

Until now we have discussed the early flowering of the science of music as a discipline within the frame of general secular knowledge that every educated person in the Middle Ages was expected to acquire. Hence works by Jews dealing with music, most of which were written in Arabic, reflected the accepted theories of the surrounding culture and to a great extent were based on texts of renowned Arab theoreticians. It is important to reiterate that in those days musical science was considered an exclusively theoretical discipline meant to train the mind for philosophical thinking, rather than to train a musician to engage in the making of music.

Nevertheless, ibn Falaqera's *The Seeker,* as well as another of his works, *The Foundations of the Sciences* (*Reshit hokhamah*)—which is to a large extent a Hebrew translation of al-Fārābī's *Iḥṣāʾ al-ʿulūm* (Enumeration of Sciences), in which the author defines the nature and scope of the known sciences. This work became known in medieval Europe through its several Latin translations (see Farmer 1939). The section on music offers a concise, factual definition of the science of music—constituting a significant departure from the earlier literature.[29] In *The Foundations of the Sciences,* written before *The Seeker,* Falaquera maintains that it is "good that we teach them [the sciences] in our language rather than that we teach them in the language of another nation." Hanoch Avenary sees this advocacy of the transition from the use of a foreign tongue to the use of Hebrew as the inception of the second period in the history of writing about Jewish music. According to him, this became "the badge of musical literature in the thirteenth and fourteenth centuries in Provence, in Italy, and in Andalusia as well" (1973, pp. 53–55).

After enumerating the texts and translations rendered by Spaniards in the first half of the thirteenth century for the Jews of Provence, Avenary adds: "Parallel with this period in the development of Hebrew musical literature, the Christian world was involved in the intellectual movement that brought the Middle Ages to their greatest heights." This movement aspired to create an intellectual European culture independent of the church framework. At the same time, the theory of musical practice was having an ever increasing influence on the literature dealing with Hebrew musical thought.

Among those who made significant contributions to philosophical works about music were poets who considered themselves "rhetoricians and musicians at one and the same time." They stressed the musical element in their poems and some of their views influenced musical thinking. Thus, for example, one of the pioneers of Jewish literature in Italy at the beginning of the fourteenth century, the poet Immanuel of Rome, in two lines expressed an opinion that became the foundation-stone for the musical thinking of generations to come: "What does the science of music say to the Christians? Indeed, 'I have been stolen from the Land of the Hebrews.' "[30] The seed of this belief in the Bible as the source of musical science had already begun to germinate in the preceding period. It now became a major motif in literature written by Italian Jews, particularly during the Renaissance, despite the growing trend toward secular humanism and cosmopolitanism.

The Bible as the original source of the science of music also found expression in the *Book of the Garden* by the well-known Spanish poet and philosopher, R. Moshe Ibn Ezra (1055–1135).[31] He was known for his liturgical poems and, after many of his verses were incorporated into the High Holiday prayers, was considered a specialist on "supplications." His secular poetry often referred to music, but such references were even more frequent in his philosophic poetical works. After citing the words of a number of philosophers about the influence of music on the soul of the individual and expressing his wonder at "this spiritual balm," he adds:

"How wonderful is this science that came into the world with Genesis, at the very beginning of the generations when human life was long and the people created these sciences with the most sublime objectives, as is told about their inventor Jubal: . . . he was the father of all such as handle the harp and organ' [Gen. 4:21]. This supreme art was created in order to integrate the four humors or natural elements of the cosmos, and to balance their conflicting differences." Ibn Ezra thus returns to a theory that was popular in the Middle Ages and was referred to above in reference to Saʿadia Gaon—the concept of harmony as a physical-cosmological equilibrium.

Writings by Jews in Christian Centers

From the third period, which Avenary has called "pre-Renaissance," we possess six original or translated works on music by Jewish authors: one in Latin called "De numeris harmonicis" by Levy ben Gershom (1343), three collections by non-Jewish theoreticians Marcetto de Padua and Jean Vaillant, and a comprehensive article translated into Hebrew from the Latin by Judah ben Isaac ha-Qadosh and a Hebrew translation of al-Fārābī's *Iḥṣāʾ al-ʿulum,* mentioned above, by Kalonimos ben Kalonimos.[32] Thus Jewish literature of this period enjoyed free access to Christian-European sources, could investigate theories dealing primarily with musical training rather than with music as a prerequisite for philosophical studies, and could offer its own theoretical contribution.

At the end of his article "The Science of Music among the Jews in the thirteenth and fourteenth centuries" Avenary writes:

> Let us conclude by saying that the attitude of Jews to general knowledge in the twelfth to thirteenth centuries did not cause a weakening of the national culture, but contributed to its intensification. Literature about music in the Hebrew language was created in order to retrieve the nation's ancient property, restore it to its proper place, and use it as one of the building-blocks in the edifice of Jewish-secular culture. In the intellectual atmosphere that prevailed during those years, the Jews could conceive of establishing their own secular culture alongside their existing religious culture; this would have meant an improvement in their existential situation and a step toward overcoming the stresses and strains of life in the dispersion. (1973, p. 55)

Musical Literature in Italy in the Sixteenth–Seventeenth Centuries

To conclude this chapter we now turn to Italy, beginning with the second half of the sixteenth century and continuing into the seventeenth. This was a glorious period in the cultural life of Italian Jewry; Jews actively participated in the intellectual life of their surroundings and adopted the prevailing modes of expression in art, theater, music, and dance.[33] Some Hebrew texts from this period are still extant; written by rabbis and scholars, most of whom were from the city of Mantua, they evince a conspicuous interest in the art and theory of music.

In his book of homiletics *Nefuzot Yehudah* (The dispersed of Judah) (Adler 1975, pp. 221–39), the rabbi and *darshan* (interpreter-commentator) from the city of Mantua, Yehuda ben Yosef Moscato (1520–90), included a comprehensive discourse on the subject of music. Like all other homiletic commentaries of this type—known as *derush* in Hebrew—this is a nonliteral interpretation of biblical words evoking new ideas and introducing new connotations. Such commentaries, dealing with religious and moral questions and often meant to give spiritual consolation and fortification, were usually delivered at Sabbath services in the synagogue. Many books from various periods contain compilations of these comments. The subject of music appears in Moscato's first *derush,* called *Higgayon bekhinnor*—a discourse on the melody of the lyre[34]—taken from the Sabbath Psalm (92:4). It is very long and deals primarily with the holiday of Simḥat Torah, which celebrates the conclusion of the reading of the Bible as the old years ends. Moscato's treatment touches on many musical subjects: harmony of man and the universe, the music of the spheres, songs of the angels, the source of music, its effect on human beings, the etymology of the term "music," rules of consonance. It is interspersed with quotations from the Scriptures and from the rabbinical literature; from the standpoint of style and of the wide gamut of ideas woven into its fabric, it is typical of this kind of homiletic work.

Generally speaking, the *derush* is organized around a central theme, the message the *darshan* wishes to transmit to his audience. He does this by tying the theme in with matters of immediate concern to the congregation which, in the particular work under discussion here, is Simḥat Torah. The message is a high point near the middle of the *derush,* the idea that belief in God and his teachings is the most perfect music. At the beginning of the *derush* Moscato refers to the invention of music and the laws of the most consonant intervals—the octave, the fifth, and the fourth. He notes that the origin of this knowledge is commonly attributed to the ancient philosopher Pythagoras, who arrived at the definition of these intervals, according to a story quoted by many medieval writers, by accident. The story told that when Pythagoras heard different sounds emanating from a smithy as the blacksmith's hammers beat the anvil, he decided to embark on an empirical investigation of the reason for the changes in pitch. He experimented by studying the weight of each hammer and comparing it with all the others. He found, for example, that the weight of one was twelve pounds, the second nine, the third eight, and the fourth six. Hence, the weight of the first was twice that of the fourth, the value called in Latin *proporzioni doupla* (double proportion) 2/1 and from this he recognized the difference in pitch called in Greek *diapason* and in other languages *Italiano ottava.* Then the other two consonants and their proportions are described in detail: the fifth 3/2 and the fourth 4/3.

Moscato then says that those who believed the legend that Pythagoras was the inventor of music and those who derived their original scientific musical precepts from him strayed far from the path of truth. By virtue of divine testimony it is known that Jubal was the father of all those who "handle the harp and organ." Indeed, development of the science of music may have occurred as recorded in the next passage of the Bible, which tells that Jubal's brother, Tubal-cain, was "the forger of every cutting instrument of brass and iron." He acknowledges that the initial discovery may have been as described in the story of the hammer and anvil, but maintains that the reference is to Jubal, whose brother Tubal-cain was a smith, rather than to Pythagoras.[35] Thus Moscato creates a harmonious combination of two traditions—one from the pagan world and the other from the world of monotheism.

Judith Cohen (1974) discusses this at length. The most important element in Moscato's homily, and the key to his point of view, is the symbolism of the number eight. Simḥat Torah—the joyous conclusion of the reading of the Pentateuch that shows the way to belief in God, is celebrated on Shemini ʿAtseret—the eighth day of the Feast of Tabernacles—which "seals all occasions." This points the way to the pre-eminence of the eighth science, paramount to the seven liberal arts that were the basis of higher education in the Middle Ages: the *trivium* (grammar, rhetoric, logic) and the *quadrivium* (arithmetic, geometry, astronomy, and music). The eighth liberal art, according to Moscato, corresponding to the octave, is considered the most perfect consonant; metaphorically, it represents harmony in the broadest sense, symbolic of the arrangement and balance that prevail in the universe and among human beings. It derives therefrom that belief in God and in His teachings is harmony—in other words, the most perfect music. The rest of the passage involves citations intended to further confirm the symbolic significance of the number eight—a discussion entailing mystical ideas that will be explored in greater detail in chapter 6.

Rabbi Abraham ben David Portaleone was a contemporary of Moscato's who also came from Mantua. He was born in 1542 to a famous family of physicians and, following the family tradition, studied medicine. He inherited his father's position as court doctor to the Duke of Mantua. Due to his position and status Portaleone had an opportunity to become acquainted with the finest musical works of the time composed by men like Gastoldi and Monteverdi. In his old age, following a paralyzing illness and a mental crisis, Portaleone turned to writing. His book *Shields of Mighty Men* (*Shilṭe ha-gibborim*) became a source for knowledge of ancient Hebrew music and instruments that was much quoted in Europe's musical literature (Adler 1975, pp. 245–83). The book has two parts: the first consists of ninety passages and the second of three "shields." The first section is an encyclopedic compendium that deals with many and varied fields of learning: philology, zoology, alchemy, medicine, etc. The second deals with the organization of Temple worship, with sacrifices, prayers, and texts concerning ritual observance.

Ten out of the ninety passages (numbers four to thirteen) and part of the first "shield" are devoted to a description of music in the Temple, the instruments used, and the musical ritual. In this early attempt at a systematic description of the music in the house of worship, the singing of the Levites, and the instruments that accompanied them, most of Porteleone's analysis derived from the musical and aesthetic scene of his own period, which he superimposed on the biblical period. Thus, for example, he identifies the quality of the Levites' singing with that of the Renaissance art song. He attributed a refined, idyllic nature to it, like that of the music performed for the barons and princes of the court in which he served; it had nothing in common with the vulgar quality of the music heard among the ordinary people and peasants. This theory of the refined, ethereal nature of Levite singing seems to have emanated directly from the creative well-springs of Renaissance thought.

The major musical themes treated in the book are the theory and practice of art music in the Temple; instruments proscribed for use in the Temple; wind instruments and their role in the musical ritual; the most perfect instruments for accompanying the Levites; the system of writing notes (based on the tablature of the lute); musicians who served in the holy ritual; musical performance from the Temple *bimah;* and discussion of the nature of biblical cantillation.

The guideline central to Portaleone's outlook has become familiar from several previous discussions: he believed that in the days of David and Solomon, Temple music in Jerusalem reached a peak of eternal perfection. As he conceived it, the Torah of Israel anteceded all the teachings of the Gentiles and was the source from which all classical writers imbibed their wisdom. With the destruction of the Temple and the tragedy of the dispersion, music was forgotten by the Jews. But it was taken over by the learned of other nations who transmitted it from generation to generation until it reached new heights during the Renaissance. On the assumption that Renaissance music was nothing more than a reflection of Temple music, in a way the identity Portaleone finds between Renaissance practice and the practice of the Levites restores its ancient glory and pre-eminent position to music. In the Scriptures and the commentaries, therefore, Portaleone finds support for various musical concepts accepted in his time such as theoretical elements, a notational system, modes, four-part singing, and division into art music and folkloristic music and their accompanying instruments—the lute, viola da gamba, clavichord, harp, organ, trombone, and others.

Descriptions of "biblical" instruments as related to their Renaissance counterparts are presented in great technical detail, substantiated by biblical verses and comments from traditional sources. One example taken from the long chapter on the *kinnor*—which Portaleone identifies with the harp—will suffice as an example. Following a detailed technical description of the instrument's structure and the technique used to play it, the author feels the need to confirm, albeit apologetically, the talmudic legend about David's harp that played by itself at midnight.[36] He gives the legend a realistic touch:

> You should cast no doubt on me or anyone else who says, that the *kinnor* is the instrument called in Italian *arpa,* since there is no other musical instrument which can play by itself when the wind blows. Moreover, all people the world over always portray King David, may he rest in peace, with such an *arpa* in his hand, and never with any other musical instrument of those mentioned in Chapter Five of this Book. Our Rabbis, of blessed memory, said (in tractate *Berakhot,* chapter *me'eymatay,* [b. *Berakhot,* fol. 1;3b]) about the verse "At midnight I will rise to give thanks unto Thee" (Ps. 119:62): "David had a sign; thus said R. Hana bar Bizna in the name of R. Simeon Hasida; a *kinnor* was suspended over David's bed; as soon as midnight arrived, the north wind blew into it and it played itself. David immediately arose and studied the *Torah* until the break of dawn." Now, if one places the *nevel,* the *ʿuggav,* the *minnim* and the rest of the musical instruments facing the wind, they will neither sing nor play. However, if one takes the *arpa* and places it facing the north wind in such a manner that the part which is not the body of the instrument is placed in the

direction of the side from which the north wind blows, and the other part which is the *kinnor* proper, is facing the direction toward which the north wind generally blows, then, when the wind strokes the strings from both sides, it will create a kind of musical whisper; not a particular melody, orderly and distinct, as created intentionally by trained harpists; that would be an absolute miracle, which is unnecessary. Our Lord, blessed be His name, will neither steal from nature nor seek miracles, except as special times, for a very special cause, in order to enhance His name, His glory, and His magnificence.

In this chapter we have attempted to present some of the more difficult problems that confront one who wishes to study the historic dimensions of Jewish music. Examples have been selected from different sources and different historical periods, starting with biblical times and ending with the Renaissance. The Bible is the main and richest source for studying music in Israel in ancient days, while the comprehensive work of R. Abraham Portaleone, *Shields of Mighty Men,* represents the first and most all-inclusive attempt of a Jewish commentator steeped in Renaissance culture, to describe systematically the musical theory, songs, and instruments that were used for ritual purposes in the Temple. Basing his work on biblical texts and Jewish commentaries, Portaleone tried to reconstruct the Temple music in light of the musical theory and practice of his own times. This anachronism can be explained away by the fundamental conviction that the origin of music, as of the other liberal arts, is found in that holiest of all books—the Bible; hence contemporary music with which the author was familiar was merely a reflection of the Temple music. In view of its speculative nature, it is hard to say with any degree of certainty that Portaleone's work made a direct contribution to research into ancient Jewish music. There is no doubt at all, however, that it is important for the insight it offers into the cultural vistas of Italy's Jews during the time the author lived. Moreover, despite some Jewish reservations about the work, Christian historians of music from the middle of the seventeenth century until the end of the nineteenth century have quoted it as a dependable source for information about the music of the Levites in the Temple. Among those scholars are, for example, A. Kircher (1719–89), Ch. Blainville (1711–77), and N. Forkel (1749–1819).

3

Music and Religion

Alien Melodies Encroach on the Prayers

Countless reciprocal threads connect music and religion; as will be shown in this chapter, various aspects of this mutual influence have left their mark on Jewish music from ancient times until today. The infiltration into sacred music of popular secular tunes from the non-Jewish surroundings was facilitated by a natural desire to increase the emotional impact of prayers by adding a musical dimension to them. Yet many religious scholars have felt that tension is created by elaborating the musical element of the prayers and borrowing tunes from sources external to Judaism, as it causes a conflict between religious norms and the desires of the worshippers. With the passage of time, this tension has been expressed in different forms and with varying degrees of intensity.

Turning for a moment to our own days, we can find quite a few contemporary examples of secular tunes penetrating the prayers, and it is interesting to examine the reaction this has evoked. For a number of years following the establishment of the State of Israel, the radio held an annual song contest as one of the events marking Independence Day. The public was asked to choose the ten best songs. As time passed and the quality of the entries deteriorated, the organizers decided to commission a song each year from one of the better-known composers. It would have its first hearing on the holiday, but would not be included in the competition. Thus it transpired that shortly before the outbreak of the Six Day War in 1967, Naomi Shemer's song "Jerusalem of Gold" was heard for the first time. Obviously, subsequent events—the war that broke out almost immediately after the celebrations of that year's Independence Day—had much to do with making "Jerusalem of Gold" one of the most popular songs in Israel. Very soon the melody also crossed the sacred threshold and was absorbed into the repertoires of synagogues representing all shades of Israel's population. The original words, of course, were replaced by words from the prayers or liturgy, such as the Trisagion (*Qedushah*) or "Come my Beloved, Welcome the Sabbath Bride" ("Lekhah dodi"), which ushers in the Sabbath.

What brought this popular secular song into the nation's most hallowed halls? Might this particular melody have been adopted by the synagogue because of its association with the historic event of the liberation of Jerusalem? Was it taken over because of its subject-matter—Jerusalem—a theme celebrated in sacred song by liturgic poets of all generations? Or might there be some quality inherent in the melody itself?

These questions are hard to answer unequivocally because, for one thing, we are not dealing with an isolated case. Many similar examples are known, from both past and present; in other words, the adoption of alien tunes touches on a most complex phenomenon that is not necessarily limited to Jewish music. This is borne out by another example, also from Israel, of something that occurred a short time before Naomi Shemer's song began its metamorphosis. Soon after the Pope visited Israel in 1965, a nun composed a hymn in commemoration of the event, adapting it to the tune of a popular Israeli song: "Go out Girls and See" ("Tsena ha-banot wur'ena"). The original words dealt with girls and soldiers.[1] True, the two cases differ significantly. The first example adopted the tune of a secular song to serve a prayer, while in the second case, despite its religious nature, the song is not liturgical and therefore falls into a less demanding framework. Nevertheless, the fact remains that the melody of a cheerful song about girls and soldiers was chosen as the setting for a hymn to be used by another culture, and the new content is diametrically opposed to that of the original. Can such a popular hit possibly find its way into the realm of prayer? Obviously it can, as further exemplified by the tune that has been borrowed for one of the important prayers, the *Qaddish* (Consecration, or prayer for the soul of the dead). The French song "Chéri je t'aime" (also called "Ya-mustafa," after its Egyptian source) acquired world-wide popularity in the late sixties.[2] Its words are "I love you my dearest, I adore you my dearest"; nevertheless, its tune was adopted to accompany this profoundly pious prayer.

Is it indeed conceivable that these three examples: "Jerusalem of Gold," "Go out Girls," and "Chéri je t'aime" represent a pattern—in other words, that highly popular songs have been adopted as prayer melodies for the very reason of their popularity? This phenomenon may well be widespread in works of a popular nature. Folk bards will set a newly created text to a tune the public knows well, thereby ensuring the text a wide audience. But methods applicable to folk songs are hardly appropriate when the subject is a prayer or religious hymn. Significantly, an Ashkenazi cantor from Alsace (France), discussing the attempt to utilize "Chéri, je t'aime" for synagogue services, described the shock and consternation with which it was greeted by the congregation. As a result, the tune was rejected by the Ashkenazi synagogue. At the same time, however, he described the adoption of other foreign tunes, among them a well known "romansa" that tells of the love between a shepherd and shepherdess. In its new transformation, this music became the melody of the Trisagion (*Qedushah*). When asked in what way the French hit differed from the "romansa," the cantor offered the interpretation that conceived allegorically, the love of the shepherd and shepherdess symbolized the love prevailing between Israel and the Congregation of Israel (*Knesset Yisrael*).[3] Thus in this case an additional element—one not always considered—has influenced the adoption of a hit tune for synagogue use: the content of the text.

From the few examples cited it is clear that in the first place, the complex, multifaceted subject this chapter deals with must be treated from various points of view. Second, the reference is to a perpetual process in the course of which different types of tunes from secular or alien spheres are absorbed into the frame of synagogue music as well as into paraliturgical poetry. In Judaism, paraliturgical songs include Hebrew devotional texts relating to religious precepts that are binding on the individual, even though they are not part of either the prescribed or expanded liturgy. Thus verses dealing with circumcision or bar mitsvah, for example, are included in the paraliturgy. Third, there is a difference of opinion with respect to the process that actually occurs, as well as to the intrinsic nature of the material absorbed.

This may well lead one to question whether all alien songs are potential candidates for absorption into some type of religious music or whether this is determined by certain crucial factors such as the nature of the melody or the essence of the original text associated with it. Is a tune that has been chosen for integration into religious music prepared for its new role by the change in its original function or by the content of the text newly affixed to it? Does it preserve its original identity or must it change either nature or structure in order to adapt to its new environment? Are transformations made to align the melody with paradigms of the ideal type of religious music? In other words, do certain religious melodies embody specific criteria to become the model for the transformation of new tunes? When attempting to answer the above questions it is important to clarify who has the deciding voice in these matters.

The Cantor's Role in Integrating New and Alien Music

Cantors have done more than anyone else to introduce alien tunes into music used in the synagogue—and outside of it as well. The responsibility of the cantor and the *payṭan* (liturgical poet-musician) for the musical aspect of the prayers goes back almost as far as the earliest synagogues. Even then the cantor—who replaced the voluntary lay reader—was one of the most important officials in the house of worship. Learned and fluent in the ritual and liturgy, he must have a pleasant voice and is under contract with the synagogue to lead the prayers. Originally he was a poet who composed and sang his own liturgies and appeared together with the lay reader. As time went on he undertook to lead the regular prayers as well as perform his own liturgies or paraliturgies, thus combining the role of *payṭan* and lay reader.

A *payṭan,* if there is one, performs alongside the cantor but his role is limited to that of a talented singer or poet-musician. He plays no special part in the prescribed prayers but does fill a particular role outside the synagogue. He participates in the performance and writing of paraliturgical and other religious songs. Both the *payṭan* and the cantor use their poetic talents and fine voices to enhance the sacred ritual, their objective being to increase the emotional impact of the prayers. Presumably, the audience is interested in the same objective. The people also influence the services, although in a different direction. They want more than just the passive role of listeners; they want to join actively in the singing. Indeed, certain passages are sung by the whole congregation and for such passages the cantors try to use familiar, or at least less demanding, melodies.

Obviously, the cantors borrowed from whatever was at hand, and some of them seem to have gone too far. Quite early on complaints were heard about the excessive number of alien tunes that were seeping into synagogue music,[4] which makes it clear that the cantor and *payṭan* have not been entirely free to do exactly as they pleased. Even when one or the other of them ignored the limitations the rabbinical authorities wanted to place upon them, other factors like the attitude and reaction of the worshippers and the officials of the synagogue were at work that tended to restrict their freedom of choice. On the whole, these factors were not evoked by musical criteria; there almost seemed to be a conflict of interests between the cantors and the rabbinical authority, and between him and the congregation. The tension between them was not caused only by the introduction of alien melodies, but by a difference in ideological approach as well. Each side had its own particular attitude to the inclusion of music in the ritual; there were times, as will be seen below, when music was rejected on the grounds of principle.

R. Judah al-Ḥarizi was a poet and Hebrew translator in Spain (about 1170–1235) who traveled extensively throughout the Orient. In 1220 he visited Baghdad and recorded his impressions in two (numbers 18 and 24) of the fifty Hebrew-language *maqāmāt*[5] of his book *Taḥkemoni* (The wise one). Al-Ḥarizi is mercilessly critical of a certain cantor-preacher who was also well-known in his community as a musician and poet—a fairly usual combination in those days. He describes the appearance of the cantor and the quality of his singing (ed. 1952, pp. 224–25):

> And here comes the cantor, the phylacteries bound around his forehead. White and handsome, two hundred cubits in size. The hair of his beard reaches his navel. He is draped in a blanket and drags its fringes along the ground, almost tripping over the edges. Upon his appearance we were all overcome with awe and bowed toward him. And we fell silent in fear of him, until he began to sing. And began to pray. And as he prayed I counted more than 100 blatant errors—outside of those not

> worthy of mention. But I said nothing, thinking it might be an accident or panic over the tribulations of the Sabbath. Or perhaps he was dead for sleep.
>
> With the advent of dawn, I rose up to go to the house of worship. And there was the cantor sitting in his great chair. He opened with a hundred blessings, organized and ready on his tongue. And he said in a loud shout, "Blessed be thou O Lord who created man an animal." And in singing he made so many mistakes they cannot be counted. Instead of "from the wicked [*zedim*] too spare thy servant" he said: "from the olives [*zetim*] too educate thy servant" [*vegam mizzedim ḥasokh ʿavdekha—gam mizzetim ḥanokh ʿavdekha*). And instead of: "And may you have an abundance of nectar of the wheat [*ḥelev ḥiṭṭim*]"—"May you have an abundance of sharp swords [*ḥerev ḥaddim*]." And instead of: "he who covers the skies with heavy clouds [*beʿavim*]," he said ". . . with clothing [*begadim*]." And instead of "And May Israel have joy in His deeds" he said "And may Yishmael [Islam] have joy with Esau [Christianity]." And instead of "Praise him with strings [*minnim*] and with organ [*ʿuggav*]" he said: "and praise him with cheeses [*gvinim*] and cake [*ʿuggah*]." And instead of "It is within your power to aggrandize [*legaddel*] and strengthen [*wu-leḥazzeq*] all," "it is within your power to vilify (*legaddef*) and harm (*wu-lehazziq*) all." Until I was deeply ashamed—to the point of regretting having come to the synagogue, but I put my hand over my mouth and was mute. And when he finished his hymns he stood there conducting his paeans of error, and he covered his face, but not in modesty. And stood there proudly, gesticulating, moving his shoulders. And raised his right foot and put it down again. And moved backward a bit and opened the hidden vaults of his wisdom.[6] And brought forth its treasures and began to recite poems and songs, all of them tattered, halt and blind, following round-about paths, without rhyme or meter, without form or content. And then his hymns fit for idiots, his ridiculous canticles fit for nincompoops and his psalms fit for asses went on endlessly. Some of the crowd remained sitting up. Others reclined, sleeping blissfully. And some fled and did not return. They left the synagogue. So the oxen fled from the herdsmen, and the cattle and flocks scattered. And only four asses remained. Bestirring themselves and shouting with the cantor, looking upon themselves as poets. And he dragged his liturgies out for them until noon. Until their tongues stuck to their jaws. And when he completed his liturgies and turned to complete the prayer, there was not a soul in the synagogue. The whole congregation was at home, sleeping.

Then al-Ḥarizi quotes a debate between one man who believes in simple, straightforward prayer with no musical embellishment and another who cites the Levites in the Temple to support his view that music in praise of the Almighty is better than the most devout, heartfelt prayer. Al-Ḥarizi speaks harshly of the quality of work composed by the liturgists and is also highly critical of the tendency to overburden the congregation with excessive musical accompaniment which prolongs the prayers and results in keeping worshippers away. Finally, he mocks the theatrical, frivolous atmosphere of the performance, in that the cantor is assisted by "four poets" (probably a reference to choral rendition).[7]

One of the targets of Judah al-Ḥarizi's criticism is taken to task by other sources as well. For example, the author of *Ḥavvat Ya'ir,* Rabbi Ya'ir ben Moshe Shimshon Bakhrakh[8] writes "The lay readers' lengthy singing of 'yoṣrot' [poetic embellishments added to the prescribed prayers; the first one is incorporated into the blessing "creator of light" in the morning prayer] is harder for me [to accept] than the solemn reading, also because the melodies are many times longer than the verbal passages" (Lemberg Edition, 1886).

From all that has been said above, then, it is clear that the cantor and *payṭan* are the focal point of ritual performance; they are largely responsible for the quality and development of synagogue music. Nevertheless, certain elements actively supervise their work and check them when they overstep what might seem to be conventionally accepted bounds. And indeed, as they represent the congregation, neither the cantor nor the *payṭan* is likely to intentionally flout the values accepted by their public. Hence it may be said that to a great extent the cantor reflects the basic views of his congregation and of the society he belongs to. A congregation that for some reason or other does not want an innovative cantor will reject his innovations. The public's judgment is influenced by ideological positions, but these are not fixed immutably; they represent a broad gamut of viewpoints that sometimes favor aesthetic considerations and sometimes reject them, as we shall see below. In other words, the cantor is answerable to his public, and the stand of both is affected by the rigidity or leniency with which the rabbinical authority is interpreted and the extent of its influence on the public. In any case, the cantor is duty-bound to explain himself, to justify his actions, and, as we have said, he is not entirely free to follow the dictates of his own will.

The late Moshe Vital, the well-known Sephardic cantor of Jerusalem who was born in Izmir (Turkey), studied with the famous Turkish cantor and musician Algazi at the School for Cantors in Rhodes, and in his youth settled in Jerusalem, expresses these matters from the viewpoint of the Sephardic cantor:[9]

> From the artistic and religious standpoint the Sephardic cantor is forbidden to introduce secular songs into the synagogue. In the synagogue one must sing only songs of praise to the Almighty, nothing else. A cantor of ours may occasionally be a secular singer who entertains others with secular songs, but it is most unusual to hear him use the tune of a love song accompanying passages of prayer such as the following examples of some of the verses sung on the Sabbath and holy days: the Consecration or prayers for the soul of the dead [*Qaddishim*] and the Trisagion [*Qedushah*], "Joyously they go forth" [*Semeḥim betsetam*], "Thou shalt be crowned" [*keter yittenu lekhah*]. He may permit himself to do so only if the tune is not familiar to the congregation. I, for example, know some lighter refrains, *coplas* (couplets of religious themes that are not included in the accepted liturgy)[10] that the congregation does not recognize, and those I can incorporate into the *Qedushah* of holy days, of the three pilgrimage festivals, Passover, etc. The congregation does not know from where I have taken the refrain, does not know its source. It simply has a slight resemblance to the *maqām* [mode or melody type] of that day's prayer."[11]

(As a matter of course, Sephardic Jewry recited all the passages of the Sabbath prayer in the specific *maqām* adapted to each particular Sabbath.)

Thus we see that according to Moshe Vital, the adoption of new melodies involves three principles:

1. Introducing secular songs into the synagogue is forbidden, but the cantor may sing such songs on festive occasions and outside of the framework of the prayers. He was referring to an example such as the *coplas* (couplets) of Joseph the Pious (telling the biblical story of Joseph) which to a great extent conform with this principle in that their Jewish subject matter gives them a suitably pious nature.

2. The use of new melodies is contingent on their anonymity: They must be unfamiliar to the public. That is, they may be used on condition that the congregation cannot identify their source. This principle obviously conflicts with the examples of popular secular songs referred to at the beginning of this chapter.

3. The melody of the original song is adapted to the characteristic mode of the particular day. Here for the first time an artistic musical component rooted entirely in the secular world is adduced and it appears to conflict with the cantor's first principle.

The Hasidim in eastern Europe evolved an interesting theory in relation to the adoption of alien tunes, as indicated by the following quotation:[12]

"The story is told by the Karlin Hasidim that at the funeral of Tzar Nikolai, the rabbi's son who would some day inherit his father's rabbinical post, the rabbi, and Zadik R. Israel of blessed memory, were all standing together with a few disciples. During the funeral a certain song was sung that the rabbi told his disciples would be worthwhile adopting; it would be good for singing the psalm consecrating the House of David. And until today it is customary to sing that song during the Ḥanukkah festival or when celebrating a house-warming."

This obviously was not just a few lone individuals surreptitiously exceeding the bounds of convention, nor was it an attempt to justify gleaning in alien fields, nor a case of some cantor seeking to publicize his talent. All is purposeful, open, and above-board. It is the rabbi who proclaims the alien tune worthy of being chosen and he is the one who issues instructions to incorporate it into his repertoire. His disciples, considering themselves redeemers in that they recognized the "holy sparks" in the foreign folk song, created collections of "tikkunim"—songs "redeemed" from an impure existence. These were new, reprocessed variations, in which entire passages were sometimes added. The renovated prayer was looked upon as bringing salvation, and therefore as more important than the usual prayer. The adopted tune was processed as a hymn of praise, its desirable "holy sparks" were reinforced, and it too was "redeemed." The process of change, grounded in ethical, mystical intentions, essentially changed the borrowed song's style. This particular conception is unique in that there is total ideological support of the very act of absorbing and changing alien songs. Hence it involves neither conflict nor apologetics.

The Attitude of Rabbinical Authorities to Alien Melodies

As indicated above, religious authorities have had reservations about incorporating musical elements into the ritual and on occasion have expressed outright objection. In discussing the extent and sources of this negative attitude, it is essential to clarify whether its only cause was the desire to prevent the secular from invading the realm of the sacred, or whether there was a principled objection to the inclusion of any music at all within the frame of religious ritual. In other words, the crucial question is whether the objection is inherent in music's very nature or can be attributed to entirely extraneous factors.

Yehudah Ratzabi (1966) cites multiple significant quotations that reflect the views of people well versed in the Bible and traditional law. Stressing their persistent objection to alien melodies, he introduces the theme as follows:

> Long ago, as far back as the time of the Second Temple, sages and scholars disapproved the Greek songs that were heard in the sanctuaries of Israel, as they considered them pagan. Of Elisha ben-Abuya who left the fold and followed evil ways, they used to say that he never ceased singing Greek songs (Bavli, Ḥagiga, 15,23). In the Gaonic period the influence of alien music increased throughout Israel's congregation in the Islamic countries, pursuant to the similarity of language and culture, and also due to the belief in the close relationship of the two peoples. From this period onward, generation after generation, judges and interpreters of traditional law have concerned themselves with the music of Ishmael.

It is clear, therefore, that alien influences were already filtering into Jewry in ancient times; they became more pervasive during the long period of dispersion which meant constant exposure to surrounding non-Jewish musical cultures. Theoretically, then, there are the following three possibilities:

1. Conceivably, there is special, appropriate Jewish religious music with roots reaching back to the period before the dispersion; in other words, some sort of ancient, archaic model exists—such as the music used in the Temple or in the earliest synagogues.

2. Music of all kinds is totally excluded from religious ritual.

3. There is a kind of music that is ideally suited for the role assigned it within the framework of the ritual, a kind intrinsically different from prevailing forms of secular music.

These possibilities are all closely bound up with the fundamental question of whether music has a special meaning in the religious sphere or simply serves to emphasize the message embedded in the text it embellishes.

Thus, from a different perspective we arrive at the same question raised previously: Are the reasons for objecting to music in religious services inherent in the very nature of music, or are they to be found in extraneous factors such as dispersed

Jewry's absorption of alien tunes during the long sojourn in foreign lands? The attempt to answer this principal question confronts us with great difficulty: available sources dealing more thoroughly with these matters generally relate to the receiving end of the process, in this case with the listener and how he absorbs and is influenced by the music. In other words, only very rarely do the sources at our disposal deal with the special message that may be an intrinsic part of the music itself; they are concerned even less frequently with the performer, the person responsible for transmitting the message.

Grief over the Temple's Destruction Rules out Music

Mourning for the destruction of the Temple is one of the main extrinsic reasons given for the proscription of music, a reason that appears in most relevant texts and has pervaded centuries of Jewish history. The most ancient source adduced by specialists in interpreting the traditional law and by commentators is the 137th Psalm, in which the Levites chant

> By the rivers of Babylon,
> There we sat down, yea, we wept,
> When we remembered Zion.
> Upon the willows in the midst thereof We hanged up our harps.
> For there they that led us captive asked of us words of song,
> And our tormentors asked of us mirth:
> 'Sing us one of the songs of Zion.'
> How shall we sing the Lord's song
> In a foreign land?

Although the subject of this Psalm is the destruction of the First Temple, it was later construed as referring to the destruction of the Second Temple as well. In his commentary on the Book of Psalms, R. Saʿadia Gaon maintains that the Levites ceased singing because their musical role depended on the fulfillment of three basic conditions: a site—the Temple in Jerusalem; a function—assisting at worship in the Temple; and finally, a status—responsibility as Levites for the singing. With the destruction of the Temple these three conditions disappeared as did the singing associated with them. The implication is that for objective reasons, as it were, the music used in the Temple did not survive in the Diaspora. But might it have been replaced by other prayer music used in the Temple alongside the Levites' songs, music that may have been more suitable for the new circumstances? The sources do not deal with these questions, which makes it impossible to answer them definitively. However, a discussion of the concept of mourning can serve as the point of departure for further pursuit of certain aspects of them. Since grieving over the Temple's destruction is the main reason given for forbidding the use of music—a reason that has spawned numerous divergent and even extremely polarized positions—it has direct relevance for the discussion.

One of the most cogent expressions of an extreme position appears in a booklet published fairly recently (1969) called *El gil kaʿammim* (from Hosea 9:1: "Rejoice not, O Israel, . . . as other people").[13] The book is divided into sections that allegedly include a distillation of everything that has been or can be said in Jewish traditional literature about the prohibition of music. In his introductory words the author complains of the decline in spiritual norms that has paralleled the rising standard of living; he bemoans the enthusiasm for "the music heard today in most of the homes in Israel," and then stresses that "to our regret we have already reached a situation in which the radio and transistor are looked upon as essential accoutrements even within ultra-orthodox circles that are considered devoted to biblical learning." Further on the author devotes a special chapter to technical innovations in the realm of electro-acoustical equipment and quotes a new rabbinical proscription. But even before this section, there is a reference to Rabbi Diskin and Rabbi Sonnenfeld, who headed orthodox Jewry earlier in the century. They decreed that the radio, phonograph, and tape-recorder are in the same category as musical instruments, since they too emit music. As both prohibitions and sanctions must have the support of traditional law, the author cites numerous scriptural statutes as well as the writings of renowned rabbinical authorities. The following quotations are of significant relevance here:

"When the Temple was destroyed it was decreed not to play any instrument of music or sing any songs and all who sing songs are forbidden to be joyful and it is forbidden to let them be heard because of the destruction, as written: 'The elders have ceased from the gate, the young men from their music.' (Lam. 5:14) and song is forbidden to cross the lips unless it is in praise of the Almighty." This prohibition, based on the end of the talmudic Soṭah, Maimonides, and all the interpreters of the traditional law, is recorded in Eliezer Azikri (1601). The author continues with a quotation from *Yosef Omets* (1929) by Rabbi Joseph Han-Nordlingen (d. 1637):[14]

"And above all, musical instruments are forbidden at feasts; they are prohibited even if there is no feast." "Hence," pursues the anonymous author, "how important it seems to me to absolutely forbid the rich to hire one who knows how to play an instrument to teach their daughters, as this is for no purpose other than to give them pleasure and make them haughty." The first quotation, which is not the only one of its kind in this collection of religious ordinances, stresses the motivating force behind the prohibition—mourning for the destruction of the Temple. Indeed, this is the subject of the first chapter, which covers several pages. The mourning must be real and perpetual, apparent even in circumstances calling for joy such as that evoked by a bridal celebration. At all times one must share in Israel's sorrow and never forget that the divine presence (*Shekhinah*) has been exiled from the land. Throughout the discussion music in all forms is identified with joy—the very antithesis of grief. Joy and music are for the future, for the time of total redemption, as in the passage "Then was our mouth filled with laughter and our tongue with singing" (Ps. 126:2).

This stern approach conflicts with the basic outlook of Hasidism which particularly stressed joy in worship of God and ecstasy induced by song and dance. The following passage castigates proponents of the Hasidic view:

> How very bad, how unbearable is the action of those men or women who assemble together to bask in the joy of friendship on the departure of the Sabbath [the reference is to the *melavveh malkah,* the festive singing that accompanies the departure of the Sabbath][15] and on all the other nights. [This is] particularly [so] in winter when there is much vain joy and music and drinking and playing and amorous singing—and alien songs are sung and woe be to them for surely their joy will turn to sorrow, if not in this world then in the world to come, if they will not give thought to repentence. . . .
>
> And in Jerusalem the prohibitions are all infinitely harsher because the [Temple's] destruction is before the eyes of the people of Jerusalem and woe to one whose dead lies before him.

Those who violate these prohibitions are warned of severe punishment either in this world or in the world to come. This type of literature makes extensive use of passages from the Gemarra that deal with punishment. Two such passages from the tractate *Soṭah,* "The ear that hears song will be torn off" and "Song in the house, desolation in the house," are quoted time and again to support traditionally grounded opposition to the use of music.

Thus we find that throughout the centuries, mourning over the destruction of the Temple is referred to as a factor of prime importance in proscribing musical instruments of all sorts. This prohibition is never violated in the framework of synagogue ritual, with the exception of synagogues belonging to the Reform movement. It is less strictly observed and sometimes completely ignored when certain religious elements are involved in events taking place in homes or even in synagogues on weekdays or at the close of the Sabbath.

The Yemenite community has been consistent in its refusal to use musical instruments; to accompany dancing on festive occasions Yemenite Jews beat on oil cans and copper trays which are not looked upon as instruments. More recently a variety of drums have been introduced into their celebrations, but the Yemenite Jews still refuse to permit the use of melodical instruments. In this case, of course, there is no absolute proof that the destruction of the Temple is the reason for avoiding the use of such instruments. Many Islamic theologists and religious authorities have forbidden the playing of instruments. There are places where this prohibition has been violated, but in Yemen it seems to have been strictly observed. We know definitely, however, that no type of instrumental music was popular enough there to either directly or indirectly influence the Yemenite Jews, or to be used by them as a model.

With this one exception, however, no Jewish community in the Diaspora has refrained from hiring musicians—whether Jewish or not—to add to the festivities on joyous occasions. To some extent these lapses have been carefully ignored, but from time to time rabbinical authorities have let their objection to the use of musical instruments be heard. An early document on this subject is the response of Rabbi Hai Gaon to the Jews of Gabes in Tunisia in which he came out explicitly against secular love songs, songs extolling an individual, etc.[16]

Music as a Force Evoking Joy

Although mourning over the destruction of the Temple is cited as a reason for refraining from the use of music or any of its related arts, in actual fact this has nothing to do with the realm of music. Had the Temple not been destroyed, can we assume that the problem would not have arisen? On the surface, that would seem to be so, but the matter is actually much more complicated. Another set of rationales enters into the discussion about forbidding or permitting music. For example, the passage quoted above from *El gil ka'ammim,* leans toward value judgment, tending to discuss the problem in accordance with criteria applicable to the inherent nature and influential power of music. In the long run this value judgment leads to divergent, even conflicting, positions that run the entire gamut of possibilities—from permitting all music to forbidding all music. In the latter case music has become identified with the concept of joy which—broadly construed—can include thoughtlessness, distraction, and entertainment in the deprecatory sense associated with taverns, drinking parties, etc. These polarized positions are expressed in the two quotations that follow, the first from *El gil ka'ammim,* the second from the great Hasidic figure Rabbi Nachman of Bretslav.

> A person who fears the word of the Almighty shares the sorrow of Israel and is pained because the Divine Spirit has, so to speak, been sent into exile. How can it be gratifying and enjoyable for him to amuse himself with the pleasure of hearing the sound of music? For in truth, we have been greatly impoverished and none amongst us knows what we lack and what we have lost and what we have caused in the evil world and what the exile of the Divine Spirit means and the extent of its sorrow and the sorrow of those above and below; for this all the anguished will grieve. . . . Indeed, it is good that we remain close to the hearth weeping and moaning like a woman over the spouse of her youth, like a lone mourner; perhaps the Lord will look down and pity his people and again gladden us as the groom gladdens the bride and then we shall be happy and joyful. (*El gil Ka'ammim,* pp. 11–15)

Such advocacy of unremitting gloom and mourning until the day of redemption is very far from the Hasidic approach that in essence preaches worshipping God with joy and believes in a close connection between music and spiritual uplift, mystical ecstasy, and "restoration" of the world. In the teachings of R. Nachman of Bretslav, for example, music fills a central and very important role. R. Nachman (1772–1870), whose followers are known as the Bretslav Hasidim, was one of the most outstanding and original thinkers of the Hasidic movement. A writer of tales, he was also known for his special attitude to and profound interest in music as part of ritual worship. As he perceived it (1951, pp. 229, 272), music brings a person nearer to serving the Almighty and to the joyful experience of aspiring to ecstatic fulfillment: "By means of song you will achieve joy and ecstasy"; "One who is fearful will allay his fears with songs of joy"; "And faith too has its own special songs." Sadness, on the other hand, puts distance between man and his God, which coincides with the words of the Zohar:

> For indeed we see that the Divinity is not present in a place of sadness but in a place in which there is joy. Where there is no joy, the Divinity does not rest. And it is written: "But now bring me a minstrel. And it came to pass, when the minstrel played, that the hand of the Lord came upon him" [2 Kings 3:25]. How else do we know that the Divine Spirit is not present in the abode of sadness? From the story of Jacob who was deserted by the Divine Spirit because he was sad about Joseph, and the moment the news of Joseph brought him joy: "The spirit of Jacob their father revived" [Gen. 45:27].

According to this approach, then, only joy brings one close to the Almighty, and the joy inherent in the sound of music can improve the world. Moreover, sadness is identified with wailing, which emanates from evil. R. Nachman writes: "Thus most of the evil make mournful, wailing music for they are a motly multitude and the mother of this teeming multitude is Lilith [a legendary figure considered one of the devil's minions. The Talmud describes Lilith as a long-haired seductress]. She wails constantly and therefore their music is baleful." It is important to note that according to R. Nachman, in Bretslav they introduced "the custom of applauding during prayers and dancing with joy every day after prayers; for by dancing and clapping hands the Masters of Judges (Prosecutors) [*dayyanim*] are appeased."

The spirit here is altogether different from the wrathful temper of *El gil kaʿammim*. In this regard it is very interesting to trace the similarity of the Hasidic approach to that of some of the Oriental rabbis. Rabbi Mordechai Abadi, a poet and musician who lived in Aleppo, Syria in the nineteenth century, writes in the chapter "The Virtue of Song" included in his book *Miqra Qodesh* (1873, p. 28): "Through the tunes you intone you rouse Almighty God to look upon this people for whom you make music and see how enslaved it is. And indeed the poets who came before us, and those of our own day, would take alien melodies and sanctify them by turning them into songs [in praise of] the Lord."[17]

The Concept of Music in Religious Doctrine

The taste and intellectual proclivities of the members of any given society are reflected in music, one of the most fundamental attributes of a culture. Religious doctrine, too, takes cognizance of music's pivotal role and therefore does not conceive of it as functioning in some separate sphere in conformity with exclusive criteria; nor are musicians free to do as they please. Thus religious music is an integral part of the general fabric of theological thought and is contingent on the meaning given by the religious authorities to the way people looks upon themselves and their place and purpose in the universe. That being the case, it is important to view attitudes to music in their broadest context and to examine them as part and parcel of the basic concepts of religious doctrine. In a way, the doctrine thereby becomes both guideline and critic of the faith and actions of those who have bound their destiny to it. Basic doctrinal tenets, however, do not always offer a clear, unequivocal approach to the concept of music, and elucidation must be sought in the comments of recognized interpretive authorities.

From the foregoing sections of this chapter it is quite clear that there is tension and often friction between musical activity and the proponents of religious doctrinal laws. Does this mean that there may be a conflict of values and interests between musical concepts and basic doctrinal concepts? The point of departure for an analysis of the tension seems to lie in the powerful influence wielded by music. Recognizing music's effective role in daily life, the sources stress its tremendous, overwhelming power. This almost magical power can evoke sensual reactions, can move people so intensely that they lose themselves in ecstasy, cannot think rationally, and abandon themselves to great emotional excitement. A state of such trance-like intoxication of the senses certainly can be construed as conflicting with purposeful, clear-headed worship.

On page 47 of *El gil ka'ammim* the anonymous author writes:

> The very basis of Hasidism and the root of pure worship is to confirm a man's obligation to the world around him. . . . And this is what our sages of blessed memory have taught us: that man was created only to take pleasure in God and to enjoy the glory of his Divine Presence, which is the true pleasure and the greatest of all available delights. The more so in that by their very nature song and gaiety are prohibited in principle and lead to all sorts of vain delusions, and through them one is swept away with the noisy, unruly multitude by meaningless loud sounds and the clanging of cymbals [a play on the words of the 150th Psalm "Praise him with the loud-sounding cymbals; Praise him with the clanging cymbals"]. [All this is] for the sole purpose of enjoying gaiety and the pleasures of the flesh—following the maxim "eat, drink . . . for tomorrow we will die," taking no stock of the purpose of life or of our precious time like the hyena who emits musical sounds by means of which it attracts humans to its lair, where, as is known, it traps and devours them.

From this passage we learn that:

1. Music distracts the mind from concentrating on the one important thing, that is, on prayer and a man's obligation in this world (as implied in "The very basis of Hasidism and the root of pure worship").

2. Music evokes sensual feelings of enjoyment that conflict with true pleasure, which is essentially intellectual (as implied in "to take pleasure in God and the glory of his Divine Presence").

3. The outcome of sensual pleasures is debauchery and thoughtlessness.

4. The magic spell is exemplified by the hyena who traps his victim in his lair.

5. The prohibition itself is the essence of the matter as in the statement: "by their very nature song and gaiety are prohibited in principle." That is to say, the prohibition against song and gaiety being an inseparable part of the traditional law, the issue is not open to argument at all. Here the author cites Maimonides, who maintained that music is prohibited not because of the destruction of the Temple, but because it can give rise to debauchery and thoughtlessness. (Maimonides's approach to music will be discussed more fully below.)

The Origin of Music According to the Homiletic Commentaries

The question of origin figures significantly in a discussion of the different ways in which music is perceived. An important debate on this issue is found in the commentaries on the stories in Genesis, particularly those connected with Jubal, "the father of all such as handle the harp and pipe" (Gen. 4:21) and his family. First of all, it should be noted that according to the *Midrash Hag-gadol* (1947, 1, p. 126),[18] Jubal invented not only the two instruments explicitly mentioned but all musical instruments, and was even the originator of the art of singing. This means that he was the inventor of music as a whole, from which we derive that music is an invention of humankind and takes its place among other human inventions such as the brass and iron tools devised by Jubal's brother, Tubal-Cain. The textual proximity of music and iron leads to speculation about a possible connection between music and armaments or between the sounds of iron and of music. Various cultures are known to identify the sounds made by iron with those emitted by Satan, or, on the other hand, with the din made to keep the devil at bay.[19]

In the midrashic literature we find another association that is relevant here: music is associated with corruption and moral degeneracy. Ginzberg (1968, 1, pp. 79) reports that Jubal, the inventor of music, is one of the sons of Cain, who was said to have been "a leader in corrupt acts . . . and so too were his progeny." It was said of Naʿama "that she would please people by playing loudly on cymbals and lured them to worship alien gods. . . . the ministering angels mistook her wonderous beauty and were attracted, led *astray* and trapped." Thus according to *Pirqe Rabbi Eliezer* (chap. 22), with song, dance, and intoxicating drink, Cain's female progeny seduce the pure offspring of the sons of Seth, the hill-dwellers: "And when they ascended the holy mountain they plucked the strings of the harp, blew the trumpets, beat the drums, sang and danced and clapped their hands, and succeeded in seducing the 520 sons of Seth who were thereby corrupted." The result was the deluge that was meant to destroy that entire tainted generation. These commentaries linked together music, earthly physical love, and wine. In this way, we believe, they established the basic conception that music has great seductive power and a magical influence over the senses that cannot be withstood. Belief in this occult power gave rise to the association of music with Satan, who figures prominently in Christian and Muslim literature of the Orient.

In any event, once the art of music is considered as a creation of human beings, it is perceived as embodying the hubris and insubstantiality of man. Its role is seen as irreconcilable with the fundamental moral and theological demands of a religion that proclaims the omnipotent rule of one God. The sole sovereignty of the transcendental God is challenged the moment music is seen as akin to satanic magic that enables the devil to control and direct the deeds and wishes of human beings. And when music is considered from the standpoint of its overwhelming power, it is found to have much in common with those magical powers that can effectively "force" themselves on the individual; religious elements, on the other hand, must be "served" or sought. In contrast to the forces of magic, religious forces are described as possessing the ability to guide and determine a man's fate. Hence, one who adopts the fundaments of this view in toto necessarily arrives at the conclusion that all forms of musical expression must be rejected.

From the standpoint of actual practice, this conclusion has not been completely borne out, as cantillation has never been rejected. It remains absolutely true, however, with regard to traditional religious conceptions about music by composers who apply the same rules and aesthetic principles that govern all music written in the hope of eliciting a favorable audience reaction. The problem exists even when the sole purpose of the melody—or the composer—is to serve a chosen text, be it a prayer or any other ritual material: the many kinds of religious music offer a much broader variety of musical possibilities than only cantillation. Were this variety to be placed along an imaginary line, at one end we would find simple, spontaneous works, very close to declamations, and at the other, creations so sophisticated as to be almost indistinguishable from art music. The very simple type of work is not generally considered worthy of inclusion in the concept of music. Indeed, it is variously described as readings, recitations, etc. Today music scholars ordinarily use the term "cantillation" to distinguish this type from more complex, organized musical compositions. Some consider cantillation as the most typical, most unadulterated expression of religious music. Moreover, as stated, in view of the fact that the musical element of cantillation is secondary and is intended to serve the text, it is accepted—either openly or tacitly—even by the most extreme opponents of music.

Conceptual Tenets as Mirrored in Reality

Essentially, the most extreme viewpoint has been held only by a minority and therefore has not had the field all to itself. There have been other conceptions, above all the approach epitomized by the world of the Kabbalah, which through the years has profoundly influenced the thinking of many people. This approach is based on belief in the tremendous power of music and its far-reaching effect on the human spirit. As against those who attribute the invention of music to Jubal, the Kabbalists maintain that music stems from more than one source and its influence is multifaceted. Because of the importance of this view and the role it has played in the development and enrichment of music, chapter 6 will be devoted to it.

A degree of flexibility was first manifested when paraliturgical music is used outside the synagogue to enhance joyous family events and holidays such as Purim, the Passover week, Sukkot—was greeted with toleration. Reality, in these cases, seems to have been stronger than ideology; people felt they should forget, even if only for a short time, the drabness and afflictions of the dispersion and on happy occasions released their pent-up tensions. Traditional religious texts were expanded to include secular songs and even instrumental music. In an early text about music, R. Hayya b. Sherira Gaon (939–1038) of Pompedita was asked why "it was usual here in the homes of the bride and groom to play drums and dance and invite non-Jews[20] who bring happiness with the harp, violin, and organ [*nevel, kinnor,* and *ʿuggav*—biblical names for instruments that were popular during the writer's time]; whether it is permitted or forbidden, and whether or not it matters which instrument is used."[21] The Gaon answers by forbidding secular love songs, and allowing laudations in honor of God, forbidding women to sing and dance in male society, and permitting only drums. The substance of this responsum was quoted by one of the greatest traditional legal scholars, R. Yitsḥaq al-Fasi (1013–1103) in his authoritative talmudic compendium. In a response to a question regarding the misbehavior of a cantor (1884, no. 281), al-Fasi went so far as to equate the song of Ishmael (i.e., Muslims) with obscene speech, and rules that if the cantor takes any part in such singing at feasts and festivities he is to be dismissed and is not to be permitted to pass before the Holy Ark. And yet, despite this extreme view, expressed in many other sources as well, it emerges that outside of the synagogue the prohibition against music was not actually put into practice. The people felt the need to enhance their festive occasions with song and music—and created facts that were hard to ignore. This situation may well have been the cause of the profusion of commentaries and variety of practical approaches suggested. Such commentaries encompass a number of all-inclusive viewpoints, as discussed in detail below.

Singing Inside and Outside the Synagogue

A fundamental distinction is drawn between songs sung in the synagogue and those sung outside it. The latter can be divided into two subcategories: the first is songs with religious content—paraliturgical songs—as against general festive songs; the second is songs with instrumental accompaniment and those without. In both cases, whether the general festive songs have instrumental accompaniment or not, there is disagreement indirectly touching on the overall question of the use of secular, particularly art, music.

Songs in Hebrew: With respect to questions of text, it is obvious and generally agreed that songs inside the synagogue must be sung in Hebrew. From the answer given by Rabbi Hayya Gaon and from the comments of many others, it appears that theoretically the same applies to songs sung outside the synagogue, although in reality, this is not so. But is it enough for the words to be in the holy language for a song to be considered permissible? Certainly not. The content of the text too must be appropriate in that it must clearly serve religious purposes.

What the Melody Expresses

Discussions of this aspect are extremely rare. First of all, it is important to clarify the associations connected with the early role of song. They involve the proscription of two main types: love songs and prayer tunes used specifically for non-Jewish religious ritual: "tunes played for idolatrous worship." The same prohibition pertains to letting Israel's religious melodies be heard by non-Jews. *Sefer Ḥasidim* (The book of the pious) (ed. 1924) by Judah he-Ḥasid (died in 1217), founder and leader of Ashkenazic Hasidism, states that just as one may not let music that is used for idolatrous worship be played before the Lord Almighty, so it is forbidden to perform a pleasing Jewish song before a non-Jewish priest, as he might incorporate it into his own ritual. As against Rabbi Judah he-Ḥasid's opinion, another wise scholar, Rabbi Israel Moshe Ḥazzan (1886) who lived in the nineteenth century, and served in Jerusalem's High Religious Court, maintained that alien music is permitted, even if it is used in non-Jewish houses of worship: "Is it conceivable that because profligate fools brought them into the house of worship, we are forbidden [to use] something that we instinctively approve?" The practice of learned cantors of his time in the city of Smyrna[22] gave support to his basic position that an attractive melody should not be prohibited just because non-Jews use it as part of their ritual.

> And I testify by heaven and earth that when I was in Smyrna, the great city of scholars and mystics, I saw some of the outstanding religious authorities who were also great creators of the science of music, headed by the wonderful Rabbi Abraham Ha-Cohen Ariash of blessed memory, who secretly used to go (behind the screen) in the Christian church on their holy days to learn the special melodies from them and to adapt them to the High Holiday prayers which require great humility. And from those same melodies they would arrange the most remarkable blessings and holy prayers, and it is clear from this that the tune is not of the essence, but the sacred words. There is a decisive argument that this is so for otherwise from whence would our pleasing tunes and voices come, since we have forgotten the songs of David and the songs of the Levites on the podium and, as is written: "How shall we sing the Lord's song in a foreign land?" Wherever Israel was dispersed we learned the music of the countries in which we settled. And in the Land of Israel and in the Arab coun-

> tries the melodies of the prayers and blessings and all the dedications are in accordance with the Arab tunes and in Turkey and Turkish tunes, and in Edom [countries under Christendom] in accordance with the voices of Edom. And who can deny that which can be demonstrated? Is it to be said that all of Israel erred, heaven forbid, by taking the utmost care to ensure that the language for serving and praising the Almighty, blessed be He, should be the holy language?" (1886, no. 10, fol. 4)

The rabbi's comment with respect to adapting melodies from the Christian church to the High Holiday prayers is most interesting. He is undoubtedly referring to the neo-Byzantine style that crystallized in the nineteenth century and acquired a dominant position in the Greek church.[23] It is also of particular interest to note that the erudite rabbi expresses rather bold ideas about the identity and sources of Jewish music, which were discussed in our first chapter.

Rabbi Ḥazzan's words as quoted above seem to supplement and support the views on this issue expressed by Rabbi Obadia Yosef, former Chief Sephardic Rabbi of Israel, and at present the spiritual leader of the Sephardi Orthodox Party *Shas,* in his *Responsa* (1976, 6, pp. 18–21):

"I have been asked if it is permissible for the cantor to graft the melody of a sensual secular song on to the blessings and commemorative or other prayers such as 'All things that live and breathe . . .' or whether a distinction must be drawn between the holy and the mundane. To the extent that approval is implicit, is it permissible to modify the text to fit the melody?" In the learned answer given by Rabbi Yosef, he makes an interesting distinction between *manginah* (melody) and *qol* (voice), which is interpreted as melody and text combined. The melody in and of itself is something abstract, or as the rabbi says: "a mere melody in which there is nothing tangible." Only the text makes it concrete and meaningful. Moreover, removing the melody from its original context is likened to the performance of a good deed (*mitsvah*): "and on the contrary, . . . it is a *mitsvah* to do so, and implies sanctification of God's name in that something has been transferred from the realm of the profane to the realm of the sacred"—a concept touched on above in connection with aspects of Hasidic ideology.

As Rabbi Yosef sees it, the transfer gives the melody a new countenance but only on condition that "the cantor chooses the songs . . . out of the purest motives, to praise and sing to the Lord, blessed be He. . . . The reference here is to the deepest inner motives, for the cantor who is glad at heart that he has been privileged to praise and thank the Almighty in a fine, pleasing voice and whose joy is awe-inspired, will be blessed. A fine, pleasant voice is an essential requirement for one who stands before the Ark of the Torah . . . but if it is his [the cantor's] intention that the congregation acclaim him personally for his beautiful voice, why, that is reprehensible."

This suggests that such musical activity is much closer in spirit to cantillation than to art music. Convincing evidence to that effect can be found in the part of the answer that deals with increasing the number of measures or going beyond the text of the prayer by introducing melodic passages and extraneous ornamentation for the sole purpose of embellishment. The rabbi warns against such practices and against excessive lengthening of bars, for fear that the word will lose its meaning, because it is "the foolish way of cantors who, to give their voices the opportunity to be heard, break every word into tiny fragments, so that not the word but the voice is heard, etc."

In conclusion, the rabbi refers to the extremely important musical issue of adapting borrowed tunes to texts. Such adaptation must be done to suit the text rather than the music: "not according to the rhythm of the secular tune; the cantors contort the meaning of a verse, put the accent on the ultimate syllable, whereas it should be on the penultimate . . . and these are boorish inversions, the way fools sing; they transform the words of the living God and subordinate the prayers and blessings to a secular tune." The borrowed tune, then, is redeemed and endowed with new life both by subordinating it to the new words and by its musical content and structure.

Musical Instruments

It seems that with respect to instruments, particularly in the framework of synagogue music, the most severe prohibitions have always prevailed. They have been strictly observed in all synagogues except those belonging to the Reform and Liberal trends. The only instrument that has always been used in all congregations is the shofar—the ram's horn, blown during the High Holiday prayers. The use of the shofar clearly contains vestiges of a magical rite, as has been explained in chapter 2. Nonconformist movements emerged during the eighteenth century and prospered in Amsterdam's Portuguese-Jewish community, in the four communities of southern France—Carpentras, Avignon, Cavaillon, and L'isle de Sorge—as well as in northern Italy. In all these communities general art music invaded the synagogue ritual and compositions in contemporary style were even commissioned for certain Hebrew texts.[24] During the nineteenth century the Reform movement developed in central and western Europe and then moved on to various centers in the United States. Among other things, this movement introduced the organ and the mixed male and female choir into the synagogue.

In almost all literature dealing with musical instruments in the synagogue, the prohibition was applied first and foremost to those used for performing art music, particularly string instruments. The poet and philosopher R. Mosheh Ibn Ezra (Spain, circa 1055–1135) discussed the use of musical instruments in his *Book of the Garden* (*Kitāb al-ḥadīqa*) which is devoted in the main to philological, philosophical, and theological interpretations and comments evoked by the metaphors in the biblical books. With respect to instruments he wrote:

"Not all musical instruments are capable of influencing the rational mind. Only those among them that are convex and have strings (similar to the lute) are likely to inspire the soul. All the other instruments are used for sundry joyous occasions as has been told about the Ark of God in 1 Chron. 13:8: 'And David and all Israel played before God with all their might; even with songs, and with harps, and with psalteries, and with trumpets' (Shiloah, 1982). Ibn Ezra would seem to be making a distinction between art music and folk music. The convex instruments which move the listener to philosophical inspiration are those that resemble the *ʿūd,* the consummate art instrument.

A similar view with respect to the role of string instruments is found in commentaries on Plato's *Republic* by the Spanish Arab Ibn Rushd Averroës (1126–98), one of the greatest of the Islamic philosophers in Spain. The original commentary has been lost but its Hebrew translation, rendered in the thirteenth century by Shmuel ben-Yehuda of Marseille, is still extant. Ibn Rushd says (with respect to what Islamic culture prohibits or permits, "the *mizmār* [an instrument similar to the oboe, used in folk music] is forbidden, the *ʿūd* and *miʿzafa* [two important string instruments used for art music] are permitted" (Adler 1975, pp. 102–4).

These two citations represent a divergent view and can be traced back to Greek philosophy, particularly to Plato. Although not widely accepted, they are further evidence of the great variety of opinions that have existed.

Rabbi Moses b. Maimon Maimonides (1135–1204), one of the major figures of rabbinical-legal literature, lived and worked in Spain almost at the same time and in the same cultural milieu that nurtured the two works referred to above. Among many other things, he bequeathed to future generations, including our own, an important discussion about music that has relevance for all deliberations on the subject. The Jews of Aleppo asked him if it is permissible to listen to regional Arabic strophic songs (*muwashshaḥāt*) accompanied by a reed-pipe instrument (*zamr*); his answer reveals his approach.[25] He makes the instrument his point of departure, saying that it must be judged as all other instruments, and all music meant for amusement is absolutely forbidden. Further on he systematically summarizes the major prohibitions in ascending order of severity:

1. Listening a song with a secular text, whether it be in Hebrew or Arabic;
2. Listening to a song that is accompanied by an instrument;
3. Listening to a song whose content includes obscene language;
4. Listening to a string instrument;
5. Listening to passages played on such instruments while drinking wine;

and then the most severe transgression:

6. Listening to singing and playing of a woman[26]

All these prohibitions are meant to help Israel be a "holy nation," as is written. And yet, Maimonides's answer does not mean a total prohibition of music, but rather forbids various types of secular music. The ultra-orthodox author of the anonymous work that we quoted at length earlier in this chapter bases his extreme approach on his interpretation of what Maimonides wrote in a letter. He says that in his answer Maimonides "did not explain the prohibition of song as due to the destruction of the

Temple, but to the very essence of the song which is reprehensible and which he very much despises, as whatever is not in worship of the Lord, blessed be He, leads one to debauchery and thoughtlessness" (*El gil ka ʿammim,* p. 42).

Thus we find that the ideological stance of the rabbinical authorities toward music derived from two fundamentals: first, from their basic view of music in principle and second, from the special circumstances incurred by the destruction of the Temple and life in foreign lands during the prolonged dispersion. Neither a uniform nor an unequivocal opinion prevails with respect to either of these fundamentals. The controversy can be summarized as follows:

• Some maintain that until the final redemption, the Jewish believer must devote himself at all times to mourning for the Temple. Consequently the use of musical instruments and organized festive song must be avoided in the house of worship.

• Others maintain that music must be avoided as it is identified with pleasure, or at least is symbolic of the normal life that was destroyed when the nation was dispersed.

• Certain people have reservations about the inherent nature of music. They claim that as a result of its power, it elicits a variety of negative manifestations: it affects the listeners' equilibrium and undermines their ability to keep all their actions under the strictest control; it distracts thoughts from study of the prayers, etc.; it causes intoxicating sensual emotions, which are irreconcilable with the basic demand to be a *goy qadosh* (holy nation).

• Some prohibit the use of music out of the desire to prevent "copying" the actions and melodies of the non-Jews.

• One type of religious song, cantillation, has been left out of the argument between the protagonists and antagonists of music in the ritual framework. This type will be dealt with at length in the next chapter.

4

Cantillation

The prime importance of cantillation is the role it plays in enhancing the words of the prayers as well as those of other basic texts not included in the liturgy. We have already noted the general consensus to the effect that cantillation is so essentially different from singing and most forms of musical activity that even its performers do not always consider it music. The recurrent use of terms such as declamation, reading, recitation, to indicate this type of presentation, shows clearly that the text takes precedence over the melody. Prior to the early days of the twentieth century, "recitative" and "psalmody" were the terms usually used, which means that the word cantillation is relatively new. It apparently is derived from the Italian *cantillare* or *cantilenare*—to murmur, hum, declaim in a tensed voice—a kind of restrained vocalizing that falls somewhere between actual singing and modulated declamation.

In effect cantillation can be defined as having a simpler, freer structure than ordinary vocal music, closer to solemn declamation than to structured, organized singing. Although on occasion this music may be ornamented with rich vocalizations, its form and flow are subordinated to the text and it is clearly adapted to the syntax and punctuation, the natural rhythm and melodic nature of the text being sung. Thus in this type of presentation, the word has absolute priority. Nevertheless, unlike declamation in which the modulations of the tensed voice are not restricted to precise pitch and melodic or rhythmic organization, there is an obvious musical component in cantillation that makes its own contribution and thereby reinforces the message of the text.

The basic principles of cantillation are universal, although their application reflects unique local attributes as expressed in language and intonation, as well as in the temperament and mores of a given population. Cantillation is primarily, but not exclusively, associated with religious rites. It may be used, for example, to foster learning by rote, a not uncommon educational tool in certain cultures; this method calls for the children to repeat specific material in unison, using simple melodic forms. Criers who announce their wares in the marketplace or on the streets also tend to repeat a rudimentary musical theme in a manner closely related to cantillation.

The principles of cantillation differ from those of the recitative that developed in Western art music during the seventeenth century. Despite the fact that both point up the stresses and punctuation of the phrase through giving undisputed priority to the text over the melody, they are differentiated by three basic characteristics:

1. The recitative is recorded in notes that indicate every pitch to be sung, whereas cantillation, a perpetuation of the oral tradition, is indicated by symbols whose interpretation may vary from one community to another and from one singer to another.

2. The use of notes determines a more or less fixed, uniform performance, while cantillation leaves the performer a broad field for improvisation.

3. The recitative is accompanied either by a cembalo (*recitativo secco*) or an orchestra (*recitativo accompaniato*). Cantillation (except within certain religious movements in Judaism) is without instrumental accompaniment.

In an exhaustive article on cantillation in the Christian ritual, the eminent scholar Solange Corbin (1961) stresses that in cantillation only the text is important as it is absorbed aurally. It must therefore be absolutely clear and thoroughly explained. In the past, when worshippers had no texts to read from, cantillation functioned, after a fashion, as oral instruction. In such a presentation, vocal tension is different from that of normal speech. In general, vocal changes depend on the type of material being transmitted, whether it be preaching, interpretive commentary, rhetoric, a legal presentation, a theatrical performance. Under these varying circumstances, speech stresses and complements grammatical and syntactic structure.

At the end of her article Solange Corbin presents an excellent summary of cantillation's numerous parameters. Although her definitions relate to cantillation in Christian ritual, they nevertheless have many points in common with its use in Jewish ritual. We shall point out the meaningful parallels and, to the extent that they exist, the differences.

1. The performer is chosen not because of his musical talent or pleasing voice, but rather in accordance with the nature of the text he is expected to perform. In the Christian church the priest, deacon, and lector are each responsible for presenting a particular text. In Jewish services the ritual functions are usually performed by two people, the cantor, who says the prayers, and another person who specializes in the reading of the Pentateuch, although occasionally the cantor fulfills both functions.[1] In describing the qualifications of the lector, Corbin writes that as he reads, he makes appropriate gestures, does not try to elicit immediate expression of the emotions implicit in the text, sings in a dispassionate voice, and transmits the message without emotional involvement. The latter comment may apply in part to whomever reads the Pentateuch, but it does not apply to the cantor. In ancient traditional texts

the ideal cantor is described as a modest, needy (*nitsrakh ve-nizqaq*) individual, with a fine presence and fine voice. It is said he must be needy so that his personal troubles will make the prayer more moving and impressive, while at the same time he will give deeper expression to the sorrows of the assembled congregation. In addition, wherever no distinction is made between the prayer leader, cantor, and *payṭan,*[2] the cantor also sings the liturgical songs.

2. The text is sanctified, evokes homage, and is always in prose, characteristics shared by Jewish ritual.

3. The musical aspect is generally akin to the oral tradition, with all that this implies. The rhythm is regular and uniform, flowing smoothly, without defined meter. The tempo is a function of local custom but under all circumstances the cadence is determined by the punctuation of the phrase rather than by precise mathematical values. Cantillation is essentially single-voiced (monodic) without musical accompaniment. Were it multivoiced or accompanied by instruments, comprehension of the text as well as the steadily flowing presentation would be hampered.

The passages from *seliḥot* songs in figure 5, recorded by A. Z. Idelsohn (1914–33, vol. 4), exemplify the above characteristics. Studying them, we find no attempt to construct a melodic line; the emphasis is on the text. All tones of each passage revolve around a tonal center—F in the first passage and A in the second.

Reading, therefore, is done on a recitative chord, that is, the melody remains primarily on a single note ending with a cadencial formula. Changes in tone or note of the recitative have intellectual, not melodic, significance; in other words, the pauses and rests derive from the text and its punctuation, not from the logic of the melody. Every pause or rest is indicated by a melodic formula. Some of the concluding formulae are given prolonged melismatic ornamentation which is usually functional, never autonomous. That is to say, the melisma[3] is not an element inherent in the structure of the music, but an expression of the desire to emphasize a particular part of the text. An excellent illustration of this is the modulated reading of the final brief verses of the Ten Commandments which in certain Near Eastern traditions are given extremely intricate, lengthy embellishment—as are other examples cited below.[4] The above-mentioned conditions find expression in a simple musical structure presented with special vocal tension that differs from that of ordinary speech, but is still something less than actual singing.

Edith Gerson-Kiwi has given the interesting name of "sounds of alienation" to the special vocal tension inherent in cantillation. In an article on the subject she stresses the function of the melody in a situation wherein the word is dominant.

> Sounds of alienation have their apotropaeic purpose during a liturgical action, but they are also produced to cover up, to distort, or even destroy the true nature of sound. . . . A more sophisticated form of voice-alienation can be produced through the conscious stylization of the spoken word into a ceremonially elevated chant or speech-melody. The prototype of these chants, or recitatives, is mainly related to the

Fig. 5. Idelsohn's example of selihot songs.

> narration of sacred texts in prose. . . . The cantor, while chanting, would limit himself to performing the main part of the text on one single tone, as if along a sound-axis, while only the points of punctuation are marked by small melodic flourishes, as preserved until this day in Eastern and Western Psalmody. (1980a, pp. 27–31)

The audience does not consider cantillation as true singing or music intended for enjoyment. It is accepted as prayer or an instrument by which a message is transmitted, but not as art; hence it is not meant to amuse or divert.

From all that has been said above it is clear that cantillation is distinguished from singing in several ways. The melody of a song is based on clearly defined principles involving scales, composition, form, and rhythm, following the conventions and rules accepted by various musical cultures. When a poem and tune are joined, the tune retains a large measure of independence and can continue to exist separately from the text. In cantillation or "melodic speech," the tune is a combination of motifs that acquire significance only when appended to the text that evokes them. From the standpoint of meter and tempo, the motifs acquire their structure from and are molded by the syntax and punctuation of the text, as well as by the principle of flow and retention—which are the reader's responsibility. In other words, this principle comes to the fore only during performance, which in itself depends exclusively on the nature of the text, the ability of the performer, and the overall circumstances. The principle of flow and retention, one of the most distinctive characteristics of cantillation, gives the performance of the oriental chant a large measure of freedom and variety. The variegation is determined by the character and structure of the text and the circumstances under which it is recited. For example, a text comprising short phrases consisting of one or two words each will be recited differently from one built of relatively long phrases. An example of a text made up of short phrases is the well-known opening prayer of the liturgy for Yom Kippur *Kol Nidrei* (All the vows). The text begins as follows:

> Kol nidrei/ve-ʾesarei/wu-shvuʿei
> ve-nidduyei/va-ḥaramei/ve-qunnamei/ve-qunnaḥei/ve-qunnasei
> di nedarna/ve-di nidar/ve-di ishtebaʿna ve-di nishtabaʿ

The example in figure 6 compares the way three different people read this text in the Sephardic tradition and shows the organization of the melodic formulae in small independent sequences that coincide with the textual formulae.

A similar type of text is the Priestly Blessing (Blessing of the Cohens):

> The Lord bless thee and keep thee;
> The Lord make His face to shine upon thee, and be gracious unto thee;
> The Lord lift up His countenance upon thee, and give thee peace. (Num. 6: 24–26)

This blessing is a vestige, so to speak, of Temple worship; after the destruction it was incorporated into the prayer. The Cohens, standing on both sides of the Ark facing the worshippers, raise their hands and bless the assemblage. The ceremony is performed responsorially, that is, the cantor says a word on a given musical motif and the Cohens repeat it on the same motif, as follows: Be thou blessed—Be thou blessed/My Lord—My Lord, etc.

On different occasions, different melodies are used for the priestly blessing. On Yom Kippur, while the cantor gives each note of the blessing intense embellishment, the Cohens repeat only the melodic motif for each word. As time passed this blessing became more and more intricately ornamented; it was no longer said in simple fashion even in ancient times when the priests sang it and greatly prolonged the music, adapting it to the text and their movements. As might be expected, there were some who questioned this custom, and echoes of their objections can still be heard today. In a conference on the Renewal of Traditional Music that was held at the Institute for Religious Music on Hanukkah, 1966, Professor Rabbi E. Z. Melamed (1966, p. 9) related that some two weeks earlier he had been asked by the central Sephardic synagogue if it is permissible for those reading the Priestly Blessing to prolong the music. The Cohens who frequented that synagogue complained that the reader went on for so long that they lost their place. For example, the reader drew out *yevarekhekhah* (thou shalt be blessed) until the Cohens forgot the word that had to be said. Rabbi Melamed said he called the cantor-reader to him and told him that the blessing of the Cohens and not his performance is the important thing. Hence he was not to draw the singing out too long.

The example of notation for the Priestly Blessing in figure 7 is taken from the Yanina community in Greece. It shows the first and last repetitions of the same musical phrase and the same fifteen words that comprise the blessing.[5]

Another interesting example of far-reaching ornamentation of individual words is found in certain performances of one of the basic prayer texts, the *Qedushah.* In the course of time the *Qedushah* became a vehicle for demonstrating the cantor's musical ability, although this would seem to contradict principles we discussed at the beginning of this chapter. The most highly developed ornamentation was associated with the most solemn occasion, that is, Yom Kippur. As can be seen from figure 8, each word becomes a lengthy musical passage. The figure shows how the Jews of Yanina, Greece render the first word of the *Qedushah, naqdishakh.*

Another type of text is one built on long phrases or phrases of varying lengths, like many of the prayers, mishnaic and talmudic texts, the Zohar, the Passover *haggadah,* and the different blessings, including those intoned during ceremonies connected with circumcision, marriage, the lighting of Hanukkah candles, etc. Here too there are both simple and embellished statements, depending on what is practicable under given circumstances. The examples in figures 9 and 10 indicate these two types of cantillation. The first is a Qiddush—the blessing of the wine on the Sabbath or holiday—recorded by Y. L. Ne'eman (1978). This is a highly ornamented cantillation in which all embellishments tend toward a major tonal center, following the basic principle of cantillation.

The second example is that of the Seven Blessings said under the bridal canopy and after the wedding ceremony in the eastern European version. The numbers mark the different musical motifs. The entire melody is built as a mosaic comprising the various motifs. In the example given, the contoural sounds of the musical phrase appear in the form of motifs. Here too the basis is a central, highly ornamented note that changes from motif to motif.

In discussing the Seven Blessings in the Ashkenazic tradition, Y.L. Ne'eman writes: "True, in our prayers we do not have 'accents' which, like the biblical accents, indicate punctuation and syntax (flow and retention) and at the same time serve as tonal guides to the musical interpretation of punctuation and syntax. But there are traditional musical motifs in every version of every prayer that facilitate the expression in music of the pause between one phrase of the prayer and the next; moreover, the difference in potential of the pause separating the following phrase or phrases is identical to that provided by the biblical Accents. Indeed, the three internal divisions of the biblical verse "and now, lest he put forth his hand,/and take also of the tree of life,/and eat and live forever" (Gen. 3:22), whose musical motifs—*revi'i, zaqef,* and *sof pasuq* respectively—[names of some of the biblical accents which will

Fig. 6. Three Sephardic readings of Kol Nidrei.

A1
רִים־פּוּ־כִּ־הַ יוֹם - מְ נָא - רַמְ - חֵ
B
רִים־פּוּ־כִּ־הַ יוֹם - מְ נָא - רַמְ - חֵ
C
רִים־פּוּ־כִּ־הַ יוֹם - מְ נָא - רַמְ־חֵ
A1
זֶה - הַ רִים - פּוּ - כִּ - הַ יוֹם עַד בַּר - עָ - שֶׁ
B
זֶה - הַ רִים - פּוּ - כִּ - הַ יוֹם עַד בַּר - עָ - שֶׁ
C
זֶה - הַ רִים - פּוּ - כִּ - הַ יוֹם עַד בַּר - עָ - שֶׁ
A1
לוֹם - שָׁ - לְ נוּ - לֵי - עָ בָּא - שֶׁ
B
לוֹם־שָׁ־לְ נוּ - לֵי - עָ בָּא - שֶׁ
C
לוֹם - שָׁ - לְ - נוּ - לֵי - עָ בָּא - שֶׁ

A
נָ - סֵי
B
נָ - - סֵי
C
נָ - - סֵי
A1
וְ - דִי נָא - נְ - דַרְ דִי
B
וְ - דִי נָא - נְ - דַרְ דִי
C
וְ - דִי נָא - נְ - דַרְ דִי
A1
וְ - דִי נָא - בַעְ - תַ - אִשְׁ
B
וְ - דִי נָא - בַעְ - תַ - אִשְׁ
C
וְ - דִי נָא - בַעְ - תַ - אִשְׁ

Fig. 7. Priestly Blessing, the Yanina tradition.

be more fully discussed below] elicit an expression of the different potential of the pause separating each segment; the same holds true for the version of the Seven Blessings, as in "Blessed art thou, O Lord, our God,/King of the universe,/Creator of the fruit of the vine." Such parallels, however, are not found in all the religious texts recited solemnly according to the above-mentioned norms of cantillation.

A. Z. Idelsohn (1923, 4, pp. 92–120) has expressed a similar, although rather more extreme opinion concerning some sort of parallel between reading done with the biblical accents and other types of reading. He maintains that there are different modes for different types of cantillation: prayer modes, psalm modes, and modes of the Mishnah. According to Idelsohn, modal frames for the various cantillations are based on a set of special, defined, characteristic motives associated with each different mode. In other words, the modes can be treated like the reading of the various biblical books, but only from the standpoint of determining the melodic skeleton and pattern. Thus, although Idelsohn uses the terms conjunction and disjunction, he does not relate clearly to the principle of flow and retention.

The rest of this chapter will be devoted to the biblical accents (*ta'amei ha-miqrah*)—which are among the most important types of cantillation. Before embarking on the subject, however, a passage from Judah Halevi's *Book of the Khazari* is of special interest as the poet offers a stepping-stone from one type of reading to another.[6] The rabbi describes the superiority of accented reading of the biblical books

Fig. 8. Qedushah, the Yanina tradition.

over the musical rendition of metrical poetry. This gives Halevi an opportunity for a unique presentation of the basic characteristics of cantillation, stressing those ways in which the musical message enriches the textual message.

> For indeed, it is the purpose of language to introduce into the mind of the listener a thought that has come into the mind of the speaker and this purpose will

Fig. 9. Ashkenazi Qiddush.

be fully achieved only in a face-to-face situation—for the things said in conversation have an advantage over the written word—following the well-known adage "as told by authors, not as told by books."[7] When speaking directly, a person takes advantage of a pause after concluding discussion of an issue, and when he goes on, he uses conjunctions that join one issue to another. In addition, by the extent to which his words are gentle or aggressive, by gestures and various nuances, he can express surprise or query, avowal, temptation, threat or supplication, which can never be expressed by the word alone. Sometimes too the speaker will use his eyes and brows, his whole head and both hands to express anger or desire, supplication or pride, in whatever measure he chooses. And here, in the small remnant of our language—a product of God's work—that has been preserved in writing, there is precision and depth that serve to fully explain the intentions of the speaker and replace the frequent hints and gestures we have spoken of in face-to-face conversation. [The reference is to] the "accents" with which we read the Bible: They indicate where the speaker meant to pause between one subject and another, and where he wanted to continue the [same] subject; and they also differentiate between question and answer, between subject and object, between words spoken quickly and those the speaker has said in measured fashion, between a command and a request—whole treatises can be written about all of this. All who aspire to attain to everything that is said above, will no doubt forego the metered poem because such a poem is read in only one way, and its reader will usually be found joining things that should be separated and pausing where he should go on; only with great effort can one avoid this.

Fig. 10. Ashkenazi Seven Blessings.

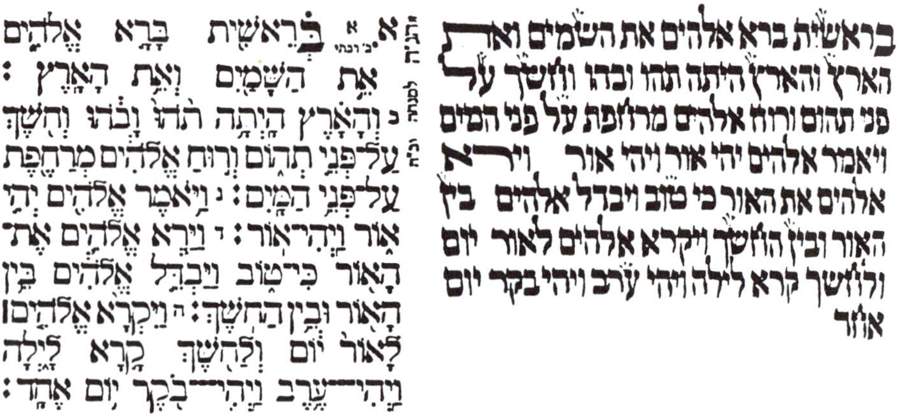

Fig. 11. Left column, Genesis 1 text with accents. Right column, Genesis 1 text without accents, vocalization, and punctuation. This is the way it is presented in the scroll from which public reading is made.

The Biblical Accents

From earliest times the people of Israel have used the biblical accents as an inseparable part of their religious ritual. There has always been meticulous concern for the precise reading of the Pentateuch and for maintaining the ancient, orally transmitted reading tradition. Acquaintance with the melodic patterns and functions of the biblical accents is of prime importance to anyone wishing to understand the musical heritage of the Jewish communities.

What are the biblical accents? Upon opening a printed Hebrew-language Bible one immediately becomes aware of graphic symbols appearing above and below the words, in addition to the vowel signs. There are twenty-six of these symbols, all different in form, name, and function. Still in use today, these symbols belong to a recognized system that was established in Tiberias in the first half of the tenth century; hence it is called the Tiberian tradition. Aharon Ben-Asher is considered the originator of the accepted version of this system of recording and vocalizing.[8] According to the tradition of the Jews of Aleppo, the *Aleppo Keter* (codex)—a hand-written copy of the Old Testament dating from approximately 920[9]—was voweled and accented by Ben-Asher himself and ever since it has been the authoritative model for redaction of the Bible. The Leningrad manuscript of 1009 also reflects Ben-Asher's Tiberian tradition.[10]

The Tiberian system—accepted and sanctified by all of Jewry—was preceded by two other systems that were rejected in its favor. One, quite similar to the Tiberian system but less sophisticated, originated in Palestine, and the other in Babylon; the Babylonian system used a letter—the first letter of the accent's name—above the words to indicate most of the accents.

The system for writing the accents was anteceded by an ancient oral tradition of accented reading. Even in the oral tradition the accent generally carried a dual meaning: In one sense it was construed as a means of revealing the more profound significance of the text, and in another it was viewed as a musical device intended to facilitate comprehension. The accent, therefore, is embedded in what is said and how it is said. The rabbinical sages believed that this type of modulated public reading began at the time of Ezra the Scribe; they found confirmation of this in the following passage from Neh. 8:8: "And they read in the book, in the Law of God, distinctly; and they gave sense, and caused them to understand the reading." The Babylonian Talmud, (tractate Megillah 3, 1) explains "and caused them to understand the reading—[refers to] the syntactical functions of the accents," and the Jerusalem Talmud (Megillah:4, 1) states: "and they gave sense—these are the [melodical functions of the] accents." This implies that even long, long ago it was believed that the Levites read the text in musical form. From the midrashic (homiletic) commentaries we learn of the importance the early sages attributed to the musical aspect involved in transmitting the textual message: "He who reads the Bible in its delightful beauty and melody, of him it is said 'honey and milk are under thy tongue' " (commentary on Song of Songs Rabba, 4:11).

According to testimony from the Talmud and other sources, in addition to the musical component, the readers made extensive use of gestures (chironomy—from the Greek *cheironomia*). It is important to remember that the public reader in the synagogue reads from a parchment scroll; the biblical text on it has neither vowel signs nor accents (see figure 11). This text is first studied from a printed volume of the Pentateuch in which both the vowel signs and accents appear. Only after one can read with complete confidence and has learned the vowels and accents by heart, is he ready to read aloud at services. To make it easier for him a "prompter" whose assistance can be depended upon stands next to him, perusing a copy of the Pentateuch in which the accents are indicated; when necessary, the "prompter" shows the reader which accent is to be used by means of a system of agreed hand signals.[11] This is accepted along with the custom of publicly reading the *Hafṭarah* (a chapter from the Prophets read after the weekly portion from the Pentateuch).

Opinions vary with respect to the origin of this custom. Some believe that it, too, originated in the time of Ezra. Others maintain that it had its inception in the days of Antioch, who forbade the reading of the Pentateuch; the people therefore began instead to read chapters of the Prophets that seemed apt and fitting for the proscribed Portion of the Week. When the edict was rescinded, it remained customary to read from the Prophets as well as the Pentateuch, a practice that is still followed today. The *Hafṭarah* generally refers in some way to the content of the weekly portion it accompanies, or to the occasion on which it is read. For example, on the Sabbath after the Ninth of Av, a day of fasting that marks the destruction of the First and Second Temples, seven consolatory *Hafṭarot* are read. The melodies of the *Hafṭarot* heard every Sabbath differ from those that accompany the reading of the Pentateuch. In addition to the Pentateuch and the *Hafṭarah,* on holidays and festivals it is also customary to read from the Hagiographa: on Passover from the Song of Songs; on Shavuoth, the Scroll of Ruth; on the Ninth of Av, Lamentations; on Sukkot, Ecclesiastes, and the Scroll of Esther on Purim. In some Jewish communities there are also special melodic motives that are used for other books of the Bible, including those that are not read publicly during synagogue services.

The Functions of the Biblical Accents

The accents have three major functions, all designed to facilitate accurate reading. The first is to indicate emphasis: by the placement of the accent, the reader knows which syllable to stress, where to strengthen his voice. The meaning of certain words changes when stress is moved from one syllable to another. For example: *ba'ah* (came) with stress on the first syllable indicates past tense, but with stress on the second syllable (*ba'ah*) indicates present tense feminine; *shāvu* with stress on the first syllable is "they returned," but with stress on the second (*shavū*) syllable means "they captured."

Punctuation is the second function of accents. As stated, the biblical scroll read at services is not voweled, accented, or punctuated; it contains a continuous series of words. The accents show the break-down into verses and then how each verse is divided internally, in accordance with the message and meaning of each segment, even each word. The conjunctives and disjunctives between words serve to clarify their meaning; incorrect parsing of a phrase may well distort the meaning of the text. For example: "Kol ha-ʿoseh melakhah be-yom ha-shabbat mot yumat" (whosoever doeth any work in the Sabbath day, he shall surely be put to death) (Exod. 31:15). This can be read (correctly) as "Kol ha-ʿoseh melakhah be-yom ha-shabbat/mot yumat" but it can also be read (incorrectly) as "Kol haʿoseh melakhah/be-yom ha-shabbat mot yumat" (whosever doeth any work, on the Sabbath day he shall surely be put to death). In this context, the system of accents crystallized an excellent set of sophisticated instructions for punctuation that facilitate maximum precision in transmitting the message embedded in the text.

The accents are divided into two main groups, each of which has a different function: the conjunctive accents (*meḥabberim*) make associative connections between words and determine the flow of reading; disjunctive accents (*mafsiqim*) are designed to show where a pause interrupts the flow. The disjunctive is not always of uniform potency: there are relatively strong pauses such as those called for by the full stop we use today, and relatively weak ones—those we indicate by use of semi-colons or commas. There are also intermediary values. Of the twenty-six accents, eighteen are disjunctives and eight are conjunctives, which gives some idea of the delicate shading made possible by the system. The pauses, some major and some minor, determine the general division of the verse into large units and smaller, secondary ones. The longer the verse, the more numerous and variegated the disjunctives.[12]

The third function of the accents is melodic. In this context the symbol denoting the accent plays a role similar to that of the neumes in the Gregorian chant: it instructs the Bible reader as to the melodic motive to be used for the word above or below which the symbol appears. Each accent has its own melodic pattern, some quite simple, others more developed and ornate. Although the musical traditions are many and varied, all Jewish ethnic groups use the same symbols. For reading biblical books other than those included in the Pentateuch, the same symbols are used, but they are given different melodic interpretation. Thus for reading the *Hafṭarah* the melodic pattern indicated by a given symbol is different from the pattern evoked by the same symbol when it appears in the Pentateuch. There are variations even in the reading of the Pentateuch itself: A special version is used for children who are learning to read, there is regular reading, and special reading for certain occasions such as the reading of the Song of the Sea on the seventh day of Passover, or the Ten Commandments on Shavuoth. Thus we see that these guides to musical reading, the symbols known as the biblical accents, have diverse musical motives; the choice of a given motive is determined by circumstances and by the book that is being read on a given occasion.[13]

With respect to adherence to the musical motives representative of each accent, it is important to note that although every Jewish congregation uses the same accents, from the musical standpoint not all congregations give true musical expression to each and every symbol. This is particularly evident in the way the Jews of Yemen read. Their disjunctives are quite ornate, and several of them use the same musical motive; their conjunctives, on the other hand, are almost tuneless. The Oriental-Sephardic version permits a large measure of freedom in the use of motives. Sometimes in the same performance a reader uses a different motive for the very same accent when it appears in a different place in the verse. Consistent use of clear musical motives is found mainly in the Ashkenazic reading tradition.

However, it must be emphasized that this wide variety of individual musical interpretations and local traditions is subordinate to one overriding principle: faithfulness to correct phrasing, as determined by the different disjunctive and conjunctive accents. In other words, the written text and its meaning, its exact phrasing and emphases—these are given values not to be deviated from or altered. They dictate the chant and the cadence. In actual fact, the biblical chant is not determined by musical standards, but is derived from and subordinate to the punctuational values already determined by the nature of the accents.

How the Tradition of Accented Reading Is Transmitted

Conscientious observance of the rules of accented reading has undoubtedly contributed a great deal to the relatively unaltered perpetuation of the musical tradition that governs the melodic patterns of the accents, but this alone would not have been enough. The fact that this tradition was deeply rooted in Jewish education has also been instrumental in its preservation: It was compulsory to learn to read with the accents in the *Ḥeder* (Jewish primary educational institution) and in other educational frameworks. Many Jewish communities resorted to the *Zarqah* Table[14] to teach the children the melodic motive of each accent. This table presented the accents in a given order, in accordance with the name by which they were known in the particular community. (The first accent is usually *zarqah*, from which the table acquired its name.) The table was printed in prayer books and volumes of the Pentateuch, the main texts studied.

Because it is meant for pedagogical purposes, the *Zarqah* Table is an artificial and schematic arrangement of the accents and therefore reflects only one aspect of their many and intricate combinations. Nevertheless, there is reason to assume that it encapsulates authentic echoes of the past. It is difficult to find support for this assumption in traditions that were and still are oral, but beginning with the early sixteenth century, the notes of the Ashkenazic tradition were written down. Thus they were preserved and have even been used in a comparative research study published by Hanoch Avenary (1976) in which he deals with the melodies of the Pentateuch in the Ashkenazic tradition from 1500 to 1900. The first notation was done in the sixteenth century by Christian humanists who were led by their critical approach to Catholicism's conventional dogmatism to seek out the Hebrew version of the Bible (Figure 12 represents the earliest known, noted *Zarqah* table made between 1505 and 1511). This caused them to engage in intensive study of Hebrew grammar and they became aware of the importance of the biblical accents for a correct understanding of the texts. Johannes Reuchlin was one of the outstanding humanists and like some others, in his Latin grammar book (1518) he included a recording of the melodic motives used by Jewish readers (figure 13). He was the only one, however, who was inspired by methodological and pedagogical considerations to append the musical notes to curricular material. He obligated pupils to learn the musical motives of the accents by heart, and then use them to read accompanying sample verses. Reuchlin's notations as well as those of his contemporaries, Sebastian Muenster (1524) and Johannes Valensis (1545), are included in a comparative table—together with nine other recordings from the nineteenth and twentieth centuries—in Avenary's study (see figure 14).[15]

More than fifty years before this, Abraham Zvi Idelsohn incorporated Reuchlin's annotations in a much more inclusive table that compared Oriental and Western traditions.[16]

In view of the fact that many different musical traditions govern the intonations in which the accents are read, the following questions again confront us: How ancient are these musical reading traditions? Can one speak of a single source for the musical motives of the accents? Can common musical motives be traced in the way different Jewish ethnic groups read the various biblical books? This discussion of the history and development of the biblical accents has, in essence, presented four fundamental hypotheses:

1. Modulated public reading apparently began as long ago as the days of Ezra the Scribe;

2. There is an obvious musical element in the reading;

3. A system of accent-symbols intended to establish inviolable rules for reading crystallized in the course of years;

4. Starting with the ninth century, all Jewish congregations everywhere adopted the Tiberian system.

Can these hypotheses conceivably offer the end of a thread that will lead us back from contemporary traditions to ancient Jewish music? Were that so, one of the gravest problems exercising students of Jewish music would be resolved. But a difficulty arises here. Jewish music is known to have been primarily the province of an oral tradition and for hundreds of years it was in constant contact with local musical cultures of many foreign lands; hence, as said before, it is not free of alien influences. Even an untrained ear can discern the miscellany of styles that characterizes Jewish music today; does this not apply to the musical patterns of the accents as well? Can one be absolutely certain that no alien influences have rubbed off on them?

As indicated previously, Idelsohn, who pioneered research into the musical traditions of all Jewish communities, concerned himself with this problem. In his time the science of ethnomusicology, then called comparative musicology, was still in its infancy. Idelsohn made extensive comparisons of the different traditions and after lengthy study he drew up a comparative table of Eastern and Western reading traditions used for the Pentateuch and other biblical books. He arrived at the conclusion that common denominators can indeed be found. It should be noted that the dependability of this table has been questioned, the above-mentioned book by Avenary, who found the notation incomplete, faulty, and gravitating toward tendentiousness, being a case in point.

It is interesting that Idelsohn initially stresses the unique, independent nature of public readings of the biblical books as practiced in the early centuries of the Christian era. In his opinion this modulated reading was distinguished from ancient Oriental singing as it was based on a set of special musical motives that were organized in specific modes. The motives were subordinate to the rigid syntactic order of the textual material, organized in groups not only of major disjunctives and conjunctives, but of secondary disjunctives and conjunctives as well, in accordance with the punctuation and parsing of the sentence. The development of the motives and their consolidation into a musical phrase follows certain accepted, fixed rules. These rules, originally expressed with the help of a few graphic symbols and finger movements (chironomics) crystallized into a sophisticated system of written symbols that reached its peak in the work of Aharon Ben-Asher (tenth century). There were, in effect, two systems of accents employed, one for a group of twenty-one books and the second for the Book of Job, the Proverbs, and the Psalms.[17] The first includes thirty accents, the second only twelve. This dual system has been accepted and

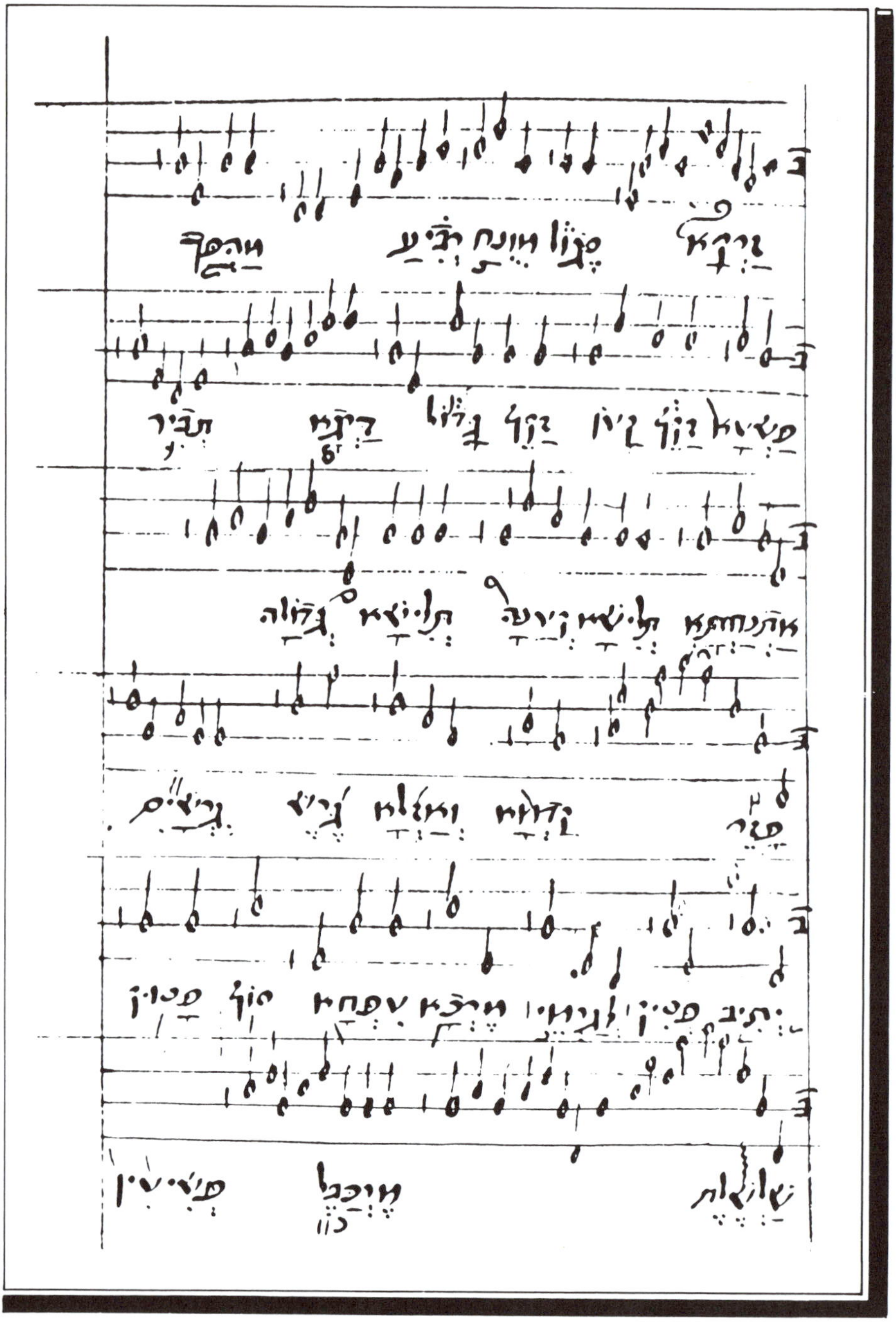

Fig. 12. Kaspar's Zarqah Table.

Fig. 13. Reuchlin's Zarqah Table.

Fig. 14. Avenary's comparative table of Ashkenazi biblical cantillation.

disseminated in its original form in all Jewish communities from earliest times until today. It did not develop into a system of musical notation as did other similar attempts in other cultures. This fact is not essentially changed by the notations of the biblical accents recorded by the humanists in the 16th century, by those of the Ashkenazic *Ḥazzanim* (cantors) in the nineteenth century, or by scholars in our own time. The musical patterns associated with the recorded accents were transmitted orally and studied under the instruction of experts in the field. The symbols serve as reminders for one who is acquainted with the musical patterns; they do not indicate the rests, intervals, or fixed degrees. However, despite the different musical garb in which the various communities attire the accents, based on a comparison of the traditional biblical reading modes Idelsohn drew the following conclusion:

> We gain a clear idea of the loose relationship between the motives and accent signs upon examining the comparative table. The comparative table of the Pentateuch mode shows how inexactly the names of the accent signs describe the impression made by the music for which they stand. But the same table gives evidence of the close relation between the motives of the various traditions, though some of these communities, due to their geographical situation and their political condition, never, or very seldom, came into contact with one another. Some of these communities, on the other hand, never stood under the influence of the Roman Catholic Church, and yet several modes are found in both Synagogue and Church. Both this uniformity of tradition and the independence of church influence prompt us to adopt the opinion that the biblical modes treated thus far, are of an ancient age, probably preceding the expulsion of the Jewish people from Palestine, and older than the Christian Church. They are the remainder of the Jewish-Palestinian folk tunes, representing the Jewish branch of the Semitic-Oriental song. (1929, pp. 70–71)[18]

Were Idelsohn's conclusions definitive, they would have revealed one of the world's oldest musical traditions, and he would have solved one of the most troubling enigmas in this field. Idelsohn's sensitive ear was surely not deaf to the obvious differences of musical styles that characterized the reading traditions of the various communities in his time—as in ours. It is also obvious that the accents evoke the same principles of punctuation and emphasis in all the traditions and thereby cause a similarity in the general structure of their melodic line. In a certain sense, all cantillations, by their very nature, represent common principles and values, such as a rising and falling of the voice, division of the musical phrase in accordance with the division of the textual phrase, certain dynamic emphases, and so forth. But particularly because this is a rather vaguely delineated musical sphere, an attempt must be made to pinpoint the stylistic differences rather than similarities; the common aspects are conspicuous, while the differences are subtle. Therefore, and because even an untrained ear can catch the different intonations and styles that hold sway in different communities, probably as a result of continuous contact with neighboring cultures—contemporary scholars no longer accept Idelsohn's theory. It is particularly hard to accept his conclusion that the melodic patterns of the accents used today represent vestigial remains of ancient Palestinian folk songs. This, however, in no way diminishes esteem for this eminent scholar whose work has contributed so much to contemporary thought in the field.

Because cantillation stands at the extreme outer edge of solemn speech, has its sights fixed on the components of music, and very gradually moves in that direction, it has become a foundation-stone of every religious ritual. Its strength lies in the fact that it contributes to the enhancement of the text being read and emphasizes the message it carries. The rules of cantillation are usually acquired by intuition and experience. From this standpoint reading according to the biblical accents is exceptional in that it is normative and is based on defined, generally accepted principles that serve as essential signposts for the reader. The biblical accents reflect an interpretive tradition of the Bible. By dint of conjunction and disjunction, through knowledge of the relative potential of the pauses dictated by the accents, by use of the traditional melodic motives, the meaning of each biblical verse becomes clear and each word is correctly pronounced.

5

The Piyyuṭ as a Factor in the Development of Synagogal Music

Originally *piyyuṭim*—liturgic poems—were written with the intention of enhancing the prayers. As time passed, however, this type of poetry found its way into other devotional texts used to celebrate occasions of a public, personal, or family nature. Between the fourth and sixth centuries *piyyuṭim* began to appear that were entirely dissociated from the prescribed prayers. By that time, the prayers themselves were becoming increasingly formalized, with the cantor reading or chanting them aloud and the worshippers quietly repeating the same text after him. There was a growing need for the introduction of some variety, above all on the Sabbath and holy days. This increasing desire for diversity, according to Ezra Fleischer (1975, pp. 49–50), prepared the ground for weaving the *piyyuṭ* into the prayers. The worshippers continued to murmur the prayer text as before while the cantor inserted the *piyyuṭ,* he and the congregation joining forces at certain points.

This poetic form had its beginnings in Palestine with the appearance of the "anonymous *piyyuṭ,*" so-called because neither the names of the writers nor the exact time of writing were known. The only *payṭan* (as the writers of *piyyuṭim* are called in Hebrew) known to us by name is Yosi ben-Yosi who apparently lived during the fourth or fifth century. From the sixth to the eleventh century was the period of the classical *piyyuṭ* in Palestine. It was then that the structural framework of most types of the classical *piyyuṭ* crystallized and flourished, first in Palestine and then in Babylonia and other countries. In the second half of the ninth century southern Italy became the first European center of this poetic form and from there it spread to the north of Italy, Germany, France, and Byzantine Greece.

In the tenth century the major creative center of this type of liturgical poetry moved to Spain. For the next five hundred years, the *piyyuṭ* blossomed with a direct affinity to the various forms of Arabic poetry. From the standpoint of content and language, the Spanish *piyyuṭ* freed itself of talmudic-midrashic content and of the esoteric, allusive language that had previously characterized such works; *piyyuṭim* were now based primarily on biblical language. From the standpoint of form, one of the major innovations of the Spanish *piyyuṭ* was that it was patterned after strophic and strophic-like poetry (see below).

It is Fleischer's view (1975, p. 340) that the innovations the Spanish *payṭanim* introduced into the structure of their poems stemmed from, among other things, the desire to involve the audience directly in the performance of prayer. Examining the *piyyuṭim* from earlier periods, we find that before the emergence of the Spanish school, the prayers were sung by the cantor alone. During the period of the classical *piyyuṭ*, a trained choir was added and prepared in advance to assist the cantor in transitional passages.[1] The congregation generally participated in the prayer with brief responses such as "Amen," "Halleluya," and "The Lord is my King." Exceptions occurred on special occasions charged with powerful religious emotion such as during the *seliḥot* (penitential prayers) on the High Holidays.[2] At such times the role of the congregation as a whole was extended; the solo parts were interspersed with refrains repeated by all the worshippers in unison.

The new patterns designed for the *piyyuṭim* of the Spanish school enabled the congregation to participate not only during the *seliḥot* and *qinot* (lamentations)[3] but also in the singing of liturgical refrains written for the Sabbath and holidays throughout the year. Fleischer believes that the tendency to include the public in performing the *piyyuṭim* also found its way into Italian-Ashkenazic liturgical poetry, although its creators preserved for a rather longer time some of the distinctive structural features of the classical *piyyuṭim*.

After the fifteenth century, when the Jews were expelled from Spain and that center was destroyed, *piyyuṭim* influenced by the Spanish school continued to flourish in the newly established dispersed communities. The kabbalist center in Safed, for example, had a powerful effect on song both in and out of the synagogue (see the following chapter). Attributing great importance to poetry, the kabbalists were instrumental in developing the *piyyuṭ* and they helped spread the form throughout the Jewish world. Thereafter, the Spanish *piyyuṭ* flowered in many communities, among them Yemen, Tunis, Morocco, and Aleppo. Little of the locally created liturgical poetry attained the widespread distribution of the Spanish *piyyuṭim*, although local *payṭanim* have continued even until today to write Hebrew poetry of this type. At the same time there was an upsurge of Ashkenazic *piyyuṭim*. In Italy, the cradle of the school, the *payṭanim* still followed patterns established by the Spaniards, but in the communities of western and central Europe—and later eastern Europe, too—prolific *payṭanim* followed a direction of their own.

These milestones indicate the various stages in the development of the *piyyuṭ* and the major centers that originally used this poetic form exclusively, because of its content as well as its place in the prayers. *Piyyuṭim* were prevalent, for example, in the *seliḥot* and *qinot* liturgy, as well as in poems linked to special holy days and festive events, the new moon marking the beginning of the month, special portions of the Pentateuch (e.g., the Ten Commandments and the Song of the Sea) or services on the Sabbath that falls on the eve of Purim, Passover, or Yom Kippur.[4] *Piyyuṭim* were also written to celebrate events in the lives of individuals such as the birth of a child, a bar mitzvah or wedding, and these songs were performed in the synagogue. Thus, in the course of time the *piyyuṭ* broke through the limitations of liturgy and synagogue song and found an accepted niche during public and private ceremonial occasions. Such paraliturgical manifestations will be discussed in chapter 7.

From its inception the *piyyuṭ* was meant to be sung. Hence, the more modification and enrichment it underwent and the more entrenched it became both within and outside of the liturgy, the more it influenced the development of music and musical life. As community life accorded ever more importance to musically accompanied poetic work, the demand for new *piyyuṭim* with which to enhance various events became more insistent. Many ideas that crystallized with the Safed kabbalists, for example, became fertile soil for the activities of *payṭanim.* Songs of supplication (*baqqashot*), such as are sung on the Sabbath after midnight from Sukkot until Passover, began to emerge in the sixteenth century—and they are still used today. The singing, which on those occasions goes on until daybreak, includes many apt *piyyuṭim,* generally organized modally. This kind of poetic creativity flourished primarily in Aleppo, Syria, and in various parts of Morocco.[5] Kabbalistic concepts, which we will discuss in the following chapter, would seem to be only partially responsible for these developments; members of the communities that instituted the supplications also seemed to harbor a love of music. Their longing for good music found conspicuous expression as supplications were often detached from their customary framework and performed at concerts of devotional music. Cantors also performed at what may be called religious concerts, where *piyyuṭim* and passages of prayer are sung to instrumental accompaniment.

Prosodic and Formal Elements in Ancient and Classical *Piyyuṭim*

The earliest *piyyuṭim* were completely without rhyme, although rhyme was a permanent element in Hebrew poetry from the seventh century on. While the Arab poets used uniform rhyme in most poetic works, the Jewish *payṭanim* preferred the diversity achieved by using strophic forms that enabled the lines to be concluded in a variety of rhymes, a technique particularly notable in the classical *piyyuṭ.* Nevertheless, uniform rhyming was also used to some extent in every period. While the poetic line is concluded by the rhyme, many poems opened with letters arranged in alphabetic order. This device, known as an alphabetical acrostic, was already widespread during the earliest period of the *piyyuṭim.*[6] The acrostic was used in many different forms: in addition to the simplest form wherein each line opens with a letter of the alphabet used in a specific order, there are lengthy *piyyuṭim* in which each word of every line in a strophe begins with the same letter.

The *payṭanim* of those periods established the rhythm of a poetic line by using a meter that was a continuation of the traditional biblical rhythmic organization, based on the number of accented words in each line. The following are a few examples of some of the metric systems typical of biblical poetry:

"Ha'azinu ha-shamayim va-adabbera/ve-tishmaʿ ha-aretz ʾimrey-fi" (Give ear, ye heavens, and I will speak; and let the earth hear the words of my mouth) (Deut. 32:1). This stanza includes two "three-unit" lines (a unit is equivalent to an accent); that is, each line has three accented words. The hyphenated construct state (*semikhut*) is generally considered as a single accent or beat (*neqishah*). On the other hand a single long word is sometimes considered two beats.

Similarly, there may be a verse consisting of two units: "amar oyev/erdof assig/ aḥalleq shalal" (The enemy said: I will pursue, I will overtake, I will divide the spoil) (Exod. 15:9). There are also three, four, and five-unit lines. Within a single stanza there can even be a varied pattern such as alternating three-unit and two-unit lines.

Elision is a well-known poetic-rhetorical device. A word (either verb or noun) is omitted but is intuitively supplied by the reader in accordance with the logic of the rhythmic pattern: "baʿerev yalin bekhi/ve-labboqer [*yaqits* or *yaqum*] rinna" (weeping may endure for a night, but joy [cometh] in the morning) (Ps. 30:6).

Another technique the *payṭanim* used frequently was to insert biblical verses or brief passages into the *piyyuṭ*. Then they used the device known as *shirshur:* links created by attaching one line or stanza to another through the repetition of a word, phrase, or motive. The writers of classical *piyyuṭim* also made use of the repeated refrain, a technique that reached superb heights in the poetry created in parts of Spain.

Quantitative Meter

Unlike the ancient and classical *piyyuṭ*, Spanish *piyyuṭ* borrowed a number of significant formal attributes pertaining to rhyme and rhythm from the Arabic—more precisely from the *qasida* (the most important poetic form used in pre-Islamic times). The classical Arabic *qasida* that developed before the emergence of Islam is built on lines of equal length and meter; the lines are divided into two equal parts called the "opening" and the "closing." The "opening," ends in a word that rhymes with the last word of the "closing." This rhyming procedure is known as "enhancing the opening." (Only the first line has this central rhyme; thereafter, the "closing" lines alone are rhymed, every one of these final rhymes being identical—even if there are as many as a hundred lines.)

Donash ben-Labrat[7] adapted to Hebrew poetry the pattern of the classical Arabic quantitative meter known as "*yetedot*[8] and *tenuʿot*." Essentially, this rhythmic system is built on distinguishing clearly between the short and long syllables that comprise a word. Quantitative meter allocates a fixed number of syllables to each line in a poem; the "long" and "short" syllables are then distributed accordingly. The lines of the poem thus become absolutely symmetrical, their overall length identical. Quantitative meter, then, disregards accents; whether accented or not, the units are equal.

In Donash's adaptation of the system, the *sheva-naʿ* (mobile schwa) and every semivowel (a schwa compounded with a vowel) is considered a short unit. A long unit is a vocalized consonant. For example the words *beni, shemi,* and *ḥashuv* each comprise a short unit (marked ˘) and a long one (marked ¯). The *sheva-naḥ* (quiescent schwa) combines with the vowel sound that precedes it and is not an independent unit. Thus for example in the word *simlah* (dress) there are two vowel sounds. As a result of the small number of short units in Hebrew, the *vav ha-ḥibbur* (conjunctive *vav*) when vocalized as "u" (in other words, when given a *Shuruq*) before the letters *bet, vav, mem* and *fey,* becomes a short unit on condition that it is not followed by a *sheva-naḥ.* In the Hebrew language a short unit is a single syllable combined with the vowel-sound that follows it; hence the grammarians of the Middle Ages joined the short vowel (˘) with the following long one (¯) to create a single unit which they called a *yated* (indicated by ˘¯), as in the word *gemar.* They called the single long unit a *tenuʿah.* A number of short and long syllables combined (no fewer than two and no more than four) forms an *ʿamud* (a metrical foot). A series of *ʿamudim* creates the meter which is therefore called the "meter of *yetedot* and *tenuʿot.*"

In view of the above, it is in place to question whether this meter is congenial to the Hebrew language. The *ʿamud* can be found in various combinations such as two *tenuʿot* (¯¯), a *yated* and two *tenuʿot* (˘¯¯¯); two *tenuʿot* and a *yated* (¯¯˘¯) and a *tenuʿah* and *yated* (¯˘¯), etc. As a metrical foot cannot comprise more than four syllables, there are eight *ʿamudim* in Hebrew. The classical meters contain different combinations of *ʿamudim* or a single *ʿamud* that repeats itself.

By virtue of the fact that the poetic line is divided into two hemistiches, a *delet* (opening) and a *soger* (closing), in addition to a symmetry of lines there is also metric symmetry between both parts of the line. Below is an example of a simple meter called *marnin.* This is one of the eleven classical meters most frequently used by the Spanish *payṭanim.*[9] It is composed of one *ʿamud* that repeats itself: ˘¯¯¯, that is, *yated, tenuʿah, tenuʿah.*

The *ʿamud* is repeated twice in the *delet* and twice in the soger:

˘¯¯¯ / ˘¯¯¯ //   ˘¯¯¯ / ˘¯¯¯ //
delet   soger

This meter is well illustrated in the *piyyuṭ* "Deror Yiqra" written by ben-Labrat, the theoretician of Hebrew quantitative meter.

˘ ¯ ¯ ¯ ˘ ¯ ¯ ¯

D̆er̄or Ȳiqr̄a l̆eb̄en ʿīm b̄at
v̆eȳintsōrk̄hem k̆em̄o b̄av̄at.
Neʿim shimkhem velo yishvat
shevu nuḥu beyom shabbat.

Fig. 15. Deror Yiqra, Iraqi tradition, version a.

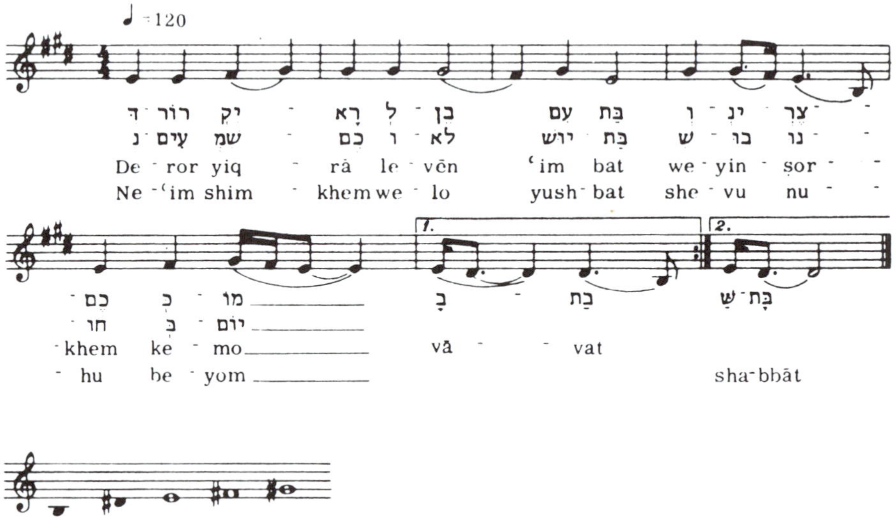

Fig. 16. Deror Yiqra, Iraqi tradition, version b.

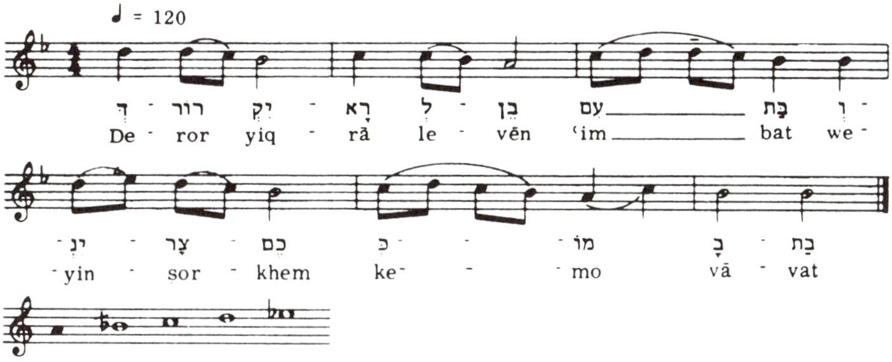

Fig. 17. Deror Yiqra, Iraqi tradition, version c.

Fig. 18. Deror Yiqra, Iraqi tradition, version d.

To demonstrate the complexity of integrating melody and text we present this same *piyyuṭ* as adapted to four different melodies traditionally used by the Jews of Baghdad (figures 15–18) as well as two versions of ibn Gabirol's[10] (figures 19–20) *piyyuṭ: shefal ruwaḥ* whose meter *ha-merubbeh* is similar to the former. It includes three *ʿamudim* in each hemistich:

˘––– / ˘––– / ˘–– // ˘––– / ˘––– / ˘–– //

Syllabic Meter

As there is something alien to the Hebrew language in the rigid meter of *yetedot* and *tenuʿot,* the *payṭanim* of Spain tended to use a different meter: the syllabic meter, which entirely ignores the *shevas* and *ḥaṭaphs.* Just as in the quantitative meter the *sheva-naḥ* combined with the vowel-sound that preceded it, so the *sheva-naʿ* and *ḥaṭaph* forms a single syllable by combining with the vowel that follows them. Thus the word *shemaʿ* is no longer a *yated* (˘¯), but a single syllable (¯). This syllabic meter did not replace the meter of *yetedot* and *tenuʿot,* but was used concomitantly.

Strophic Songs

From the standpoint of structure, content, rhyme, and meter, poems with refrains and other strophic forms undoubtedly lend themselves most readily to being sung. From the beginning of the eleventh century, when this form developed in Spain, it dominated poetic creativity and greatly enriched the repertoire of songs. The different kinds of strophic poetry developed as a reaction to the classical forms in which, as Ezra Fleischer (1975, pp. 344–45) writes: "The two elements of the classical Arab poem, the quantitative meter and the uniform rhyme, were quite foreign to the spirit of Hebrew poetry; . . . since traditional Hebrew poetry

Fig. 19. Shefal ruwaḥ, Iraqi tradition.

אֲ - נִי נֶחְ - שָׁב בְּ - עֵי - נַי
ʾa - ni neḥ - shāv be - ʿēy - nay
כְּ - תוֹ - לַ - עַת קְ - טַ - נָּה בָּ - אֲ - דָ - מָה
ke - to - la - ʿat qe - ṭa - nā bā - a - dā - mā
מְ - לֹא עוֹ - לָם אֲ - שֶׁר אֵין
me - lo ʿo - lām ʾa - sher ʾēyn
קֵץ לְ - גָדְ - לוֹ הֲ - כָ - מוֹ -
qēṣ le - god - lo ha - khā - mo -
- נִי יְ - הַ - לֶּל - ךָ וּ - בַ - מָּה
- ni ye - ha - llel - khā u - va - mmā
Fine

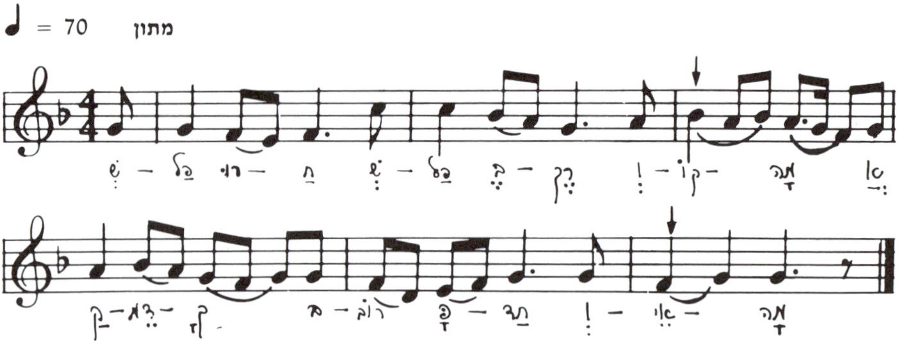

Fig. 20. Shefal ruwaḥ, Moroccan tradition.

preferred—particularly for long poems—the more frequent rhyme that constantly changes the strophic structures."

The strophic song (*shir-'ezor* in Hebrew)[11] describes the form that developed in Spain in or about the year 1000. In Arabic it is called *tawshiḥ* or *muwashshaḥ,* which mean "belt" (as both noun and adjective)—a belt inset with various precious stones. The *muwashshaḥ*[12] is divided into strophe after strophe, in accordance with a range and number determined by the *payṭan.* The rhymes can change from one line to the next, but they must be metrically equal. The *'ezor* (refrain-recurring unit) comes between one stanza and the next and can consist of one line or two, but is always shorter than the stanza itself. Its rhyme usually differs from that of all the other stanzas, and occasionally it even has a meter of its own. The first rhyme is repeated in all the refrains that appear in a given poem. Sometimes the refrain is at the beginning of the poem, before the first stanza, in which case it is called a *madrikh* (guide). This is very common in folk poems where the refrain is sometimes repeated time and again.[13] Examples of this can be found in "Tsur mishello," and "Yah ribbon ʿalam," among others.[14]

Hebrew strophic poems were already being written in the tenth century,[15] but they flourished mainly in the eleventh and twelfth. Many were created by poets of the remarkable period known as the Golden Age. Among them were Shmuel Hannagid (993–1056), Shlomo ibn Gabirol (1021–70), Moshe ibn Ezra (1055–1140), Judah Halevi (1075–1141), and Abraham ibn Ezra (1092–1167). After the expulsion from Spain strophic poetry continued to be a major form of Hebrew *piyyuṭ.* New centers of Hebrew poetry that emerged after the expulsion also continued to develop this form, primarily in North Africa, Salonika, Constantinople, Rhodes, and Egypt. It also flourished in places where Jews had settled before the expulsion, such as Yemen, Palestine (in Safed), and Kurdistan.

The Arab *muwashshaḥ* which was originally a light, cheerful, secular folk song, flexible in form, offered a good deal of freedom and opened very interesting possibilities for integrating text and melody. As the themes revolved around love, wine, etc., this form first entered secular poetry and was quickly accepted; it soon secured a respected niche in the sacred liturgy as well, becoming one of its mainstays. These achievements can be attributed primarily to the fact that because of its simple rhythms, musical rhymes, and short lines, strophic poetry is highly suitable for singing. Indeed, this became a very popular form for Hebrew *piyyuṭim* that were sung both in and outside of the synagogue.

The Ashkenazic *Piyyuṭ*

The Ashkenazic *payṭanim* retained the patterns set by their classical predecessors. Although some of them—under Spanish influence—used the quantitative meter, they somewhat modified its form. In common with most other trends followed by writers of liturgical poetry, Ashkenazic rhyming tends to be strophic. However, unlike the Spanish school in which biblical language and grammar predominate, the Ashkenazic *piyyuṭ* is interspersed with the esoteric allusive language and emblematic appellations endemic to the classical *piyyuṭ,* and this is overlaid with mishnaic and talmudic idiom. The acrostic reappears in a variety of forms and sometimes, particularly in Italian and German works, a lengthy signature is affixed to the poem (for example, "Shlomo, the modest rabbi, may he be upraised by Torah studies and good deeds, amen"). The performance of Ashkenazic *piyyuṭim* is characterized by a wealth of responses and refrains, while strophic patterns are almost nonexistent.

The *payṭanim* of Italy and Germany held the classical *piyyuṭ* in highest regard and interjected it into the prayers. For these innovative works they focused on material that had had limited distribution in classical *piyyuṭ,* including primarily three types: the supplications (penitential prayers) and lamentations; the creative *piyyuṭim* that enhance the benedictions associated with the morning prayer "Hear, O Israel"; the festive "evening" *piyyuṭim* meant to enhance select prayers for the Sabbath and the eve of holidays. Fleischer's reference to the German *piyyuṭim* has particular significance for our discussion here: "The central European *piyyuṭ* . . . is a reflection of its time and place; it is the poetry of gloomy, oppressive days. Even when expressing joy, the best poems and most elevated thinking are somehow faltering and lackluster. This is (or this poetry is) possibly the one and only room in the temple of sacred Hebrew song that expresses more than a slight patina characteristic of its time and place" (1975).

In the penitential prayers and lamentations the gloom and depression are conspicuously present. The penitential prayers known as *ʿaqedot* because they are associated with the sacrifice of Isaac, bear this out. Others are referred to as *ḥaṭanu* (we have sinned), so-called because of the recurrent refrain: "ḥaṭanu Tsureinu, selaḥ lanu yotsrein" (We have sinned against the Lord, forgive us, our creator). A special type of pentitential prayer are the *gezerot* (edicts) which include descriptions of the traumatic suffering of central European Jewish communities during the Crusades and all through the Middle Ages. The *gezerot* appear primarily in Ashkenazic *piyyuṭim;* in Spain they are found only during the doleful oppression of the fourteenth and fifteenth centuries. Many of the lamentations that mark the Ninth of Av also contain oblique references to painful contemporary events.

Works of poets who recounted the sufferings of Jewry during the Middle Ages led to the creation of a musical pattern typically used by Ashkenazic Jewry—the *mi-Sinai* (from Mt. Sinai) tunes—an allusion to the antiquity attributed to this pattern (see below).

Integration of Melody and Text

The mutual adaptation of text and melody is a complex artistic task requiring skill and talent; not every text automatically fits every tune. The *payṭan* or cantor, those who are responsible for liturgical and paraliturgical singing, are called upon to make these adaptations. In olden times the *payṭan* performed a three-fold task: he wrote the text, adapted the words to the melody, and performed the work as part of the prayers or other religious rites. Once a body of *piyyuṭim* had acquired an accepted place within the regular prayers, fewer and fewer new poetic works were absorbed into the liturgy. This limited the function of the *payṭan* to aspects of musical adaptation and performance. At the same time the writing of *piyyuṭim* continued to flourish outside the framework of prayer and ritual worship, *piyyuṭim* being sung with the Sabbath Psalms, the lamentations, the penitential prayers and supplications, as well as at paraliturgical events such as circumcisions, weddings, and so on.

Even today, therefore, one can find three types of *payṭanim:* One who still fulfils the three functions: he writes the text, adapts it to appropriate music, and performs the integrated work publicly. Then there is the *payṭan* who, as a talented musician, does not write but adapts an existing text to music and performs the work. The third type makes do with playing the role of performer. Nevertheless, in a throwback to traditions based on oral transmission, both the act of adapting a tune to a text and the act of performing it require creative musical talent. Indeed, according to Near Eastern conceptions of music, all adaptation, even if it makes use of a well-known tune, is in the nature of a creative work that stands on its own merit. Although in this process almost no new melodies are created, most being drawn from exisitng music (even if this is not always admitted), in the course of adaptation both structure and rhythm are changed; the performer, too, makes his own contribution. Adaptations, therefore, can be looked upon as acts of musical composition, which is what the *payṭanim* maintain they are. It should be remembered that in the process of adaptation, not only the melody but the text as well absorbs changes: There is an occasional change in the natural accent of a word, or a single phrase expressing a poetic idea is divided into two melodic phrases.[16]

If he so desires, the *payṭan* can announce the identity of the melody he has chosen by indicating its original name at the head of the new work. This practice was widespread in Spain and was transplanted to countries abroad together with the exiles.[17] An excellent example of this can be found in Israel Najjara (1550–1620), an outstandingly talented poet-musician who left a strong impression on the work of all generations that followed him. He became a symbol of the revival of Hebrew poetry in the East after the expulsion from Spain.

Najjara's father had been among the Spanish Jews who were banished, but Najjara himself was born in the kabbalist center of Safed. He had a strong artistic bent and highly developed musical taste. His rare creative power also expressed itself in virtuoso performances. He borrowed freely from the folk music of his time, and the names of hundreds of Turkish, Arabic, Spanish, and Greek melodies head his songs. His songs are innovative as compared with those of his predecessors in that each and every one of them was written for a specific tune to which he adapted his original text. He considered it almost a sacred task to make his poem and the foreign melody fit each other perfectly. Jews of his time were attracted by the songs of their alien surroundings but had difficulty reconciling the appealing foreign tunes with the different syllabic structure and rhythm inherent in their native poetic language. According to Najjara (1587, introduction), this situation could be remedied only if the Hebrew poems were made to conform to the alien syllabic configuration. It was his hope that if he wrote in this fashion, the Jewish public would eschew the foreign songs in favor of his. And indeed, his book *Songs of Israel,* first printed in Safed in 1587, was very well received and widely distributed. During his own lifetime it was reprinted in three editions, the one hundred songs included in the first edition growing to three hundred. To a great extent the enthusiasm with which these new songs were received derived from the popularity of the melodies and the integral syllabic adaptation of the Hebrew words.[18]

One method adopted by Najjara (as well as other poets of his own day and later) was to use particularly popular *shirei dugma* (model songs). He tried to make the Hebrew words of the songs' first lines sound very similar to the original words of the song that was being used as the exemplary vehicle. In other words, the Hebrew imitated the original, as in the famous Spanish romansa that begins

Arbolera Arbolera Arbolera tan gentil

Najjara used another version of the Spanish words, replacing the "Arbolera" by "Arboleda," and he starts his song:

(Spanish) Arboleda arboleda arboleda tan gentil
(Hebrew) Ḥil yoleda Bi soleda Qeshurah ʿal lev Biftil.

This technique, of course, is different from merely tacking an existing text onto a melody; it borders on creating a new musical composition and can be found in the *piyyuṭim* of various ethnic groups.

Avenary (1979, p. 186), dealing with the Gentile songs as a source of inspiration for Israel Najjara, writes about the above-mentioned practice:

> The aim at vocal concord between model and new creation is another feature of Najjara's working process. In general it accompanies the limitation of metre and rhythm, and the majority of the Hebrew songs fulfil these demands. We shall quote one example for each of his polylingual sources:
>
> a) (Spanish) Partome d'amor
> (Hebrew) Yaʿalat hamor
>
> b) (Turkish) Yalan se ey felek/yalan sen yalan/.
> (Hebrew) Yihroq shen zar doleq/holam lev holam/.
>
> c) (Arabic) Ana al-samra/w-sammuni sumayra/.
> (Hebrew) Anna el shamrah/nafshi mil'vaim/.
>
> The first half of the Arabic-Hebrew example is even written with the same letters in both languages!
>
> These Hebrew poems are distinguished by a rich variety of rhythmical structures. It may be supposed that Najjara followed his models in this respect; for in his Preface he postulated an identical number of accents as the first condition for successfully joining a foreign melody with a Hebrew text.
>
> In exploring the field of borrowed melodies for Jewish hymns, we have become aware of the intrusion of Spanish, Turkish and other poetic forms into Hebrew literature and their full assimilation, while the medieval metrics of Arabic origin were abandoned. These poetic forms' connection with agreeable tunes and their smoothly flowing rhythm assured them a great measure of popularity; they enjoyed uninterrupted continuity of performance down to the present. A contemporary Jew from Baghdad, for instance, when asked today about Jewish folksong, will spontaneously refer to the songs of Israel Najjara and his school. We also discovered an occasional close relationship between the Hebrew work and its foreign model, and observed that this must have contributed to the creative conception of the author. This feature should certainly not be overlooked, but it should be regarded as only one of several artistic elements mastered by gifted poets like Najjara. Thus the knowledge of music and poetry together will lead to a fuller evaluation and deeper appraisal of a fertile period in Hebrew poetry and song.

Creativity in the Singing of *Piyyuṭim*

We have noted that in the course of adapting existing tunes to a liturgical text, the artist was sometimes tempted to demonstrate his creative powers. One example of this is the use Moroccan *payṭanim* made of nonsense syllables for the sake of *taʿmīr*—embellishing the music. Where the musical phrase is longer than the verbal one, the *payṭan* supplies the missing syllables with meaningless na-nas, yi-lis, etc., a technique known as *shughl.*[19] The problem of the discrepancy in length of the verbal and musical phrases—passages in which the rhythmic musical organization behaves independently of the textual phrasing—is recognized by *payṭanim* of other ethnic groups as well. The phenomenon is most apparent in the opening or introductory sections of songs. These slow, ornamental openings which are also of an impromptu nature, precede the rhythmic *piyyuṭ* itself and require great skill and creativity on the part of the performer. The audience usually listens to this improvised section very attentively and the unexpected nature of its development creates an element of tension among the hearers. This tension is released as the congregation participates in the following rhythmic portion of the song which is rapid, popular, and easy to perform. The audience can easily take part either by singing along or clapping hands, depending on the occasion. As the rapid part of the song is performed, several disparate elements are reconciled: tension is relieved, an artistic performance gives way to popular folk participation, solo singing is replaced by group performance.

This dual form seems to be a crystallized, fairly common structure and the slow introductory opening has been given various names, the most popular of which is the *mawwāl*—an opening musical passage associated with improvisation. In Moroccan Jewry's songs of supplication this section is called *bitayn,* or "two lines," a reference to the two brief initial lines that leave adequate room for embellishment. Such short texts appear in the songs of several ethnic groups, their ubiquity largely a result of their easy applicability. Each opening can be sung before any *piyyuṭ* and in whatever musical mode the particular community is accustomed to. There need be no direct connection between this introductory text and the rest of the poem. As time went on, therefore, a repertoire evolved consisting of very brief *piyyuṭim* that serve as "introductions" or *mawwāls,* texts used for the improvisations that introduced the main body of the text, the *piyyuṭ* itself.[20]

In what fashion does the impromptu nature of these introductory passages find musical expression? In actual fact, the performer bases his improvisation on the material of the *maqām,* which represents a modal conception uniquely characteristic of music of the Near East and other countries dominated by Muslim culture. A *maqām* or "mode" is a complex musical entity given distinct musical character by its given scale, small units, range and compass, predominant notes, and pre-existing typical melodic and rhythmical formulas. It serves the musician as rough material for his own composition. Each *maqām* has a proper name that may refer to a place (as *ḥijāz, ʿirāq*), to a famous man, to an object, feeling, quality, or special event. Emotional or philosophical means and cosmological background are attached to a *maqām* and also to the rhythmic modes. The equivalent of the Arabic term *maqām* is *dastgah* in Persia, *naghmah* in Egypt, and *ṭbāʿ* in North Africa. Against this background, both composers and performers benefit from a relatively high degree of freedom. The artist is permitted, and indeed encouraged, to improvise spontaneously. The Oriental artist is fond of the details constituting a work; it is as if he were less concerned with a preconceived plan than with allowing the structure to emerge empirically from the details.

The *maqām,* then, can be defined as the basis for composing music that is in a fluid situation, steadily emerging. Oriental music paraphrases the patterns of ancient melodies; these patterns coalesce to form a musical continuum with differing but defined tonal centers. As time passed, local modal styles developed based on this conceptual principle, styles that are different dialects, as it were, of the same language. As a result, the same modal scale can appear in a variety of places and under a variety of names. Moreover, even when the scale is identical, there are differences on the stylistic level. Generally speaking, we may say that the technically talented musician of the Near East takes considerably more liberty in the use of patterns than does his Western colleague.[21]

The *Steiger*

The *Steiger* ("scale" in Yiddish) in the music of eastern European Jewry is parallel to the *maqām*—or mode—in the music of oriental Jewry. The *Steiger* also supplies the raw material on which the singer—usually the cantor in this case—bases his improvisations. Such raw material includes musical motives identified with the modes. Certain modes are used for the opening, others for endings, and still others to form a link between beginning and end. Appearing in the middle of the musical work, these links behave in accordance with the special laws that govern the *Steiger* itself.

Steigers generally have predominance within different groups of prayers. Eric Werner (1976) maintains that a *Steiger* is fixed in a given spot in the prayer as a result of considerations of how it corresponds to a given mood. The names of most of the *Steigers* are taken from the first words of the prayers they are identified with:

- *Adonay Malakh*—the accepted mode for prayers of thanksgiving and praise;
- *Magen Avot*—most widespread among western European Jewry, found in anecdotal and didactic texts;
- *Ahavah Rabbah*—appears most frequently in eastern European tradition and is mainly used to request mercy;
- *Seliḥah* (penitential)—used for different types of penitence, entreaties, supplications, and lamentations but it does not have a motive typically used for openings or endings. (Figure 21 illustrates the skeleton of the four Steigers.)

The *Ahavah Rabbah* is identified as a Jewish mode and in Hasidic singing (*niggun*) it is the dominant—virtually the only—*Steiger* used. One fairly well-grounded opinion, however, maintains that it originated in the Orient and reached eastern European Jewry with the cossacks. It is almost exactly the same as the *ḥijāz maqām,* with corresponding notes and intervals. Nevertheless, it can reasonably be assumed that despite the tonal similarity, the typical motives of the mode will vary from culture to culture. It should be understood that the *Steigers* fulfill many and diverse functions, and are not limited only to the *piyyuṭ*. They create a continuity linking the various prayers and, with the *mi-Sinai* tunes,[22] form the basic musical pattern employed by the cantor.

Fig. 21. The Steiger.

Ways of Performing the Songs

Synagogue hymns can be performed by a solo voice, by several soloists, by a soloist with the audience participating in a responsorial capacity, or by a chorus. Traditionally the men do the singing although in our day, under Western influence and with the growing tendency to hold concerts of liturgical music that stands on its own merits, a revolution has been taking place in this sphere. Women accompanied by musicians have begun to appear on the podium and perform liturgical songs.

There has been a considerable measure of "democratization" in the ritual performance of this music. The *payṭan* and cantor perform parts of the *piyyuṭ,* above all the opening and closing lines, thereby endowing these sections with the special festive embellishment discussed above. To the extent that the tune of the *piyyuṭ* is complicated and soloistic in nature, individual worshippers who have good voices perform certain verses; musically talented children are also encouraged to take an active part in this type of performance. With the exception of the first and last verses, certain *piyyuṭim* that have simple folk melodies are performed in their entirety by the whole congregation. *Piyyuṭim* that include answering words or phrases are sung by the cantor, with the worshippers intoning the responses. It is interesting to note that among the Jews of Yemen the group performance predominates. While group singing generally tends to be heterophonic, the Yemenite Jews seem to imbue theirs with rudimentary elements of polyphony.

Responsorial Singing

The Spanish *payṭanim* considered it important to ensure that the *piyyuṭim* would be performed with active audience participation—known as "responsorial singing." The congregation either sings certain passages or repeats lines that have just been sung by the *payṭan* or cantor. The length and frequency of the response varies, as does its place in the structure of the *piyyuṭ,* but there are certain overall common attributes: The response almost always consists of a brief, simple, rhythmic repetition of a melody and a few words—sometimes no more than one or two. The New Year prayers, the Yom Kippur prayers, and the *seliḥot* are rich in responsorial singing; the congregation's response ranges in form all the way from the repetition of a single word to the repetition of a whole line. This audience response is an important part of the prayer-singing. It enables the general public to play a significant role in what is going on: it keeps the people alert and attentive while the cantor sings and they await their cue to join in. The response can be antiphonal—that is, two-part—or choral, the worshippers singing in unison.

In responsorial singing the congregation either joins the cantor or answers him by singing well-known lines. There are editions of the prayer books, particularly those that include the High Holiday prayers, in which certain verses are preceded by the instruction "cantor," while others are marked "congregation." It is essential to distinguish carefully between the part sung by the *payṭan,* cantor, or some other trained individual, and the general congregation. Obviously, a solo performed by an individual can be more intricate and sophisticated and require greater technical and musical talent than is expected of one who sings as part of a group. In many cases, the role of the congregation is highly stylized in form: throughout a given passage the worshippers answer with an unchanging melodic and rhythmic phrase, even though the text itself may vary.

There are times when the passage being sung is divided into two parallel parts such as: "Give ear, O ye heavens, and I will speak;/and hear, O earth, the words of my mouth" (Deut. 32:1). Such a division is expressed in the performance as well: part of the congregation sings the first half of the verse, the other part of the congregation sings the second half. Alternatively, both parts can be sung by cantor and congregation or by two cantors.

This review of the background of some aspects of the development of the *piyyuṭ* as a creative work coupling words and music is intended primarily to point up the central role this artistic form played in the evolution of liturgical and paraliturgical singing. At its inception the *piyyuṭ* had indeed been intended to adorn, expand, and enrich the prayers. It is eminently clear, however, that even at the earliest stages of development it embodied a new musical dimension, one that was essentially different from the chanting that had previously characterized the performance of simple prayers. This dimension, influenced by the rhythmic element of the poetic words, sought to reinforce the religious experience with the uplift induced by the power of the music. Despite the ideological conflict noted in previous chapters, a conflict engendered by this development, natural love of music and the reality of Jewry's daily exposure to the music of the non-Jewish surroundings required a measure of compromise, even if only for the purpose of channeling sensual pleasures into a religious experience. The same need to compromise elicited the necessary search for a proper equilibrium between text and music. In this context, the *piyyuṭ* was a provocative source of musical inspiration.

6

Music in the World of the Mystic

Should chance bring you to Jerusalem's ancient Western Wall at midnight you are likely to witness the strange rite of *tiqqun ḥatsot*—the midnight vigil—being performed by Hasidim. They fervently recite prayers and *baqqashot* (supplications) aloud, lament the destruction of the Temple, and bemoan Israel's exile and dispersion. In the synagogue, on the eve of the Sabbath when the sun is about to set, one can see all the worshippers turn toward the entrance to greet the "bride" as they reach the line "Welcome O Bride, welcome O Bride, the Sabbath Queen," that is part of the hymn "Lekhah dodi." Thus the congregation, likening the Sabbath to a queen and bride, invites her to enter; some even dance before her as one dances before a bride. Or should you venture out after midnight on a Sabbath during the winter months that separate the Sukkot from Passover, you will find the synagogues of Jews from Syria, Morocco, Bukhara, and Turkey crowded with devout worshippers. With earnest enthusiasm they sing *baqqashot* hour after hour until the dawn approaches and they make their way home.

These and many other customs evolved under the influence of Jewish mysticism and the kabbalistic lore that emanated from Safed in the sixteenth century.[1] The various scenes described above are evidence of the continuing vitality of that influence as exercised through the exaltation of music in ritual as well as in daily life. In the mystic's world, prayer and the singing associated with it were perceived as elevating the soul to celestial realms where it could bask in the supreme glory. Such spiritual uplift flavored the believer's miserable life in this world with a taste of the splendor of life in the world to come. The mystic hears singing everywhere. In his imagination the entire universe incessantly sings the praise of the Lord, as is written: "Kol ha-neshamah tehallel yah" (Let everything that has breath praise the Lord) (Ps. 150:6). This special attitude deriving from the cosmic meaning inherent in the kabbalist's approach to song also encouraged the use of song as an enhancement to ritual.

Concepts relating to the importance and virtues of music that developed in the mystical doctrine and contributed to the enrichment of the musical repertoire, are so interwoven with the symbols and concepts comprising the world of the kabbalah that it is often difficult to treat them separately. Hence in the writings of the kabbalists not only is there no systematic discussion of music or expression of opinions about it, but even in the few cases where these matters are explicitly raised, the focus is not on music in and of itself. Nevertheless, as we shall see, these ideas affected practical musical activity, and on the conceptual level may have had even more important implications. Thus, for example, as against the extremist theological belief that music issued from a diabolical source and was intended to confuse the mind of the believer, diverting his thoughts from sober contemplation of the wonderful acts of the Creator, the mystics maintained that music has its source in the divine; in their view, God created it on the third day, making angels out of his own breath to sing his glory, day and night. Therefore the constant repetition of that revealed and divine music through mystical intention increases one's knowledge of the secrets of the creation and strengthens the believer's outlook.

Isaac ʿArama[2] (d. 1494) says that the secret of music was delivered to Israel together with the Torah (Adler 1975, p. 94). The thirteenth-century Spanish poet and kabbalist Isaac Ben Shlomo ibn abu Sahulah[3] wrote in his commentary on the Song of Songs that: "Knowledge of the secret of music leads one to knowledge of the secret of the Torah" (Adler 1975, 172–74). In the heated discussion about possible deleterious effects of music, one finds even stronger emphasis in Muslim mysticism of the Middle Ages on the view that music is neither monogenetic nor monovalent, that is, it oscillates between the divine and the satanic, the celestial and the terrestrial. The impact of music on the listener depends on the individual's virtue as well as the degree of mystical cognition of God and His revelation. According to the Spanish Muslim mystic Ibn al-ʿArabi (1165–1240), in its highest form the listening experience becomes entirely spiritual.[4]

The great flowering of music and the firm status it acquired in religious life as it found its way into widely varied activities was inspired by the symbols of the mystical doctrine, symbols that underpinned the ideological support emanating from the kabbalistic circle in Safed. At the same time this flowering emphasizes the disparity between the impulse immanent in the striving for a profound spiritual experience and the expectations of established institutions regarding the perpetuation in word and deed of the normative *mitsvot*. In the tension between the two, the drive for spiritual uplift prevailed, probably as a result of the trials and tribulations Jewry was suffering at the time, and also because it had earned the ideological approval of the most authoritative kabbalist scholars. In addition, these developments were undoubtedly fostered by the conceptual and behavioral changes engendered by the expulsion from Spain in 1492, an event that sent shock waves through all of Jewry.

With the decline of Spanish Jewry, the mystic teachings of the kabbalah and the messianic apocalyptic ideas it embraced became the expression of yearning for redemption and seemed to offer a spiritual lifeline to salvation. After the expulsion the singing encouraged by various esoteric doctrines became increasingly important, as a reaction to the rationalistic philosophy that had held sway among the Jews of Spain. The newly founded centers of Jewry were receptive to music as an element fortifying religious-spiritual aspects of life. The eminent scholar Gershom Scholem says about the movement that established itself in Safed some forty years after the expulsion from Spain that the linking of mysticism with apocalyptic messianism made kabbalism a highly important historic force, one possessing great creative strength. It was: "the last movement in Judaism to have had such a broad scope and such a decisive and continuous influence on the whole of the diaspora—in Europe, Asia and North Africa" (1971, p. 541).

From the Safed period onward, *Sefer ha-Zohar* (Book of splendor) became the major source of esoteric studies. The nation sanctified it as a canonical text and used it to guide Jewry through the labyrinthine byways of life. When it appeared in print in the first half of the sixteenth century, its widespread distribution was assured and its influence gradually penetrated into many and varied circles. The Zohar marks a lengthy process of development undergone by the kabbalistic doctrine; its roots lay in the esoteric and theosophical schools of thought subscribed to by Jews in Palestine and Egypt during the time of the Second Temple. It originated in ideas of a mystical nature that appeared in apocalyptic literature dealing among other things with divine revelation, the End of Days, the celestial world and its residents, the Divine Throne and its occupant. We have texts from the period that coincide with the beginning of Christianity (they were edited somewhat later) that were called *Sifrei Hekhalot* (Books of the Chambers) and *Sifrei Merkabah* (Books of the Throne-Chariot).[5] These books are exegetical treatments of the *Merkabah,* the chariot on which the Almighty, blessed be He, reveals himself. The revelations described are based on the prophetic visions described in chapter 1 of Ezekiel and chapter 6 of Isaiah.

The mystic's ecstatic ascension to the higher chambers (*hekhalot*) where he would be able symbolically to see the Divine Spirit, required preparation, primarily exercises in concentration. These were performed by lowering the head to the knees and singing hymns of an ecstatic nature—presumably replicas of the hymns the angels sing to God in heaven. A constantly recurring theme of these hymns was the *Qedushah*—the Trisagion—from Isa. 6:3: "Holy, holy, holy is the Lord of Hosts." At a later period the singing of the *Qedushah,* the highest point for both the angels and Israel, led to crystallization of the important themes of the resonances between the micro- and macrocosmos, culminating in the parallel singing of the *Qedushah* by the angels and Israel (see below).

With respect to the *Merkabah* mystics, Gershom Scholem (1975) maintains that in this context one may speak of the "threshold" of mysticism, as these theorists of God's Chariot-Throne never come near the Creator. The line of separation is never obscured, there is no interaction; a concept such as *devequt* (devout adherence) which appears later in the kabbalah, the Hebrew mysticism of the Middle Ages, is extremely remote from the *Merkabah* literature. And something else is missing as well: the symbolic attitude to religious matters, which is such an important part of the kabbalah. In the main, these are descriptions of visions and of the behavior necessary to reach the ecstatic state desired by the visionary. Nevertheless, from the historic standpoint the *Merkabah* literature must be viewed as an important foundation stone, a stage on the way to creating the doctrine of the kabbalah, difficult though it may be to find its traces in the writings of the kabbalists. Scholem goes on to explain that for chroniclers of Israel's history and religion, as a historic phenomenon the kabbalah begins in the twelfth century of the Christian era, when the earliest kabbalistic text, the *Bahir Book,* appeared (in Provence, France). This book is also known as the *Preachings of Rabbi Nehuniah ben Ha-Kaneh*—one of the greatest of the *Merkabah* mystics. Attribution of the *Bahir* to this tanna (a scholarly Mishnaic authority)[6] seems to be the tenuous thread that leads from the *Merkabah* mystics to the kabbalah (Scholem, 1971).

In the twelfth century the doctrine of the Kabbalah made its way into Provence; from there it spread to Spain where it reached its peak in the city of Gerona in the thirteenth century. Gerona offered fertile soil for the germination and growth of the ideas of the early kabbalists, their work culminating in the *Sefer ha-Zohar* written by Moshe de Leon between 1280 and 1286. "The Zohar," according to Isaiah Tishby (1957, 1, p. 17) "is not one single book, but a large literary treasure-trove embracing many and varied parts." Bibliographically, the Zohar includes three books, divided in all the known editions into five volumes: The first includes discussions of the biblical book Genesis; the second, the book of Exodus; a third volume includes the rest of the Pentateuch; Zohar Amendments (*Tiqqunei Zohar*) and the New Zohar complete the five volumes. The *Zohar* (p. 23) does not present its ideas in the systematic, orderly fashion of the kabbalah, but expresses them through commentaries and homiletics. Issues are discussed in confused disorder and subjects that seem to have only the remotest affinity are often interwoven. The Zoharic commentaries and homiletics are not limited to the biblical themes that make up the frame of the work; they encompass all manifestations of Judaic thought and feeling.

These introductory comments, meant to establish very general milestones that serve as the background essential for an understanding of some musical subjects found in the kabbalah, can best be concluded by again turning to Gershom Scholem. In his attempt to discover—beyond the purely historical connection—a common denominator underlying the different currents of thought characterizing respectively the early mysticism of the talmudic period, the Spanish kabbalah (thirteenth century), the school of Safed (sixteenth century) and the Hasidic movement, Scholem writes: "Such a common denominator can, perhaps, be discovered in certain unchanging fundamental ideas concerning God, Creation and the part played by man in the Universe. Two such ideas are the attributes of God and the symbolic meaning of the Torah" (1967, p. 18). Indeed, through the mystical interpretation of the Torah, the believer might find the way to mystical cognition of God and His revelation. In this respect, it is relevant to repeat ibn Sahulah's statement that "Knowledge of the secret of music leads one to knowledge of the secret of the Torah."

Music and Meditation

Unlike the Muslim mystics who usually describe in great detail the decisive role played by music and dance in rousing the devotee to ecstasy, the Jewish kabbalist normally abstains from revealing his personal experience and from providing autobiographical details. He describes the objects of his contemplation objectively, for he considers meditation an intimate act, not to be exhibited publicly.

For the kabbalists the ecstatic experience does not mean a state of confusion and complete self-effacement—which would correspond to the Arabic *fanā'*, the highest degree in the process of mystical union;[7] this type of ecstasy is the province of the vulgar. The kabbalist's ecstasy can rather be described as a profound meditation through which the mysteries of the Divine Name reveal themselves to the illuminated. This state can be reached by prayer with intention (*kavvanah*), the singing of hymns, and the science of letter combinations. In every respect the sounds of speech and the speech associated with musical sounds are invovled and together they imply, in our case, recourse to the pre-eminent language, Hebrew. In the chapter of the song of Creation in the tract called "Perek shirah" (The song of Creation),[8] we read that all beings are granted the gift of language for the sole purpose of singing—in biblical words—the praise of their Creator. The prevailing idea of the pre-eminence of the Hebrew language, its superiority over all other languages,[9] is founded on the concept that it is the one and only language of God; its mystical value arises from the fact that all that lives is an expression of God's language.

Music and Prophecy

In thirteenth-century Spain a school of "Prophetic Kabbalism" developed that wished to demonstrate the practical method of acquiring the spirit of prophecy through exercises such as studying letters and names as well as by means of the science of letter combination and numerology. Abraham Abulafia (b. Saragosa, 1240), was the outstanding proponent of Prophetic Kabbalism.[10] He had journeyed to distant parts and considered himself a disciple of Maimonides, maintaining that his own teachings were a continuation of those of the master. The literature of the kabbalah was much influenced by this school, although its effect is hardly reflected in the published texts.

The school of Prophetic Kabbalism developed special ways of progressing to spiritualization and prophetic revelation. In his search for a way of freeing the soul from the bonds of ordinary perception, Abulafia developed a theory of the mystical combination of Hebrew letters (*ḥokhmat ha-tseruf*) in which the alphabet takes the place of musical notes. He compared this type of intellectual exercise based on pure thought to musical composition, maintaining that it exerted the same influence on the soul as music does. In his *Gan naʿul* (Closed garden) he writes:

> Know thou that the combination of letters can be compared to listening to music, for the ear hears and the sounds are combined in accordance with the [required] form of a melody, or the syllables [of speech]. The proof can be found in the combination formed by the *kinnor* and *nevel* [biblical terms for instruments designating two types of lyres][11] whose voices when mingled cause the listening ear to perceive a variety of emotional meanings. Through their vibration the strings touched by the right and left hand bring a sweet sensation to the ear. And from the ear this sensation travels to the heart, and from the heart to the spleen, and enjoyment is continually renewed through the recurrence of sounds, and the same is true of the combination of letters.[12]

Thus we learn that the combination of letters gives the soul the same pleasure as musical harmony, because these combinations unveil hidden secrets. This kinship between the meaning of letter combinations and musical harmony, as well as their effect on the soul, apparently is not restricted to pure theoretical speculation, but extends to practice. Abulafia himself establishes rules concerning the use of particular intonations and vowel pitches in the performance of certain forms of recitation. A disciple of his compares the pleasant voice of one reciting to the pleasant sound of the *kinnor,* stating that they exert the same influence on the soul.[13] Another disciple offers a concrete example to demonstrate the overwhelming power of a good melody. After having stated that King David and the Levites received their musical art through divine inspiration, an indication that their melodies were indeed those sung by the angels, he refers to the art of the cantor. When a cantor is good looking, has a pleasant voice, is eloquent of speech, and his melodies are harmonious, he brings enjoyment to the souls of the worshippers. Since the souls are spiritual and emanate from the Holy Name, the Holy Name shares their enjoyment. It is to him (the cantor) that the verse "He who rejoices God and men" refers.[14]

According to this theory music is metaphorically conceived not only as the technique of letter combination, or a means of attaining prophetic revelation, but also as a direct tool for acquiring the power of prophecy. In dealing with this topic, Abulafia and his disciples referred to such biblical verses as: "And there, as you come to the city, you will meet a band of prophets coming down from the high place with harp, tambourine, flute, and lyre before them prophesying" (1 Sam. 10:5); or: "But now bring me a minstrel. And when the minstrel played, the power of the Lord came upon him" (2 Kings 3:15). These examples illustrate how prophecy is achieved thanks to music, and how the receptacle of prophecy, the intellect, is prepared.

Moreover, in the writings of this school, this secret power of music does not seem to be considered a lost science retaining only historic relevance.

Man as Protagonist of the Drama of the Universe

"If the whole universe is an enormous complicated machine," writes Gershom Scholem, "then man is the machinist who keeps the wheels going by applying a few drops of oil here and there at the right time" (1967, p. 30). This beautiful simile placing the kabbalist in the center of the world's dramatic stage is directly related to some of the most important roles assigned to music in kabbalist writings. But first, let us see how man is animated by a spirit emanating from God, implying that it is the divine spirit that causes man to sound in perfect harmony. A talmudic legend quoted in the Zohar—one we have referred to before in these pages—recounts that David's *kinnor* suspended over his bed plays of its own accord when the north wind blows through it. A symbolic commentary on this legend compares the *kinnor* to the human body. And just as with the *kinnor,* the divine spirit (i.e., the north wind) blows through the orifices of the body, making it resound and sing. Hence a man animated by the divine spirit is like a vehicle for the divine melody and message received by emanation.

Commenting on the same legend, Judah Moscato (d. 1590) transposes the content into the concept of resonance between David's soul (his *kinnor*) and the north wind (i.e., the divine spirit), concluding that just as the *kinnor* player has to master his art to obtain perfect harmony, the spiritual *kinnor* (the human soul) has to abide by the laws of harmony and music (Adler 1975, p. 230). Almost the same concept is to be found in certain Muslim mystical writings. In his work "The Lightning Flashes Concerning the Refutation of Those Who Declare Listening to Music Is Forbidden," Abu Ḥāmid al-Ghazzālī (d. 1121) describes the mystical meaning of the instruments used in the ceremony of *Dhikr.*[15] Speaking of the flute, he says that "its nine holes correspond to the nine orifices of the human body, and that the air which penetrates the flute to make it sound is comparable to the divine light entering the reed of human existence" (Shiloah 1979, pp. 112–13).

But man is not just a passive receptacle or vehicle; he is a protagonist capable of influencing his own destiny and that of the universe through prayers and the singing of hymns. One of the prevalent themes of kabbalistic literature is God's predilection for Israel's prayers, for its chanting of the Torah aloud in a pleasant voice, and its singing of hymns and prayers. The *Zohar* is full of references of this kind: On the night of the Exodus God orders the angels to stop singing because Israel is singing on earth; the angels stop and listen. At midnight when the Holy One, blessed be He, enters the Garden of Eden to delight with the righteous ones, the choir of angels, the trees of Eden, and heaven and earth sing his praises. But at this time God hears the voices of those who are studying the Torah on earth, and this sound is more beautiful to him than the singing of the angels. Hence, the extreme importance of singing and studying the Torah in a beautiful voice at midnight. This concept was probably influential in the development of the midnight vigil (*tiqqun ḥatsot*) as well as the nocturnal singing of various associations (e.g., "Watchers of the Dawn") and the singing of *baqqashot* in Oriental communities (see below).

The sublime nature of Israel's singing is related to another important theme, that of the communal or parallel singing of the angels. These latter may join in only when Israel has sung but, on the other hand, the power of this singing achieves its highest expression only when both choirs simultaneously intone the praise of God. So it is that whenever Israel gathers to sing hymns, the angels in the celestial realm do likewise. This acquires particular importance in the performance of the *Qedushah*—the Trisagion.

According to mystical theories, the *Qedushah* as sung concurrently in the synagogue and in the heavens is a supreme moment for both the angels and the people of Israel. The concept of mutual resonance between the microcosmos and the macrocosmos (in other words, between man and the angels) eventually evolved from this simultaneous singing. What is said by man here on earth has an echo in the heavens and vice versa. such mutual resonance is expressed in a belief in the interrelation of the celestial *Qedushah* and the *Qedushah* said on earth: to attain full potency it must be said in both places at once. Three groups—or choirs—of angels in heaven participate in the *Qedushah* while the people of Israel are singing it on earth. One group comprises those angels who intone songs and praises during the day together with the earthly worshippers; the second consists of the angels who accompany the people of Israel at all times, whenever they say the *Qedushah*. The third, the "supreme choir," sings in the highest, most exalted realm.

Thus when the people of Israel sing in praise of the Almighty they are accompanied by the angels. This parallelism extends not only to the *Qedushah*, but implies full concordance between the singing of those on high and those below. A passage of the *Zohar* that attributes great importance to the parallel singing of the *Qedushah*, also describes its performance by three choirs posted in different places within the celestial orbit.[16] The *Zohar* describes one group of angels that declaims the first "Holy" in full, high voices. A group on another side chants the second "Holy" in pleasant tones and from somewhere else a group simply intones the third "Holy." Each choir has its own leader. On still another side the waves of the sea billow and subside and the angels placed there intone sweetly "Barukh kevod Adonay mi-meqomo" (Blessed be the glory of the Lord from his place). These describe figuratively the rendering of the words of the *Qedushah*. Indeed, after the opening sentence: "Naqdishakh vena'aritsakh ke-no'am siyaḥ sod sarphei qodesh" (Thou shalt be hallowed and adored as in the pleasant secret converse of the holy Seraphs) come the words "Ha-meshaleshim lekha qedushah ve-khen katuv 'al yad nevi'akha ve-qara zeh el zeh ve-amar qadosh qadosh qadosh" (who thrice bless thee, as is written by Thy prophets, and called to one another and said holy, holy, holy). And in response those paying homage intone "Barukh kevod Adonay mi-meqomo." This multi-choir performance so beautifully described by the author of the *Zohar* is therefore based on the words of the *Qedushah* itself, wherein there is a conspicuous parallelism between those above and those below.

The *Qedushah* of the *Musaph* (added prayer) known as *Keter* (Crown—so-called because of its first word) also gives forceful expression to this parallelism. Its opening sentence is: "Keter yittenu lekha Adonay Eloheinu mal'akhim hamonei maʿala yaḥad ʿim ʿammekha kevutse maṭṭah" (A crown will be given thee, our almighty Lord, [by] the multitudes of angels in heaven together with the congregations of thy people on earth).[17] The form and words in which the *Keter* continues evoked an interesting responsorial song: the descriptive passages are sung by the cantor and the answers of the angels are sung by the congregation. There is a difference between the *Qedushah* of the morning prayer and the *Keter* of the *Musaph,* which, as we have said, is always sung responsorially and has a popular, almost folk nature. On the other hand, in many Sephardic communities, particularly in the Balkans and eastern regions of the Mediterranean, the *Qedushah* has become almost a bravura passage in which the cantors exhibit their full talent for improvisation and melismatic embellishment. Because of the special sublimity with which the mystics invested the *Qedushah,* the Zohar (in *Tiqqunei Zohar,* 12:27a) refers to this prayer as one of the songs associated with messianic redemption. At the End of Days all the animals will awaken and sound their voices and the birds will trill sweetly to greet the maiden (the *Shekhinah*—the mystical Congregation of Israel, sometimes given female identity) with joy and song, and to be granted the blessing (of union) with the groom. The song heard then will be the *Qedushah.*

To return to the simile of man as machinist, we can now carry it further and define some of the objectives attainable through his powerful influence. First there is the basic concept that considers the earthly community of Israel as formed according to the archetype of the mystical congregation called *Shekhinah.* Hence, everything that is done by individuals of all communities on earth is magically reflected in the celestial regions; or, as this concept is often formulated, the impulse from below calls forth the impulse from above. This influential force or impulse can be used in the struggle against the satanic powers of the devil and to restore the primordial harmony that was destroyed with Adam's fall. Two primary concepts are connected with this purpose: the *kavvanah*—the mystical intention or act of concentration, directly linked to the inner cosmic process, and the *tiqqun*—restitution or reintegration with the original harmony that was destroyed when Adam transgressed, causing the emergence of diabolical forces. It becomes one of the tasks of the illuminated to fight against the evil that tries with all its might to disrupt the harmony sought by those who have seen the light.

The Struggle against Evil Forces and the Realm of Darkness[18]

These forces dwell in the depths of the great abyss and become potent in the darkness of night, particularly during the first watch. This realm of darkness is considered identical with the *sephirah* (celestial region) of stern judgment and punishment. The music of the evil forces consists mainly of discordant notes, wailing, sobbing, lamenting, and the blowing of horns, all of which caused horrible discord in the world and brought forth stern judgment. The Zohar calls these evil forces "Masters of Sobbing" or "Masters of Wailing." Their power expires with daylight, which corresponds to the *sephirah* of love or God's mercy, although according to one passage they even succeed in silencing the marvelous choir of the angels. When God's Chariot-Throne—*Merkabah*—moves, countless myriads of angels intone songs, evoking a sound pleasant to the ear and delightful to the heart. To the left stand two hundred thousand Masters of Sobbing. Then the Master of Judgment appears; he stands among them and the singing ceases. The blowing of the ram's horn and the singing emanating from the right side silence the wailing of the left side and the stern judgment is transformed into mercy.

We repeatedly find the idea that music comes from the north, that is the left, the side of judgment, while speech arrives from the right, the side of mercy. However, there is another conception of the source of song. In an exegetical treatment of the verse, "I will sing of the mercies of the Lord for ever" (Ps. 89:2), the question is raised as to whether song emanates from the side of mercy, that is, the right side; the answer is that it is included in the right-hand aspect of the left side.

The realm of darkness of the *siṭra aḥra* "other side" (a term designating evil), symbolizing the imperfection due to the fall, is like nocturnal darkness and the darkness of Israel's dispersion. All of these symbolize imperfection and joylessness. Midnight singing causes the angels to weep and imbues them with a feeling of profound sorrow; then God shakes those above and those below. Only thanks to people who study the Torah at night does the Holy One, blessed be He, enjoy any gratification; the souls of the righteous also take pleasure in listening to the singing of those who are studying the Torah. Noctural singing is supremely effective both in the struggle against the forces of darkness and in eliciting divine mercy; hence this singing receives extensive treatment in the Zohar.

At night, when the Master of Judgment rules the world, the Masters of Sobbing blow the ram's horn and wail. When they blow the horn a second time they waken song, the *ba'alei trisin* (shield-bearers) rise—and Judgment wakes up. Human beings are asleep and their souls leave them to bear witness on high; judgment having been passed, divine mercy permits the soul to return to the body.

Midnight is a turning-point. At that hour the Holy One, blessed be He, goes into the Garden of Eden to enjoy the company of the *tsaddiqim* (the righteous). All the trees and perfumes sing before him, the *tsaddiqim* intone: My love enters his garden.[19] Great are the rewards of those who rise to study the Torah at that hour; God offers them a thread of mercy because then they give voice to the words of the Torah and the sweet waters of the river of Eden will quench their thirst. Furthermore it is said: "The Holy one, blessed be He, prefers this sound over all the hymns and praises recited on high." And when the north wind begins to blow at midnight all the spheres and all the heavens and the holy animals and *ofannim* (a mystical appellation for one of the groups of angels) and all the heavenly host—are roused and animated and they all burst into song in praise of Him who said "Let there be a world," until He enters the Garden of Eden with the righteous. And with respect to the north wind—it is at midnight that the *kinnor* over the bed of David wakens him to praise the Almighty in full-throated song.

But this is not all that happens at midnight. A spark issues from within the "wheels" of the animals: it touches the rooster under his wing—and he cries out. The crowing of the rooster at midnight is a call to wake up and weep for the destruction of the Temple. The Almighty, blessed be He, takes part in this weeping and it is in this context that the following verses are recited: "O God, the heathen are come into Thine inheritance" (Ps. 79:1), "They have given the dead bodies of Thy servants" (Ps. 79:2), and "By the rivers of Babylon" (Ps. 137:1).

The singing continues into the third watch (*ashmoret shelishit*): David, with the angels, plays for God, as implied in the passage in Job (38:7). "When the morning stars sang together,/And all the sons of God shouted for Joy." The result of the human activity is widely pervasive—not only does the Almighty enjoy it and shower his mercy on the living, but when human beings burst into song, the celestial creatures add the cognitive power that enables them to know and to attain.[20]

The Shofar[21]

Many passages of the Zohar deal with the shofar: its shape, the material it is made of, the sounds it emits, and its various functions. In reviewing some of its functions we necessarily refer to motifs associated with cosmogonic theories, that is, with the study of processes and reasons that brought about the creation of the world and the relationships between divine and mundane forces. A theme that constantly recurs in different forms is the role the shofar plays in dissipating harsh judgment. It is within the power of the shofar to change the nature of celestial judgment from punishment to clemency; the blowing of the shofar can interrupt and even silence the accusers on the day of judgment (the New Year). When the Holy One, blessed be He, is sitting on the seat of Judgment and the litigants—the Masters of Sobbing and Wailing—bring their denunciations to him, by dint of prayer and blowing the shofar, the people of Israel turn God's decision from punishment to merciful forgiveness.

How is this accomplished? The sound of the shofar, which is compounded of fire, wind, and water blended together, rises to the seat of Judgment and strikes it, creating a sound on high that is described in mystical terms as the "voice of Jacob." The blast reverberates loudly and the devil becomes confused, while the Almighty's compassion is aroused. Satan cannot exert his dominance by eclipsing the moon (at the beginning of the month the demonic forces of the serpent are the ruling power) and compassion mitigates the severity of the judgment. By the interesting procedure described below, the sound rises to the Judgment Seat and a harmony is created as the voices from earth mingle with those from above. Just as compassion aroused below encourages the awakening of compassion in the celestial regions, so the sound of the shofar below awakens the sound of the celestial shofar. A sort of mutual affinity exists between the world above and the world below. Through this affinity the blowing of the shofar is able to reinforce the power of the Almighty, blessed be He, and bring about *tiqqun* (the restoration of harmony) in the world.

As the New Year begins God wants the shofar blown to strengthen him; if it is blown *bekavvanah*—with mystical intention—its sound rises and aggrandizes the Patriarchs. Each blast of the shofar rises to a celestial sphere where it remains until the next blast arrives; together they rise to the next sphere, where they again wait; then they move on, fortified anew at each sphere, until they have reached the highest sphere, the one that towers over the rest and is the place of residence of the Almighty, blessed be He.

In this context the concept *kavvanah* is most important. In order to blow the ram's horn with *kavvanah* one must know the symbolic secrets of the different sounds. It means knowing the esoteric significance of each sound and drilling it into one's memory, which is much more than merely blowing into the shofar to evoke its three basic sounds—*teqiʿah, shevarim,* and *teruʿah* (blast, tremolo, and fanfare).[22] In this connection it is said that Rabbi Shimon[23] would not permit a man to blow the shofar unless he was "wise enough to know the secret of blowing" (Zohar 3:18a–b). This is also the sense of the passage: "Ashrei haʿam yodʿei teruʿah" (Happy is the people that know the joyful sound) (Ps. 89:16). Such knowledge includes, among other things, the symbolic meanings of the three basic forms of blowing the shofar. The *teqiʿah,* derived from *hoqaʿah,* is based on the verse "And the Lord said unto Moses, take all the chiefs of the people and hang them up (*hoqaʿ otam*) in face of the sun, that the fierce anger of the Lord may turn away from Israel" (Num. 25:4). When the guilty are kept far away from the gateway to the King, prayer and song can rise thereto. The living things spread their wings to receive them, God hears the wings flapping to announce the coming of the queen (symbolic of *Knesset Israel*), and opens the Temple, receiving her with joy. All of this occurs at the time of the eighteen benedictions recited daily—the *ʿAmidah* (standing) prayer—and therefore this is the most appropriate occasion for making requests.

Moreover, important historic events in the life of the nation are associated with the blowing of the shofar, as well as events of the future—that is, the redemption. The *teqiʿah* symbolizes the continuation of the *galut* (dispersion), the *shevarim* symbolize the approach of redemption, the arrival of which is announced by the jubilant *teruʿah.* The *shevarim* shatter the tombstones of those being punished; their pillars stand in the gateways and prevent the prayers from entering the world above. This interpretation is based on the passage in Exod. 3:24: "Thou shalt not bow down to their gods, nor serve them, nor do after their doings; but thou shalt utterly overthrow them, and break in pieces their pillars." The *teruʿah* shackles the provocateur in chains, because it produces trill-like sounds suggesting the links of a chain.

The concept of *zikhron teruʿah* that appears in prayers implies remembrance of important past events. When the people of Israel sound the shofar with the advent of the New Year, they remember the fanfare that saved them by bringing down the walls of Jericho, and they are saved again (Josh. 6:1–6). As a result of Joshua's victory, they will be victorious over the angels who bear witness against them. The *teruʿah*—likened to a chain—symbolizes both the chaining of the forces of evil and liberation from the chains; the people of Israel will be freed as slaves are freed of their chains, when the shofar of the final redemption blows.

And indeed, both past and future are associated with the shofar of redemption. This is a recurrent motive in the literature of the kabbalah: the millenial *shofar* of redemption is symbolic of the shofar that brought the people of Israel out of Egypt; the shofar of the revelation of Sinai is the great horn that will be blown at the end of days, as stated in Isaiah: "And it shall come to pass in that day,/That a great horn shall be blown;/And they shall come that were lost in the land of Assyria,/And they that were dispersed in the land of Egypt;/And they shall worship the Lord in the holy mountain at Jerusalem" (27:13).[24]

A rather detailed description of the role of the shofar at the End of Days appears as follows in the *New Zohar:* "Then they will carry the banners of the Messiah and the noise of the sounds of the shofar will fall upon the world and all the people of the world will hear and see" (*Zohar Ḥadash,* 56a). At this tremendous event the most important happenings in the history of the people of Israel will return and be crucially significant—and they will close the cycle of the generations. The Song of the Sea will be heard on the day of redemption. At that time there will be many who will sound the shofar and many singers and makers of lightning, about whom it is said in the revelation at Sinai: "And it came to pass . . . that there were thunders and lightnings and a thick cloud upon the mountain and the voice of a horn exceeding loud."[25]

Throughout the ages the shofar has tantalized those who believe in its magical power. They have been fascinated particularly by the idea that Satan tries to interfere with the blowing of the shofar in the hope of preventing the blasts from rising to heaven. They even attribute any unsuccessful attempt to bring forth sound, to diabolic intervention. To thwart the devil's intentions, the shofar blower seeks ways of confusing him. When the shofar stubbornly refuses to produce sound there are those who whisper into its wide end the verse: "And let the graciousness of the Lord our God be upon us:/Establish thou also upon us the work of our hands;/Yea, the work of our hands establish thou it" (Ps. 90:17). Others simply soak the shofar in vinegar to remove the sting that is making it rebellious and to chase the devil out of it—as there is no doubt that his presence is what is blocking the instrument's opening.

In two illustrated prayer books produced in the fourteenth and fifteenth centuries there are stereotypical drawings of a man blowing the shofar.[26] The artist depict him performing his function: the shofar in his mouth emits magical sputters and sparks of sound. The shofar player's right foot is raised to rest on a three-legged stool. It is commonly assumed that the function of the stool is to separate the player from the ground, which is the source that nourishes the corrupt powers of external forces. As time passed these popular beliefs gave rise to humorous anecdotes, one of which appears in Droyanov's *Book of Jokes and Wit.* This tale tells of the original way in which an "official rabbi" suggests subduing a rebellious shofar—but first the concept of "official rabbi" requires explanation. According to the laws of the Russian monarchy, every Jewish male was permitted to serve as an "official rabbi"—the only condition being that he was well-educated and practiced a profession such as medicine, the law, or engineering. The face that he might have been totally ignorant even of the Hebrew alphabet was of no concern. Consequently, many small communities that did not have the means to support both a doctor and an "official rabbi" would appoint the doctor as their rabbi. The story told by Droyanov is as follows:

> On the first day of the New Year the shofar rebelled and only ear-piercing shrieks issued from it. The synagogue officials sat down to take council. What should they do to divert the shofar from its perversity on the morrow as well?
>
> One of the officials said; "I know for sure: When a shofar rebels, one recites: 'Let there be sweetness' " [a charm against mishaps].
>
> A second official responded: "And I have heard it said by the well-informed: a rebellious shofar must be soaked in vinegar." Then they approached the "official rabbi," the doctor, to decide which course to follow.
>
> The doctor-rabbi listened to the argument, thought matters over and said: "My advice is to combine both remedies: One dose of 'Let there be sweetness' to one dose of vinegar." (1963, 1, p. 143)

The Universal Harmony

In his book *The Binding of Isaac* Isaac ʿArama[27] discusses the musical meaning of universal harmony. He maintains that the perfection of the world is the outcome of the tuning of the different strings of the minor instrument (the microcosmos) in perfect consonance with the strings of the major instrument (the macrocosmos). Harmonic proportionality of the instruments is established through observance of the laws of the Torah, while nonobservance of the laws impairs this proportionality, causing the world to degenerate. It is therefore the task of man to concentrate his whole inner purpose on the reintegration of the original harmony and the primordial spiritual nature of all creation. This means, in effect, salvation.

In a commentary on the first word in the Bible *bereshit* (in the beginning), the *New Zohar* 5b–6a tells us that God created the world in song (that is, harmony), because the word *bereshit* suggests *shir ta'ev,* which is a rearrangement of the same letters (in Hebrew the "b" and "v" are signified by the same alphabetic symbol, the vocal aleph after the r is quiescent). In *bereshit* the *sh, i,* and *r* constitute the word *shir* (song); the *t, e,* and *v*—the word *ta'ev* (desire). *Shir ta'ev,* then, means song of desire, expressing the longing of the whole universe to glorify God, the desire of heaven and earth to sing the praises of the Holy One, blessed be He. It is said that *shir ta'ev* corresponds to the Song of Songs, the finest of all songs, which shall be heard when the chief demon Samael and all his hordes[28] disappear from the world, that is to say, at the End of Days. Then all the beasts of the Chariot-Throne will bestir themselves and sing aloud and all the winged creatures will whistle tunes, welcoming with music and gladness the daughter (the mystical archetype of the community of Israel) on her way to the bridegroom to receive the wedding sanctification. They will sing the *Qedushah*. It is then that David's *kinnor* will waken him and sing ten kinds of melodies, the first of which is *'Ashrei* (Blessed is—the initial word of the Psalms), the equivalent of *Bereshit*.

The Whole Cosmos Sings

A recurrent theme in the Zohar is the music of angels. In the process of creating the world, God made the angels out of his own breath and they sing his glory at all times. They are organized into different classes and choirs according to their attributes and to the hours and watches of day and night. Among the various classifications, there is one that divides the choir of angels into three bands. The first is assigned to sing together with Israel during the day; the second is said to join Israel in the singing of the *Qedushah* and is subdivided into three choirs, each intoning the word "holy" alternately and in different renditions. Each choir has its own leader. As to the third band, it is constituted of the upper maidens, is the highest of all the choirs, and upon it devolves the task of establishing blissful union and harmony between the *sefirah* of *Malkhut* (Kingdom of God) and that of *Tif'eret* (Beauty). This is not the only female choir in the upper regions; other choirs and even soloists dwell in the female *hekhalot* (chambers). In Yokheved's chamber myriads and multitudes of women sing the Song of the Sea three times a day. After the passage "Then Miriam the prophetess, the sister of Aaron took a timbrel in her hand," (Exod. 15:20) the rest of the women are silent and Yokheved sings alone. The righteous ones in the Garden of Eden listen to their song and some of the angels join in. In another chamber Deborah and a women's choir intone the song Deborah sang in this world.

The song of the angels in the three watches of the night, as against the three daily prayers of the Jews, is a favorite theme, repeatedly described in various versions. In their song the angels seek to unite with their Lord, but the proximity of diabolical forces interferes. Those forces have to be driven away by guile. Not only the angels sing: the stars, the spheres, the *Merkabah*, (the Chariot-Throne) and the beasts, the trees in the Garden of Eden and their perfumes, indeed, the whole universe, sings before God. No one on earth, with the exception of Moses and Joshua, can hear this music. As to Joshua, it is said that he heard the pleasant melody of the sun in the middle of a battle and was seriously disturbed, which is why he said: "Sun, stand thou still at Gibeon" (Josh. 10:12), meaning "stop singing." Moscato

(d. 1590) quotes this tradition to prove that not only Pythagoras was capable of hearing the music of the spheres.[29]

The music of the spheres and planets has led to several speculations that are included in *Midrash ha-ḥokhmah* by Judah ben Shlomo ha-Cohen ibn Mitka (mid-thirteenth century). In his "Speculation on Psalm 150" he establishes parallelisms between the nine classical instruments mentioned there and the nine spheres or planets: the *tof* (frame drum) corresponds to Jupiter; *maḥol* (interpreted as dance) to Mars; since this latter is considered baneful, its association with dance indicates negative aspects and imperfection. The *minnim* (string instrument) corresponds to Venus; the *ʿuggav* (wind instrument) to the sun; the *tsiltselei shamaʿ* (sounding cymbals) to the moon. The other instruments and their corresponding planets are missing.[30]

Commenting on the same Psalm, a passage of the Zohar declares that all these praises with the diverse instruments are as nothing compared with what is said in the last verse of Psalm 150, which also closes the book: "Let everything that breathes praise the Lord./Praise the Lord."

Influence of Kabbalistic Mystical Theories on Song

Theories dealing with the power and function of song were extensively developed and given important practical application by the kabbalists of Safed. This kabbalistic school had its wellsprings in the teachings of Isaac ben-Shlomo Luria, reverently called the "Saint Ari" (*ha-Ari ha-qadosh*).[31] Born in Jerusalem in 1534, Luria died in Safed in 1572 at the age of thirty-eight. Despite his youth and the brief time he spent in Safed, he made a profound impression on the religious center there and subsequently on all of Jewry. The Ari left very few writings of his own, his doctrine having been transmitted and expanded in the works of his disciples, particularly R. Ḥayim Vital (1543–1620), whose book *Ets Ḥayim* (Tree of Life) is considered the standard rendition of the Lurianic kabbalah.[32]

The kabbalists, among whom were talented poets, believed in fostering poetic creativity, as it could raise the individual and help him overcome the drabness and mundane tribulations of life in this world. They believed that the heavenly gates opened to receive one who intoned a Psalm, a portion of the Mishnah or Zohar, and conscientiously sang hymns and supplications. He became a part, so to speak, of the universal singing of the celestial angels, of the moving "wheels," and of the wind that stirs the trees in paradise. Leading kabbalists would often take their students on long walks, during which they would sing hymns of praise and adulation. Some of the devotees taught these songs to women and children.

The Sabbath

The theme of the sanctity of the Sabbath influenced the development of song. The Sabbath was a kind of small-scale paradise with sweetly scented delights that enveloped the pious. According to the mystical doctrine that emanated from Safed, the Sabbath was personified as a heavenly queen imprisoned in the sky; she descends to earth once a week to dispense her holiness. This idea gave birth to one of the fundamental rites associated with the day: *Qabbalat Shabbat*—receiving the Sabbath. As the sun set on Friday the kabbalists dressed in festive apparel and filed out to the fields in a proccession worthy of a queen. They would chant Psalms and verses of the Song of Songs and would sing "Lekhah dodi liqrat kallah, penei Shabbat neqabbelah" which was written by one of their devotees, the poet Shlomo Alqabetz.[33] This song was lauded by the Ari, who also contributed poetry of his own: three *piyyutim* in Aramaic. One of them—"Azammer bishvaḥin lemeʿal go pitḥin"—was acclaimed like "Lekhah dodi" and accepted by all communities in Israel. While "Lekhah dodi" is sung to welcome the Sabbath in the synagogue following the reading of the Song of Songs and several Psalms, the *piyyuṭ* "Azammer bishvaḥin" and the two other *piyyuṭim* composed by the Ari are sung before the Three Meals.

The prescribed Three Meals are associated with another concept introduced by the Lurianic kabbalists: *ʿOneg Shabbat* (Sabbath enjoyment). One honored the Sabbath through engaging in pleasurable activities—lighting the candles, blessing the wine, eating and drinking well, and dressing in fine raiments. Even a poor man must feel like a prince and is commanded to show his respect for the Sabbath by dressing well, eating good food, and singing. The three obligatory Sabbath meals are times of supreme joy and exaltation. The meal partaken in common and the *niggunim* sung while eating bring great joy to the members, rousing them to ecstacy as intense as if they were tasting of the fruits of paradise.

The idea of the *Qabbalat Shabbat* at which *piyyuṭim* composed by the Safed kabbalists were sung, was adopted by all Jewish communities. "Lekhah dodi" is one of the *piyyuṭim* that has been given many different musical guises. In some communities, if the cantor so chooses, he periodically sings it to a different tune. A good example can be found in the notebook of the cantor Isaac Offenbach, father of the famous opera composer, in which he recorded dozens of melodies that he himself created for "Lekhah dodi."[34] The *piyyuṭ* is readily adapted to folk melodies; even within the framework of a single tradition, it easily conforms to various tunes.

Although at the *Qabbalat Shabbat* in the synagogue the Psalms are usually chanted, some of the traditions give them more developed treatment. An interesting example is the Psalm "The Lord reigns, he is clothed in majesty" (Ps. 93:1) as sung by the Jews of Yanina, Greece. The conclusions of the verses are marked by a second voice singing a third higher. (Whereas in most communities, this Psalm is simply chanted, in Yanina it is usually sung in a fairly well-developed version. From figure 22 it is quite obvious that the melody follows the verses into which the text is divided by prolonging the note of the last word of each verse.) Some passages of the Sabbath evening prayer are given more developed treatment, such as three-part singing.

The Three Meals—the first following the evening prayer, the second after the morning prayer, and the third following the afternoon prayer, before the Sabbath has

Fig. 22. "The Lord Reigns," Yanina Sabbatical hymn.

ended—have gradually become occasions spent singing in the bosom of the family. Many texts of the hymns sung today are taken from the poets of classical Spain or of later periods. Almost all the *piyyuṭim* have a strophic pattern with a repeated refrain, which invites varied kinds of performances. Those *piyyuṭim* that were composed specially for the Sabbath acquired many different musical accompaniments—largely of a simple folk nature—that lend themselves to group singing.

The Sabbath is received as a queen and is given a royal send-off when she departs. The custom of *Melavveh Malkah* (accompanying the departing queen) acquired special significance with the Hasidim, who often gather together to sing *niggunim.* At the close of the Sabbath, after the *Havdalah* (which includes in the following order the benediction over the wine, perfumes, and candle, blessing the distinction between sacred and profane, between light and darkness) they would sing special songs, most of which were concerned with the redemption and its harbinger, the prophet Elijah. Because the figure of Elijah stirred the popular imagination and was the theme of countless legends, songs were written about him not only in Hebrew but also in the vernaculars used by various different ethnic communities. The example in figure 23, "El Dio alto" (Supreme God) is in Ladino, the Judeo-Spanish used by Sephardic Jewry, set to the lively march-like tune in which it was sung by the Jews of Salonika.

Indeed, very soon there was a great proliferation of songs and hymns appropriate for the synagogue and for prayers said at home or around the table during the Three Meals. *Piyyuṭim* were also written for services on special Sabbath days.[35] It is not hard

Fig. 23. El Dio Alto, Salonika tradition.

to understand why Sabbath songs acquired a predominant position in the collected works of the kabbalist poet Israel Najjara, whose book *Songs of Israel* was discussed in the previous chapter. As noted there, three editions of this book were published in the poet's lifetime, which is further evidence of the public's demand for hymns and songs. This was further confirmed by one Menachem ben Moshe Levy who published the Salonika edition of Najjara's book in 1599. He wrote that he was inspired to print the poems in response to the great demand on the part of the public "to seek the countenance of our Lord in the [prayer] watches" (Yahalom 1982).

Nocturnal Singing

Under the influence of the Zohar and the Safed kabbalists, the idea of rising at the midnight hour to sing became very popular. In the book *Shivḥei ha-Ari* we read

> And Rabbi Abraham Halevy [who settled in Jerusalem in approximately 1515, and dealt primarily with apocalyptic indoctrination] would rise at midnight every night to go from street to street and weep in a loud voice and shout aloud in harsh wailing tones . . . calling each scholar by name and would not leave him until he saw him rise from his bed . . . and at the same hour they would all rise to go to the synagogues and houses of learning and would chant the *tiqqun ḥatsot* [the midnight vigils] and then would study, each man according to his understanding. Some groups would study the Zohar and the Kabbalah and some the Talmud and Mishnayot and some the Bible, and then they would sing hymns from the Psalms and refrains and *baqqashot* until the light of day. In so doing, they roused compassion. (Kfir 1982, pp. 72–73)

From this quotation we learn that in kabbalistic circles they would rise at midnight to engage in study and *tiqqun*—even to sing *baqqashot*. Influenced by them and particularly by the Ari's pupil, Ḥayim Vital, various associations were formed in both the East and the West that instituted customs such as *tiqqun ḥatsot* (midnight prayer), *shirat tehillim* (singing psalms), and singing *shirei baqqashot* (songs of supplication) and other prayers. These groups called themselves by names that related to their nocturnal singing such as *Shomerim Labboker* (watchmen of the morning), *Meʿirei Shaḥar* (awakeners of the dawn), *Ḥadashim Labeqarim* (renewal each morning). Other groups chose names referring to song-types such as *Ḥavurat Baqqashot* (association of suppliants) or *Shirat Tehillim* (Psalm singing). The traveler Benjamin the Second,[36] who visited Aleppo in 1849, wrote about one of these groups:

> On the Sabbath eve all members of the community sing pleasant songs composed by wise scholars. The European Jew will be filled with wonder upon hearing the beautiful singing of the whole community together. Most of the songs and prayers were written by the great poet Israel Najjara of Damascus—author of the book *Songs of Israel*. In addition, you find a special company of vocalists intoning King David's Psalms in pleasant voices. These stirred my emotions and upon hearing them, my soul soared on the wings of the remote past to the time when God's inspiration put the words into the mouth of David, sweet singer of Israel. (Benjamin 1859, pp. 14–15)

This singing was apparently highly embellished, full of heartfelt longing, and had roots deep in the art songs of the region.

The *Baqqashot*

The great importance the mystics attributed to singing from midnight on led to the establishment of choral groups of early risers and Watchmen of the Morning. To keep such groups adequately supplied—prosaic though it may sound—there was need for large quantities of *piyyuṭim* and other musical material. The demand created an encouraging climate for poets and talented *payṭanim* who had absorbed the doctrines of the mystics; they wrote copious, beautiful poetry. The *baqqashot* were given extensive and sophisticated development, particularly in Syria and Morocco, the two major centers.[37] On Sabbath eve in the wintertime between Sukkot and Passover week, men, women, and children would go to the synagogues after midnight and spend the entire third watch (*ashmoret shelishit*) in solo and choral singing until break of day. These major traditions still maintain their vitality and are observed to this day—which does not mean, of course, that they were the only ones. It is of interest to note briefly that from Morocco and Syria this custom spread to many other places, one of them being Yugoslavia. In an article entitled "R. Israel Najjara and His Hymns," M. D. Gaon records having found evidence of the custom in Sarajevo: "In the bitter, freezing winter days, all those who rose early would come [to the synagogue], particularly the members of the regular *minyan* [the ten adult males necessary to conduct prayers]—the *Baqqashah-jis*—for the purpose of sweetly singing the hymns of the Kabbalist-poet [Israel Najjara]" (Gaon 1930–32, pp. 145–46).

In the seventeenth century the custom was brought to Italy by envoys and kabbalists. Before long, various cities had groups called Awakeners of the Dawn, Renewal each Morning, and Watchmen of the Morning. All these groups put special emphasis on music and in the course of time they even composed in Western art music style. A cantata called "Watchmen of the Morning" was printed in Venice in 1681 (Adler 1966, pp. 89–109; Schirmann 1979, 2, p. 51). A similar phenomenon occurred in Amsterdam's Portuguese community where a collection of songs by a group of Watchmen of the Morning appeared under the title *Night Watch* (Amsterdam, 1767–68) (Adler 1966, pp. 208–9). And finally, mention must be made of the group of *Mafṭirim.*[38] In the Turkish city of Adrianopolis they sang hymns for a large audience on the Sabbath and holidays and on special occasions before the afternoon prayer, as well as before the morning prayer (when there was a cantor with a fine voice).

Although the singing of *baqqashot* is traditional in many communities, it evolved into a strictly organized form of poetical, musical, and social importance only in Syria (Aleppo and Damascus) and Morocco. *Baqqashot* meetings are held in the synagogue every Friday after midnight from Sukkot to Passover. A group of accomplished singers, including professionals, executed a standard repertoire of *piyyuṭim*—most of them written by local poets but supplemented by the hymns of the Safed mystics (such as Azikri's "Yedid nefesh" which is included among both the Syrian and Moroccan *baqqashot*). The melodies are extremely heterogeneous, containing artistic and popular idioms, the latest novelties, and archaic traditions that had long since disappeared from the surrounding culture. The musical factor is prominent and often tends to overshadow the basic religious purpose of the meeting. The *baqqashot* may thus be considered as part religious concert and part prayer, with attendance motivated equally by religious, aesthetic, and social considerations.

The Aleppo *baqqashot* consist of certain fixed *piyyuṭim* and a large number of optional ones that are selected each night according to circumstances and the character of the audience. Each *baqqashah* is performed antiphonally (by two groups). Between one *baqqashah* and the next a soloist or smaller group takes turns in singing the so-called *petiḥah* (ouverture), which is a Psalm or the last verse of the preceding *piyyuṭ;* the *petiḥot* melodies are improvised, highly melismatic, and constructed in a way that creates modulation from the *maqām* (mode) of the preceding song to that of the subsequent one. The concluding *baqqashah*—"Yedid nefesh," is sung in the *maqām* of the current Sabbath. In the Moroccan *baqqashot,* the repertoire is entirely fixed and arranged in sets of different *piyyuṭim* (except for two recurring ones) for each *baqqashah* night, which is also assigned its particular dominant *maqām.*

The *piyyuṭim* used in Morocco for the *baqqashot* were collected in anthologies. The anthology called *Shir yedidot,* published in Marakesh in 1921 and still in use, was an attempt to create uniformity. The book contains 550 *piyyuṭim* to be sung on twenty different Saturdays; each group or series to be used for a given Sabbath is written in the mode in which all the *piyyuṭim* are sung on that particular day. The first two *piyyuṭim*—"Dodi yarad leganno" and "Yedid nefesh"—are repeated every Sabbath, but each week they are in a different mode, as they too are adapted to the musical mode of the week.

The general structure and musical content of the Moroccan *baqqashot* are inspired by the Arab Andalusian model, the *nūba*, as it developed on Spanish soil from the eleventh to the thirteen centuries. The *nūba* is a set of pieces performed by a small orchestral ensemble, a choir and solo singers who also play instruments. Each *nūba* is composed of five movements or parts and is executed in a particular mode. Each of the parts is called a *mīzān* (meter), designated by its dominant rhythmic pattern. Every *mīzān* is based on a poetic structure patterned after strophic songs and called *ṣanʿa* (craft). There are several *ṣanʿas* to each *mīzān* and they range from very slow to very fast (*inṣirāf* [departure] is the name given to the last fast *ṣanʿa*). Improvised solo passages are sung between the verses; they are called *bitayn* (two verses).

The singing of *baqqashot* by the Jews of Aleppo is organized in a pattern similar to that of Najjara's books, in other words, according to a modal key. In Aleppo, however, there is not a fixed mode for each Sabbath, and *piyyuṭim* can be sung in a variety of different modes. While the *baqqashot* songs of the Moroccan Jews draw their inspiration from Andalusian music and in part are derived directly from the *nūba*, those of the Jews of Aleppo are taken from music of the Middle East. Their modes are very different from those used by the Jews of Morocco. The melodic content, style of performance, and vocal technique required of the performer also differ greatly.

Social Aspects of the *Baqqashot*

From this brief description of the institution of *baqqashot* as it evolved in the course of centuries, it becomes clear that their musical component and degree of sophistication reflect an emphatic affinity with the art music of surrounding cultures, as well as a leaning toward the mystic ideology that engendered them. This is particularly apparent when the *baqqashot* are extracted from their normal framework and schedule, and are performed on ordinary weekdays at what might be called religious concerts. On such occasions they are performed with instrumental accompaniment that is otherwise nonexistent because of the sanctity of the Sabbath and the tacit ban on music in the synagogue. This development, discernable almost from the time the *baqqashot* songs were originally introduced, is indicative of an endeavor to strengthen social cohesion and enhance a sense of group identification.

Indeed, objective observers happening to witness the rites of *baqqashot* singing for the first time, might well be confused and think that in the middle of a winter's night they have come across a mass communal folk celebration. They will see crowds of people of all ages, children under foot, the women bunched together in the women's section, men hurrying around serving cups of hot tea and coffee and tasty refreshments, sweets and strong drinks. Well-known singers in the center of the multitude sing intricately embellished passages and compete with one another in the creation of heart-warming improvisations.[39] Sometimes one even hears familiar tunes of secular folk songs and the crowd enthusiastically joins in to produce a rousing, if rather disorganized, chorus. Observers seeing all this for the first time may well wonder what this occasion has to do with the mystical content that gave birth to the customs.

It would seem that very early in the period we are dealing with, the need was already felt to create an attractive alternative that would keep the ordinary Jew from seeking diversion in foreign cultures. Israel Najjara discusses this explicitly in the introduction to his *Songs of Israel.* He admits that his purpose in writing in Hebrew was to counteract the tendency of Jews to express love and longing in songs written in Arabic and Turkish. To encourage them to eschew foreign songs, he prepared similar ones in Hebrew, setting them to tunes the people were familiar with. Moreover, it was not always possible for Jews to participate freely in the musical life of the communities they inhabited. Hence those events that endowed music with an important role became, as it were, religious concerts in an unquestionably Jewish-religious framework, the music being performed for Jews by Jews. In our own day the *baqqashot* have become a medium through which the individual indentifies with the community in which these rites are performed. For those who participate in them or encourage them, the *baqqashot* have become something of a musical-cultural event that represents the classical tradition developed by our ancestors in the course of hundreds of years.

Kabbalist rabbis who composed *baqqashot* poems also set them to music and published them in anthologies. These activities have not always been looked upon with approval; many of those anthologies, therefore, include somewhat apologetic introductions. Rabbi Menahem Di Lonzano, who was born in Constantinople circa 1550 and died in Jerusalem, writes in his collection *Refrains and Verses* (published about 1575), which included alien Turkish tunes that he adapted to his own *piyyuṭim:* "Almighty God knows . . . that I did not write [words] to enhance the tunes of Ishmael in order to mock them or so that jokers would abuse them with drum and pipe and drunken playing, but I chose the tunes of the Ishmaelites because in them I saw melodies of broken hearts and oppression and I thought that with them the impure heart would be conquered and thus I would pay for my offence . . . and this is the reason that many of [the songs are] not to be said on the Sabbath and holidays." In his most famous book, *Shetei yadot* (published in Venice in 1618), he wrote: "The author said: my beloved friends have asked me to record with my heavy pen a few jingles and *baqqashot* I have composed so that with them they too can praise and exalt God and when I saw that this bequest of theirs is in homage to the Almighty, I hastened unhesitatingly to fulfil their request."

Closer to our own time, there is Rabbi Mordechai Abadi, a man of the nineteenth century who lived and worked in Aleppo. He wrote many *piyyuṭim* that were included among the *baqqashot* songs. In 1872 he issued a collection called *Miqra qodesh* which is the main book of *baqqashot* used by the members of the Aleppo community. In a long introduction entitled "Shaʿar ha-shir" (Chapter on song), as if defending himself in the face of criticism, he stresses the importance of singing in general, and of nocturnal singing in particular. In support of his thesis, he quotes the Zohar and words of our ancestral sages.

Kabbalistic Symbols and Ideas Penetrate Paraliturgical Song

Continuing to examine customs that were born and flourished under the influence of the doctrine of the kabbalists, it is now in place to discuss briefly the penetration of kabbalistic symbols and ideas into songs meant for secular and paraliturgical occasions, primarily weddings. This was particularly notable in the work of the greatest poet of Yemen, Shalem Shabazi (1619–80). He was learned in astronomy, astrology, and healing, and was well versed in the Bible, kabbalah, and philosophy. Some five hundred of his poems are extant; they deal with *Knesset Israel,* the Torah, redemption, and the world to come.[40]

Persecuted Yemenite Jewry, suffering incessantly from repressive edicts, enthusiastically embraced Jewish mystical literature, above all the Zohar. In addition to studying the secrets of the Creation and of the heavenly spheres, the Jews of Yemen were particularly exercised by questions of life in the Diaspora (*galut*) and redemption. Dreams of redemption are implicit in many of the songs sung at weddings and other festivities. The wedding song "*Ayyelet Ḥen*" (Lovely doe), attributed to Shalem Shabazi, exemplifies this:

Lovely doe in *galut* supports me
And at night, my resting place is in her bosom,
I am always ready for her glass of wine
And her desirable wine mingles with mine.

This is the beginning of a poem in which the bridegroom and bride are being led to their nuptial couch.[41] On the face of it, the poem refers directly to a given situation and event. The "lovely doe" is the bride and the speaker whose wine will mingle with hers is the groom. But the charming woman is not only a beloved bride; she is also the embodiment of the *Shekhinah* that gives the groom—a metaphor of the people of Israel—support in the *galut* (analogous here to the darkness of night). And indeed, in his book *The Doctrine of the Zohar* Tishbi maintains that in her merciful devotion the *Shekhinah*—who nourishes the world and protects its creatures—can be compared with a compassionate doe who assumes the burden of finding sustenance for the rest of the animals. The *Shekhinah,* then, is the mother of the world, and above all, mother of Israel. Tishbi writes:

> The bonds of the *Shekhinah* with Israel, which are like those of a divine mother to the nation below and to *Knesset Israel* [the celestial Congregation of Israel] above, find quintessential expression in the development of the idea of the *galut* of the *Shekhinah* which has its source in the legends of our revered sages. "Come and see how beloved Israel is unto the Almighty, blessed be He, for wherever they have been dispersed, the *Shekhinah* is with them. . . . And also when they will be redeemed, the divine presence is with them, as it is said that then the Lord thy God will turn thy captivity," (Deut. 30:3) and it is not said "he turned" but "will turn" which teaches us that the Almighty, blessed be He, will end captivity in the Diaspora together with his people. The sages who introduced this idea into the legend intended to stress God's eternal love for Israel and His maintenance of the covenant He made with His chosen people, even when in their iniquity they deceive him. As a sign of His love He shares their sufferings as they wander in the *galut.* (1957, 1, p. 228)

There can be a different interpretation as well: the groom is a metaphor for the sphere *tif'eret* (beauty), known also as *Israel Saba*—literally Grandfather Israel, but understood as the traditional People of Israel. In this sense there is an analogy and resonance between the upper and lower worlds: as against the earthly coupling of male and female, there is a heavenly coupling of the "kingdom" and the "glory" or of *Knesset Israel* and *Israel Saba.* Here again it is in place to quote Isaiah Tishby: "The male and the female divinities are the father and mother of Israel, and not only of the nation as a whole, but of each and every individual, for the sanctified souls of the people of Israel are the offspring of the heavenly coupling and they spread throughout the world from the bosom of the *Shekhinah.* The strong bond of these spheres with Israel is marked by special national symbols. *Tif'eret* is called *Israel Saba* and *Shekhinah* is called *Knesset Israel*" (1957, 1, p. 227).

Summary

We have tried to complete the circle by surveying some of the many symbols that developed in Jewish mystical theory and practice. We have attempted to show how those symbols evolved, made their mark on, and were bound up with daily activities of the past several hundred years, particularly since the sixteenth century. Here and there, as in the matter of the *baqqashot,* we have noted the wakening of earlier bonds and the partial or total replacement of original content by new content and sometimes even new values in response to the times. But about one thing there can be no doubt at all: the world of the kabbalah acted as a catalyst of prime importance in the flowering of poetry and song. It also served to arrest the onslaught of an extremist minority that objected to music, as we have seen in chapter 3.

At the same time, the kabbalists made a contribution of incalculable value to the democratization of the religious song. This was expressed in poetic structure and pattern, in melodies and social aspects; singing, which had been the preserve of the aristocracy, henceforth would find its epicenter among the masses. From the standpoint of the poet, there was a clear, almost total transfer to lighter genres based on rhythm and form that were in general more appropriate for singing in public and particularly for singing by the public. The extensive use of refrains was one of the main characteristics of these more popular genres. And perhaps the most outstanding change: From the outset the *piyyuṭim* were written to be sung and therefore the maximal consonance of text and melody was taken into consideration.

On the other hand, an interesting process was set in motion that may be called sanctification of the secular through the medium of song. In an article by Yosef Yahalom about Israel Najjara, the process is described in the following passage, which is a fitting conclusion for this chapter.

> In the Kabbalah the power of symbols has always been great. They were often derived from very intimate realms and highly emotional situations that are not usually discussed at length in public. But here, strangely enough, these things were used to serve the holiest aspects of religious thought. During the time of the Ari the audacious symbols that until then had been used in deepest secrecy, became generally known. Imaginative people who dealt in mystical speculation seem to have sublimated the coarse materialistic element by attiring it in symbolic garb. Against this background it is also easier to understand the sudden increase and rapid spread of poetry rooted in imagery borrowed from the poems and songs of the Oriental nations in whose countries the Jews had settled. Credence must be given to Najjara's words about the great attraction Turkish love-songs had for the Jews and it is just possible that he himself was slightly tainted by the same weakness. Be that as it may, it was the spiritual atmosphere of sixteenth-century Safed that made Najjara's creative activity possible, that lifted the holy sparks from "Satan's camp" to the "hallowed camp." (1982, pp. 91–92)

7

Non-Synagogal Music
Between Sacred and Secular

Whereas the foregoing chapters have focused on the basic forms, ideological background, and status of liturgical music, this chapter will introduce the reader to the instrumental music and song that is an integral part of Jewish daily life. Being a more inclusive body of music, compounded of extremely diverse elements, it is not easily classified. It accompanies individual Jews as they perform their mundane chores or celebrate special family occasions, as they participate in public ceremonies or mark festive events with neighbors—sometimes even non-Jewish ones. Yet one cannot unequivocally describe this music as secular, in contradistinction to the sacred song of the synagogue. Classification is difficult here not so much because of the incursion of the secular into the sacred (which we discussed at length in chapter 3) but rather the contrary: not infrequently, sacred music invades the realm of the secular.

In his book *Jewish Music in Its Historical Development,* written some sixty years ago, A. Z. Idelsohn already noted this, although he drew rather farfetched conclusions. In the original edition, the first part—which includes sixteen of the book's twenty-three chapters—deals with the various aspects of synagogue singing (*Ḥazzanut,* biblical accents [*taʿamei miqra*], reform of *Ḥazzanut,* etc.). The second part contains only four chapters, in which the author discusses the folk songs of Oriental Jewry, the folk songs of European Jewry, the Hasidic song, *badḥanim* (merry-makers), and *klezmerim* (music-makers). The final chapters deal with Jewish art music and the place of the Jew in music as a whole.

In his opening remarks to the section of the book that discusses music outside of the synagogue, Idelsohn raises the issues of sacred and secular in Jewish song. His discussion centers on the fundamental question of whether the Jews have folk songs in the true sense of the term. He starts with the basic assumption accepted by students of music: every nation that has created its own history and lives on its own land has its own folk songs. The opposite side of the coin is that the folk song necessarily has its source in a nation. This being the case, Idelsohn poses the question of whether the Jews are a nation. On the surface, the answer would have to be negative, since for two thousand years they have been scattered throughout the world. But, he explains, this is an exceptional situation. Palestine never ceased to serve as a source of inspiration for songs sung by Jews. Wherever they were, the Jews kept their spiritual homeland and their longing for it alive in their hearts, perpetuating a special kind of nationhood nurtured by religion and the concept of the sanctification of life. Here Idelsohn arrives at an interesting conclusion: "Thus, life as the Jew visualized it, has no room for what is commonly denominated 'secular.' " The Jewish folk song, according to him, is therefore rooted in the sacred: "This spiritual nationality brought forth a folk-song as distinctive as the people itself. Just as to the Jew religion meant life and life religion, so to him sacred song has been folk-song, and folk-song, sacred song" (1929, pp. 357–58).

Idelsohn bases his contention on the frequency with which melodies based on the *ta'amei miqra,* prayers, and *piyyuṭim* are used for songs sung outside of the synagogue. And he adds: "Even those types of songs common to all people, which are designated as 'secular,' such as cradle and love songs, humorous songs and ballads, received in Jewish folk-song a different complexion; they recieved an impress of the religious life-concept that flowed in the blood of the Jew. And because of this conception, vulgar songs that sought to insinuate themselves never did become rooted in Jewish folk-song. If by folk-song we understand words and tunes of war and drink, of carnality and frivolity, then the Jews have no folk-songs. Jewish folk-song, like Jewish life in the last two thousand years, nestles in the shadow of religion and ethics."

In actual fact, the situation as we know it is much more complex; our folk songs indeed may not be quite as colorful as those of other nations, but many unquestionably bear the stamp of Jewish values—songs of prayer and longing for Zion, songs of suffering, of hope for redemption, songs that extol the sanctity of the Jewish way of life and are interspersed with biblical stories and ethics as well as with concepts from Jewish philosophical literature. Nevertheless, among the thousands of familiar folk songs (most of them, incidentally, in languages other than Hebrew) there are also descriptions of acts perpetrated by Jewish murderers, cheats, and scoundrels, tales of unfaithful husbands and lonely, miserable women, emotional outpourings and songs of carnal desire, of old men attempting to seduce young girls. In short, Jewry has songs that express all conceivable tenors and hues of normal human activities and describe the entire gamut of upheavals that constitute the experiences one is likely to undergo in this world. The Sabbath hymns, holiday songs, and *piyyuṭim* that accompany the most basic events in a person's life, represent only one tributary—overwhelmingly large and important though it may be—of the great effusion of songs Idelsohn may unfortunately have ignored or overlooked due to a language barrier.

Singing in and out of the Synagogue—Basic Distinctions

Traditional synagogue singing of all Jewish ethnic groups has three elements in common:

1. Hebrew—the language of the Bible, prayers, and *piyyuṭim.* Because of its sanctity and its use by all generations and all ethnic traditions, Hebrew has remained the only language (except in the Reform movements)[1] in which the ritual may be conducted.

2. Basic texts—the biblical books, the weekly portion and *Hafṭarah,* the prayers, etc.—became the sacred possession of the nation as a whole.

3. Occasions and events marking the cycle of the Jewish year—from daily and Sabbath prayers to the numerous special and holy days—have been shared by all Jews everywhere. Ethnic differences, it should be noted, were expressed only in the optional *piyyuṭim* appended to various prayers.

Extra-synagogal song presents a much more complex and diversified picture than synagogue song. Taking as our point of departure the three common elements designated above, we immediately become aware of the great difficulty involved in an attempt to pinpoint definitive common denominators underlying the different traditions.

Language. Hebrew is used in songs sung outside of the synagogue, but is certainly not the only or even the predominant language. In addition to the prayers, Hebrew is used primarily for ceremonial occasions, many of which relate to the annual cycle such as the Sabbath hymns, the Passover *haggadah,* and traditional holiday songs—"*Pirqei avot,*"[2] and others. It is also the language of certain rituals that mark events in the life cycle of the individual. This is the paraliturgy that accompanies events and ceremonies established by religious ordinance; every Jew must observe these ordinances, as he observes the prayer sequence, although they are not included in the prayers. The term "paraliturgy" refers to aspects of ritual that apply only to the part of the ceremony that is associated with a given ordinance (for these Hebrew is always used) and not to the larger part of the festivities that can include any kind of music. But one must bear in mind that very many of the songs sung outside of the synagogue are in the diverse languages and vernaculars spoken by the non-Jews among whom Jews lived, or in special dialects such as Judeo-Arabic, Judeo-Spanish (Ladino), Aramaic, Judeo-German (Yiddish), Judeo-French, etc. There are also many songs that use two or three languages, one of them Hebrew: Hebrew and Aramaic or Spanish, Persian, Yiddish, Ukrainian, and so on. Hence the language of extra-synagogal song reflects both something of Jewry's unity and something of its pluralism.

Texts. Here, too, one can find a common ceremonial core, but outside of that, the differences are great. Indeed, each ethnic group crystallized a characteristic repertoire encompassing a body of songs, themes, and ways of performance that reflect the particular cultural situation and creative power of the community in question, and of it alone. Even functional *piyyuṭim* in Hebrew, such as the ones sung at the circumcision ceremony or in honor of a bridegroom, are likely to differ from group to group, to say nothing of the non-Hebrew repertoire. Moreover, a new element enters the scene here, one that is totally nonexistent in synagogue singing: women take part and even create texts that are performed in circumstances and on occasions that have unique reference to them and their world. (Progressive movements in Judaism that do not separate the men and women in the synagogue and give the women an equal and active part in the prayers, even permitting female *ḥazzans* to read the Torah aloud, are still few and far between.)

Above all, it is important to note that alongside the liturgical songs there are not only secular but even non-Jewish songs. So we find that parallel to the accepted rituals sanctified by Judaic tradition, individual creativity manifested itself and drew its vitality and substance from the alien traditions that impinged on Jews wherever they resided. This presents us with another essential difference: The sacred Hebrew texts—both prayers and *piyyuṭim*—became known to most communities and were recorded for posterity, which contributed to their permanancy and sanctification. As time passed, not only prayer books, but anthologies of *piyyuṭim* and ballads were published. Some of these collections, organized by seasonal events or important dates in the life of the individual, contained the works of a single poet, some of several. Certain anthologies were arranged according to musical criteria, that is, according to the mode of the accompanying melody. In addition, *piyyuṭim* unique to a given ethnic group were often recorded by their composers in the notebook of a *payṭan* or *ḥazzan* who would thus have the text available when he wanted to practice.[3] *Ḥazzanim* and *payṭanim* would also record verses they learned from others or had written themselves, and their notebooks often contained their personal comments as to which poems were appropriate for which events, many of these comments being of a musical nature. Obviously, the reference here is to the texts; the *payṭanim* referred to their notebooks only as a means of refreshing their memories or as a way of ensuring that some of the poems would not disappear with the passage of time. An interesting situation was thus created: From the standpoint of text, a written tradition was emerging; from the musical standpoint, the emerging tradition was an oral one. With respect to folk songs in different languages, including the women's songs, they were and continued to be part of the orally transmitted tradition, with all that is implied thereby.[4]

Special events. Piyyuṭim touching on personal events in the life of an individual are only a marginal part of synagogal singing, most of which relates to significant dates and occasions of importance to the general public. In contrast, singing outside the synagogue emphasizes happenings affecting the individual's life: childbirth, circumcision, bar mitsvah, arranging engagements and marriages, wedding celebrations, and mourning. The events themselves are common to all, but in each place and each ethnic group their content and scope, the manner in which they are conducted, their attributes and accretions, are different.

Songs associated with public occasions of a perennial nature should also be mentioned. Some have a generally shared religious ritual character such as Sabbath hymns, seder-night songs, Ḥanukkah songs, and so forth, while others belong almost exclusively to certain ethnic communities, such as the *hillulot* (jubilee) festivities at the graves of saints, the *mimuna, seherane,* etc. (These will be discussed in greater detail below.)

A minority of the songs accompanying these events are associated with the *mitsvot*—positive commandments—or with specific functions. These songs do not change and, with the exception of those involving women's rites, they are in Hebrew. Most of the songs, however, are of an informal, entertaining nature, containing verses in various languages and dealing with every subject imaginable. There are also Hebrew *piyyuṭim* alongside foreign-language poems that may be on religious Jewish themes or unquestionably secular ones.

We therefore find that the three elements shared by synagogue song of every culture—language, text, and occasion—are not unifying elements in extra-synagogal singing. This is particularly so with respect to music and its performance.

Music and Musical Performance

Extra-synagogal singing has two major parts. One part, the distinctly paraliturgical, is almost indistinguishable from synagogue song. The benediction and *qiddush* are chanted just as they are in the synagogue; the *piyyuṭim* are sung in the same or similar tunes as the prayers. Moreover, the synagogue's cantor or reader often performs some of these ceremonial rites.

Specific musical interest appears in the second, less formal kind of extra-synagogal singing. Almost unlimited use is made of secular music of the surrounding society, including instrumental accompaniment, despite the fact that musical instruments continue to be banned inside the synagogue. The accompaniment for both male and female voices is often no more sophisticated than simple rhythm instruments; only rarely is it performed by musicians recognized locally as an ensemble. Since a certain amount of skill and talent is required to play an instrument and many who have attained artistic proficiency expect compensation when asked to play for a particular occasion, in many places a professional level of musicians emerged. Such professionals included both instrumentalists and vocalists, and they demanded and received appropriate remuneration for the pleasure they bestowed on those who hired their services.

The status of professional musician for those who earn their living by their talent usually refers to performers of art music, although occasionally folk musicians also receive such recognition. With respect to art music, however, an interesting phenomenon developed, one that had far-reaching implications. Gifted artists burst through the confines of the ghetto walls and made names for themselves in non-Jewish society. Their major income eventually came from outside of the Jewish community. The general acceptance of these Jewish musicians was abetted in Islamic countries where religiously observant Muslim rulers forbid Muslim citizens to play in public for religious reasons.[5] At the same time it should be noted that where there were no professional Jewish musicians or where the Jewish community refused to condone their activities, on joyous occasions Jews employed non-Jewish, usually Christian, instrumentalists.[6]

Events and Occasions

Synagogue song is constrained in scope and essence by a framework of content and time. With respect to singing outside of the synagogue, the bounds of time and place are vastly expanded and the proportions and essential nature of happenings are infinitely more complex and variegated. At times the singing outside of the synagogue is associated with events and occasions that touch upon the life of the community in general; at other times it focuses on the private life of the individual. There are times when the singing has a defined function, but it may also be entirely dissociated from any specific happening. Individuals may express themselves in lyrical song even if there is no apparent relation between the song and whatever evoked the urge to sing. The themes and contents of the songs are as extensive as the range of occasions that inspire them, and in most cases the accompaniment of instrumental music adds a further dimension.

Events Associated with the Jewish Calendar

Certain activities are almost an extension of the formal ritual and liturgy. One example of this can be found in the Sabbath songs and hymns discussed at length in the previous chapter. The many songs in Hebrew and in folk dialects that celebrate the departure of the Sabbath belong in a similar category. The core theme of these songs is the redemption and the figure of its harbinger, Elijah the prophet. Some of the same songs are included in the circumcision ritual as well, since Elijah is also known as the "angel of the Covenant," one of his tasks being to attend every circumcision and observe the ceremony with his own eyes. And indeed, on these occasions it is customary to set aside a special chair for him, known by all as Elijah's chair. Elijah is associated with another most important event: the Passover seder. Each participant at the seder is given four glasses of wine, and a special glass is always filled for Elijah. According to Maimonides, the hymns of praise in the second part of the *haggadah* that is read on Passover eve in every Jewish home are said over Elijah's glass.

The *haggadah* contains a relatively short description of the Exodus from Egypt, some biblical verses, passages from the Midrash, religious laws and prayers, hymns of praise and gratitude to the Creator for the great miracles He performed for the people of Israel, and appeals for redemption. The word *Haggadah* apparently derives from the biblical passage: "vehiggadta lebinkha bayyom hahu lemor" (And thou shalt tell thy son in that day, saying: It is because of that which the Lord did for me when I came forth out of Egypt) (Exod. 13:8).

The custom of telling the story of the Exodus from Egypt on the eve of Passover already existed in ancient times, the oldest part of the *haggadah* having been written while the Temple was still standing. As the generations passed its contents were constantly re-examined and new passages were added. Among the later additions that appear at the end of the text, two songs merit special mention: "*Eḥad mi yodeiyaʿ*" (Who knows one) and the Aramaic song "*Ḥad gadia*" (The little kid). Both belong to the cumulative type of song in which new items are added after each verse, with the refrain consisting of a repetition of all the items in reverse order, from the last back to the first. These songs, which seem to have originated in Christian Europe, and are perhaps modeled after such well-known songs as "The Twelve Days of Christmas" or "Alouette," were translated into the various vernaculars used by the Jews and set to many different local tunes.[7] The text of the *haggadah* read by Jews as they sit around the family seder table is basically the same everywhere; the reading, however, is in the cantillation traditionally used by the ethnic group to which the family belongs. Outside of Israel it is customary to print a translation in the local language alongside the Hebrew text, to enable all those participating in the seder to understand what is being said.

Passover—and its allied customs—has inspired folk songs in many languages and dialects. In the Balkan communities, on the days preceding the actual holiday, the women would sing Ladino romances (ballads) about the life and deeds of Moses and his central role in Jewish history, about the Exodus from Egypt and related themes; a selection of these can be found in M. Attias (1961, pp. 179–87). Appropriate songs are also performed during the preparations for Passover in the eastern European communities, particularly while baking the *matsot* eaten instead of bread for the eight days of the holiday.

Other holidays and festivals also were marked by songs sung in vernaculars the Jews used locally. The songs usually centered on or developed aspects of the procedures and customs followed in the course of celebrating the holiday. These songs inspired elaboration and constant reworking of biblical stories and legends. They were thus imbued with a quasi-educational character, one of their prime functions being to reinforce fundamental tenets that would strengthen the faith of the individual Jews. Hence it is not surprising that the first collection of songs printed with their musical scores—*Simhath ha-nefesh* (The delight of the soul) by E. H. Kirchhain (1727) was largely devoted to the Jewish holidays. The collection contains thirteen songs in Yiddish for Sabbath and festival days, three of them about circumcisions, weddings, and daily subjects.[8]

General Festive Gatherings

Until this point we have discussed types of songs sung outside the synagogue but that nevertheless serve specific religious functions such as holidays and memorial dates celebrated by all of Jewry. In this section we shall discuss the vocal and instrumental music that play a central role at various publicly celebrated folk events. Out of the large number of such occasions, we have chosen to expatiate on interesting and widely popular ceremonies observed by Jewish Oriental and Western communities both in Israel and abroad. The *hillula* (jubilee) is one of the most interesting of these. It entails a ritual pilgrimage to the burial site of a "saint," on whose grave the believers prostrate themselves. Other exotic customs imported to Israel with certain ethnic groups—such as the *seherane* and *mimuna*—are also being renewed in Israel.

The Hillula

This custom has three major elements: it includes celebrating the sanctification of a revered public figure, a mass pilgrimage to the site of his burial, and a jubilant festive reunion of people who originally came from the same community abroad but may now live in widely separated areas of Israel. The word *hillula*, which is Aramaic in origin, implies a joyous celebration. Certain orthodox Jewish sects use the term to describe the annual ritual of visiting the grave of a *tsaddiq* or *Ḥasid* on the actual or reputed day of his death. In the *kabbalah* a death is conceived as an esoteric mating of souls with the divine essence, and is therefore a kind of wedding of man and God. In actuality, the celebration of the rite of consecration sometimes bears the solemn stamp of a ritual act, but sometimes is an occasion for folk festivities. We find this dichotomy explained in an interesting fashion by Issachar Ben-Ami: "It should be added that the *ziyāra* [literally "visit," but usually used to mean pilgrimage] is also an expression of the Jew's desire to break away from the drudgery of everyday life and spend time in the bosom of nature. The atmosphere at the saint's grave is one of jubilation and joy" (1975, p. 196).

The concept of *tsaddiq* that rooted itself in the popular mind was a kind of middle-man, one who mediates between the nation and its God. This gave rise to the belief that physical proximity with the *tsaddiq*, such as prostrating onself on his grave, can evoke a magical cure for hopeless invalids, the mentally ill, or barren women. One may go on pilgrimage to the holy site throughout the year, but it is most usual to observe the ritual on memorial days that fall on fixed dates. Such days then become joyous reunions and the pilgrims spend their time eating and drinking, singing and dancing.

Broader aspects of this picture have been dealt with in Ben-Ami's *The Veneration of Saints among Moroccan Jews*, some passages of which we quote:

> The glorification of saints is a universal phenomenon; it is a dimension of religious observance that can be found in all monotheistic and polytheistic religions. It finds expression in religious, historic, sociologic, folkloristic, economic, cultural, political, and other manifestations. Only recently have scholars begun to try to fathom the full significance of these ramified manifestations, but their research has not yet afforded us a comprehensive understanding of the phenomenon.
>
> The ritual of sainthood among the Jews of Morocco is one of the most important

> cultural attributes of that community and is deeply entrenched in all strata of the people. It should be pointed out that from several standpoints Moroccan Jewry's collective perception of saints is an exceptional manifestation. I am of the opinion that their sanctification of certain individuals can serve as an excellent model for an extensive study that will be of importance both intrinsically and for research in general. (1984, pp. 11–12)

Moroccan Jewry's idolization of saints originated, of course, in North Africa, but they brought it with them to Israel, where the traditional rituals are perpetuated while new customs are being added. Here many thousands eagerly participate in the *hillula,* a major event in the lives of Jews of North African origin. A Moroccan Jewish family is generally attached to one particular saint, the bond being formed as the result of assistance the family has received from him, because a member of the family had a dream about him, or due to geographical proximity. This saint is commemorated by the lighting of a candle in his honor annually, on the first of each month, or even once a week, as well as by evocation of his name when trouble occurs in the normal course of life. The most tangible manifestation of the bond is the visit to the saint's grave. If his burial place is nearby, those who revere him light a candle at his grave every week, usually on Friday or on Saturday night.

An important means of expressing adulation for the saint is through *piyyuṭim* and songs heard at the *hillula* that takes place at the graveside, in the synagogue, or at home. These songs express the gathering's spiritual exultation and love for the revered saint. The liturgy usually includes a variety of types of songs. One type is the *piyyuṭ* written entirely in Hebrew and sung by the men only. Its objective is to extol and aggrandize the saint; it may have been inspired by the belief that the *tsaddiq* helped the composer recover from an illness, the composer may have witnessed a miracle attributed to the *tsaddiq,* or he may have been deeply impressed by a visit. *Piyyuṭim* of this type are usually circulated in hand-written single sheets of paper; very few of them have been collected and printed in anthologies. Another type is the *piyyuṭ* written both in Hebrew and Arabic, with the Hebrew verse immediately followed by the one in Arabic, or with the first verses in Hebrew and the final ones in Arabic. This type too is sung mainly by the males, although the women usually know the Arabic passages. The third type is written entirely in Arabic, in the form of a *qaṣīda.*[9] This is sung in the saint's honor primarily by the women and it is characterized by a marked rhythmic beat that inspires the assembled crowd, including the men, to join in. Participation is widespread particularly when the *qaṣīdas* being sung are well known to everyone who has ever participated in a *hillula* (Ben-Ami 1984, pp. 99–101).

Usually each *qaṣīda* and *piyyuṭ* is dedicated to a given saint, although many of the songs name more than one. There are special songs for the ceremony surrounding the auctioning of glasses of wine or *maḥiah* (literally "water of life"—an arak prepared by Moroccan Jews from dates and figs) in the saint's honor. In the hope of encouraging the bidders to raise the price for a glass of the *tsaddiq*'s wine, these songs tell about miracles he performed and the benefits that will accrue to those who drink the liquid. Certain well-known melodies and musical patterns constantly reappear in the songs, although the text frequently undergoes changes.

As stated, adoration and reverential commemoration of the saints, as well as faith in their successful mediation between the believer and his God, is fairly prevalent among Jewish ethnic groups. But distinctions must be drawn between local saints, recognized primarily by those in a given vicinity, and those who have acquired recognition by the entire nation. The latter are generally figures from the Pentateuch, Mishnah, or Talmud who were buried in Israel.

There is also a group of saints from those ancient days who are buried abroad; they are treated like local figures, although they are known far and wide. Such famous local saints, for example, are the Baʿal Shem Tov[10] and R. Nahman of Bretslav,[11] both buried in what is now the Soviet Union. As might be expected, Morocco probably has the largest number of such "local" saints.

Among those whose sanctification has been recognized by the entire nation, the outstanding figure is certainly Shimʿon Bar-Yoḥai,[12] whose grave at Meron attracts great masses from all Jewish groups to a *hillula* on the thirty-third day of the Omer. This *hillula* is the climax of celebrations that begin four days earlier at the grave of R. Me'ir Baʿal Han-nes in Tiberias.[13] Moshe Shokeid writes in his chapter devoted to the pilgrimage to Meron:

> The memory of Rashbi [R. Shimʿon Bar-Yoḥai] also serves as a source of inspiration and faith for the Hasidim and of hope for the oppressed and suffering. The sick and lame believe they will be cured at his graveside. Children are taken to Meron for their first haircut, and their shorn locks are tossed into the burning torch on the roof of the tomb. Into the same flame pilgrims toss other items such as handkerchiefs and scarves, as well as candles to feed the flame. They also throw coins and candles on to the grave to be collected by individuals or religious institutions that are in need of financial support." (1977, pp. 98–99)

The song extolling Shimʿon Bar-Yoḥai is popular today in many communities and in most places it is sung to the same Sephardic melody. The *hillula* at his grave is a time-worn custom; Joseph Caro (1485–1575), author of the *Shulḥan ʿArukh,*[14] fiercely attacked the *mustaʿrabim* (old Arabic-speaking Jewish communities in the Middle East) for their custom of making mass pilgrimages to the grave of Shimʿon Bar-Yoḥai.

Rachel's tomb near Bethlehem and the "Tomb of David" on Mt. Zion in Jerusalem fall into the same category: they too are sites to which all Jewish ethnic groups make pilgrimages. Another biblical figure universally revered by Jews is the prophet Elijah. Numerous sites throughout the world as well as in Israel are associated with his name and have been sanctified. There are putative graves of somewhat less renowned personalities that folk tradition locates in a variety of places abroad.

They became the focus of pilgrimages for communities in their particular vicinity, although some believers would even come from far away to prostrate themselves at the grave. An interesting note on the subject has been published by S. D. Goitein:

"In a letter written in about 1176 that was found in the Cairo Genizah,[15] a salesman who was in India writes to his younger brother in Alexandria, Egypt, telling him that although it is very good of him to want to postpone his wedding until his [the elder brother's] return, it were best not to do so, for, as an experienced traveler, he intended to make a detour to Baghdad where he would prostrate himself on the grave of Ezekiel" (1981, pp. 13–18).

Indeed, the graves of Ezekiel (Iraq), of Ezra the Scribe (Iraq),[16] of Mordekhai the Jew[17] (Iran), and of Nahum the prophet in Elqosh (Iraqi Kurdistan) were revered as holy sites by the Jews in their vicinity. In those regions it was the custom to visit the graves during the Festival of Weeks Shavuoth, which was called instead *ziyāra* (pilgrimage) because it was the time of pilgrimages to the holy sites. It may be that this derives from the popular belief that King David was born and died on the Shavuoth holiday, which explains why pilgrimages are made on that day to his tomb on Mt. Zion in Jerusalem, as well as to the burial places of other saints.

Among the Jews of Iraq, pilgrimages to the graves of saints inspired many songs in which the sacred and secular became inextricably meshed. Worthy of special mention are the songs in Judeo-Arabic called *kunags,* songs of the way-stations, that reflect the difficulties pilgrims encountered along their arduous route.[18] The *kunags* that were best known and even published were those describing the pilgrimages to the graves of Ezekiel and of Ezra Hasofer, as well as to the Land of Israel. The *kunags* are also known by the name *Tsuri goali yah* because these Hebrew words open each song and function as a refrain (see figure 24). An example of a *kunag* celebrating the pilgrimage to the grave of Ezekiel follows (in a free translation):

The first day's station is Dura.
May God grant that the houses of the enemy will be deserted

and we will go to prostrate ourselves before our lord,
may our beloved be joyful and may our enemies die.
Zuri goali yah . . .

The second day's station is Khān el Zād,
may God grant that the enemy will be few and will not multiply
and even that his clothes be sold publicly,
and may our beloved be joyful and may our enemies die.
Zuri goali . . .

The third day's station is Bir el Netz.
May God grant that all the enemy die and pass away
and also be cut to pieces, and drown.
And may our beloved be joyful and may our enemies die.

Fig. 24. Kunag, song of way-stations.

Throughout the period that the pilgrims remained at the graveside they sang songs of this kind. Among them were also professional musical groups whose playing and singing helped make the time pass pleasantly.[19]

The ethnographer Erich Brauer describes a special custom followed by Jews of Kurdistan:

> The holy place that attracts the largest crowds is the grave of the prophet Naḥum in Elqosh [near Mosul]. Every year thousands of Jews from Mosul, Basra and all of Kurdistan, come here. A detail typical of this "ziyāra" is the "ascension to Mt. Sinai" that takes place on both days of the holiday. Not far from the grave is a hill called Mt. Sinai which the people climb. When they reach the top they read the Ten Commandments. . . . After that the whole crowd descends in great joy and gladness. Orchestras accompany them and the strongest men lead, dancing the Sword Dance. (1948, p. 247)

The sword dances that are popular throughout the Near East are performed only by men. Although actually vestiges of war dances, they are now done exclusively for entertainment.

Mimuna and Seherane

Among the traditions that have been revived in Israel are the celebrations of the *Mimuna* and *Seherane*. Originally, the *mimuna* did not necessarily include a pilgrimage to a *tsaddiq*'s grave; both customs clearly bear the earmarks of mass outdoor festivities. Brought to Israel by Moroccan Jews, the *mimuna* is gradually acquiring the character of a general folk celebration with masses of people spending a day together in the open. Other aspects of the celebration take place in homes and are of a family nature.

The *mimuna* starts at the end of the Passover festival when guests—invited and uninvited—are received at tables laden with food and drink. The refreshments have symbolic meaning: vegetables (symbolizing renewal), sweetmeats (success, pleasure, satisfaction), eggs and fish (be fruitful and multiply), etc. Ceremonial greetings are exchanged among the celebrants, the salutation most frequently heard being "May you be granted success." The songs associated with the occasion also refer primarily to happiness and success.

The origin and significance of this joyful holiday with its sacred and secular songs and music-makers, is not entirely clear. One theory is that it is in the nature of a *hillula* in honor of R. Maimon—the father of Maimonides. In the wake of repressive campaigns led against the Jews by the Muwaḥḥidūn rulers, Maimon left his birthplace, Spain, and settled in the city of Fez, then an important Jewish center. Tradition tells that R. Maimon died the day after Passover and since there are no pilgrimages to graves in the month of Nissan (in which the Passover festival falls) the *mimuna,* held after Passover, is in his honor. Hence Fez is the city in which the *mimuna* was first celebrated. A slightly different version is attributed to one of the wise men of Lybia. According to him, word of R. Maimon's death arrived during the holiday period so the mourners' meal was postponed until after Passover. There are, however, several other equally plausible explanations of the *mimuna.*

Similar customs exist in other ethnic groups as well. One such is the *seherane* celebrated by the Jews of Kurdistan. The literal meaning of the word *seherane* is "walk" or "trip". The first day after the Passover seder in Kurdistan was a day for going out walking, a day on which, with the advent of spring, the non-Jews went out to relax and enjoy nature. They would eat and drink as well as sing and dance. The *seherane* too is a spring festival, very much like the official Persian holiday that is still celebrated in Iran today. There were places where it was customary to celebrate the *seherane* the day after the Sukkot holiday, because according to talmudic sources, on that day one must be happy. In recent years this custom has been renewed in Israel and indeed takes place at the time of Sukkot, to avoid its overlapping with the *mimuna* (see Halper-Abramovitz 1984, pp. 260–70).

The Life Cycle

A person's lifetime, from birth to death, is filled with a succession of outstanding occasions, many of which are celebrated in song and dance. In the past, when means of entertainment were limited, if a family or ethnic group had extensive social ties, the celebration of various ceremonies would extend over several days. Gatherings honoring given occasions—whether happy or sad—were very popular. Songs sung at those times reflected the life and happenings in the community; they mirrored the people's character, culture, way of thinking, beliefs, aspirations, and longings. At such times the folk song reaches its fullest expression and greatest diversity, as we shall illustrate below.

Birth

The first event in the life cycle is birth, and its celebration sometimes starts even before the event itself, with the pregnancy of a young wife. With the Jews of Amadia in Kurdistan, when the wife discovered that she was pregnant it was customary to bring her to her family's home where the women gathered to celebrate. Accompanied by musical instruments, they sang and danced in her honor.

The birth of a boy always elicited great joy. In many communities, the mother and newborn son were the center of special events that started with the birth and continued until the circumcision. During those eight days constant vigil was kept around the mother and her son, because they were considered easy prey for devils until the actual circumcision. Everyone, therefore, was on guard to prevent harm from coming to mother and child. The women of the family, as well as the female friends and neighbors, spent day and night there, singing special songs for a new mother. Those who watched over the bedside at night, led by the young wife's mother, sang incessantly both to keep themselves awake and to ensure that the young mother's sleep would be safe and sweet. The songs gave expression to the painful experience of childbirth as in the Judeo-Spanish song "When birthpains rack the expectant mother," paraphrased below:

"When the expectant mother was racked by pain, she sent for the midwife to come quickly. Sweat trickles down her soft downy cheeks; her mother dries it with her shirt. Then the midwife says: 'Give now, give now' and the woman in childbirth begs the emerging one: 'Please stop pushing so hard! Oh, God save me!' and the blessed arrival says 'Please help me.' Alive and blooming is the welcome body. Long life to the newborn and to the mother. She has given birth to a son" (Attias 1961, pp. 231–32).

According to popular belief the demons—headed by Lilith—are jealous of those blessed with a son who soon would fulfill the *mitsvah* of the circumcision (*brit*—the "covenant"). So they seek a propitious moment in which to harm the mother and child. According to a medieval story reported in J. Dan (1980, p. 21), Lilith maintains that God created her only to afflict babies with fatal disease and that she has permission to harm the male baby to the eighth day and the female to the twelfth. This belief, held by all the ethnic communities, maintains that the demons are increasingly dangerous as the circumcision approaches, particularly the night before it is to be performed. On that night, therefore, the vigil is even more important; it is customary to read chapters of the Zohar and to take other precautionary measures such as burning incense and myrtle. In Kurdistan the midwife strikes the new mother three times, wrings her own hands three times, and intones: "Lilith leave." The women color the mother and son with blue and yellow paint to chase away the evil eye.

In Morocco they would perform the *taḥdīd* ceremony. (The term *taḥdīd* is apparently derived from the word *ḥadīd,* which means iron. Some people believe the ceremony is so named in reference to the sword that is made of iron.) This is a ceremony conducted the night before the circumcision in which a sword is used to banish the evil spirits. The sword is brandished in all corners of the house and around the beds of the mother and child, while a selection of biblical verses and appropriate Psalms are sung: "Vihi noʿam eloheinu" (And let the beauty of the Lord our God be upon us) (Ps. 90:17); "Yoshev beseter ʿelion" (He that dwelleth in the secret place of the Most High) (Ps. 91:1); "Lo tira mipaḥad laila" (Thou shalt not be afraid for the terror by night) (Ps. 91:5); "Ha-mal'akh ha-goel" (The angel which redeemed me from all evil) (Gen. 48:16); "Birkat Cohanim" (The priestly blessing) (Num. 24–26); "Hinnei miṭṭato she-lishlomo shishshim gibborim saviv lah" (Behold, it is the litter of Solomon; Three score mighty men are about it) (Song 3:7); and others. All verses are repeated three times either in the cantillation of the *taʿamei miqra* or as if one were taking a solemn vow. After this ceremony, which is of a clearly ritual nature, throughout the night *piyyuṭim* dealing with circumcision and Elijah the prophet, as well as general folk songs, are sung in Judeo-Arabic.

The Wedding

Of all family events, the wedding and its colorful attendant ceremonies probably is most important in the life of the individual and the community. In every traditional society, particularly if the reference is to a national minority group such as Jewry has been in the Diaspora, perpetuation of the family means the survival of the community and the nation. For that reason marriage is a supreme and fundamental value, playing a vital part in strengthening group bonds. In Judaism the wedding acquired a religious coloration, and participation in the joy of the bride and groom is considered a *mitsvah*—a good deed. From this derive the concepts, among others, of "*mitsvah* dance," "Mitzvaweiver" ("*mitsvah* women" who lead the bride to the bridal canopy).

The wedding marks a sharp turning-point in the life of individuals, who move from dependency on their families to a more independent life in which they establish families of their own. This dramatic transition is accompanied by feelings of fear and threat, and in all ancient societies rites of passage are instituted for the purpose of allaying those fears and preparing the individual for his new life. Many customs stemming from the superstitious belief in a bond between marriage and death are connected with the transitional nature of these events.

In chapter 2 we quoted the words of the Mishnah, "ḥalil la-kallah ve-lammet (The pipe is for the bride and the dead); in other words, the flute (pipe) is played at the wedding and the burial. The tie between marriage and death symbolizes the continuation of a person's existence through the family: the new generation is born after the wedding and this is, so to speak, the rebirth or eternal life awaiting the *tsaddiq* after death. The tie between marriage and death, between joy and trepidation, finds expression not only in the fast observed by the bridal couple on their wedding day, but in the special customs associated with crucial dates in the life of the individual, customs that relate those dates to religious ordinances. In an article about a Jewish wedding in the outlying town of Alsace in the second half of the nineteenth century, Freddy Raphael writes:

"Birth, the bar mitsva ceremony, the wedding and death are most important events in the life of the community. One finds the following blessing on the strip of material used for the circumcision which is later embroidered and tied around the Bible: 'May God raise us for the Law, for the nuptial canopy and for good deeds.' This blessing attests to the centrality of the wedding in the hopes every father has for his son, hopes that encompass observance of Jewish law, study, and love of one's fellow-man" (1974, p. 181).

When describing the wedding day (p. 193), Raphael tells that the clarinetists who played while the marriage contract was being signed (figure 25) then accompany the bridal procession through the streets of the town, the two fathers leading the groom and the two mothers the bride: "The bride's face was veiled and she was dressed in a lacey gown. Here too joy and solemnity go hand in hand" (see figure 26, a wedding song that enhances the event).

The colorful ceremonies that begin with the matchmaking and engagement and end in the parties held for a week or two after the wedding thus represent a major crossroad at which song, dance, processions, and merry-making combine to create a rich tapestry containing something of everything—religious and secular elements, concepts associated with marriage, and seemingly extraneous matters as well.

In an article entitled "The cancelled wedding motif in Yiddish Folk Song" Meir Noy begins by saying:

> The wedding theme in the folk song of Jews of Eastern Europe is multi-dimensional and omnipresent, being found in almost all categories of songs that reflect a person's life: starting with visions of marriage in the cradle-songs, through children's rhymes and playful songs, the search for the partner, the choice, the difficulties confronting the couple before the wedding, the marriage ceremony with dance music and songs sung by merry-makers, songs about family life and everything it entails—all the way to the golden wedding. One may also add to this songs about

Fig. 25. Ḥuppah niggun, Alsace.

Fig. 26. Ḥuppah Lied, Alsace.

> the allegorical wedding of the people of Israel and the Torah, retrospective songs about the wedding, humorous and satiric songs, weddings of animals and so forth. (1974, p. 53)

The tendency to include songs on general themes and not only those about weddings is widespread in all Jewish communities. Thus, for example, Yosef Tovi (1978, p. 17) writes about the singing of the men in his article, "Wedding Songs of the Jews of Yemen":

"At weddings they sing *shirot* [a type of strophic song popular among Yemenite Jews][20] even if the themes do not relate to weddings, but have general content; their subject-matter is primarily the galut and redemption, which for the past hundred years have been the main themes of Yemenite Jewry's songs. They also include other themes such as exaltation of the Torah, the body, soul and mind. There are lamentations, songs of praise and adoration, and even historical songs."

Wedding songs in Hebrew or other languages and dialects had broad thematic scope, touching upon many aspects of the life of the individual and the community and accurately reflecting their experiences, beliefs, and desires. They were performed by individuals or groups, the singing either solo or responsorial. Some of the songs were accompanied by dancing and instrumental music provided by an individual musician or by an ensemble. In many communities the men and women had separate repertoires of songs, instrumental music, and dances.

The wedding theme in all its ramifications holds a position of central importance in the world of Jewish music outside the synagogue. Some of the songs sung by the women that have particular interest both intrinsically and from the musical and social standpoint, are described in greater detail below.

Songs of the Women at Wedding Ceremonies

Many of the wedding songs indicate an attempt to offer the frightened young girl a measure of psychological preparation and assistance at this crucial turning-point in her life. It must not be forgotten that in traditional societies the girls get married at a young, sometimes very young, age and lack all experience of life. They are attached to their family customs and home life, have been closely sheltered, and know very little about the world outside. The upheaval involved in going to live with a man the girl does not know, leaving the house in which she was born and grew up and moving to the home of the groom's parents who are still strangers to her—all of this is certainly cause for trepidation. During the relatively long period (it sometimes extends over several months) before this sharp change, a variety of rituals and above all, songs, help to fortify the girl's spirit and prepare her for what is to come.

On the Sabbath following the engagement the women of Bukhara would play a game called "The Singer and the Drink" in order to bring together the families of the recently engaged couple. The hostess would raise a glass containing a drink and would start to sing. When she finished she passed the full glass to the woman next to her. If this woman knew how to sing, she did as the hostess had done, and if not, she had to drink the contents of the glass down to the last drop. This game lasted for hours on end and helped form a bond between the two families that were about to be related by marital ties.

Playing games and having fun are good ways of alleviating tension and bringing hearts together. The songs of the women prove this in different ways. In Morocco it was customary to play entertaining games on the second Sabbath after the wedding day, known as "the Sabbath of the swing" because of one of the games played. On this day the bride's friends and many other women would come to her house where a swing was put up in the garden or courtyard. The bride is the first to swing, each of her friends then following her in turn. Throughout the swinging an old woman, who receives gifts from all those present, sings songs extolling the bride's beauty.

An amusing collection of songs included in the women's repertoire is the "Songs of Curses," ostensibly meant to entertain the women by introducing a light atmosphere. Two singers exchange juicy curses for the edification of all those present. These songs are usually concluded with conciliatory verses in which the singers ask forgiveness, express contrition, and try to end on a more acceptable note of good will. These songs may well express hidden protest or criticism of practices that under ordinary circumstances may not be spoken of openly.[21] Some of the songs, for example, vilify old men who want to marry young women—either as a first wife or to replace an older one.

In all Jewish ethnic groups there are similar basic preparations for marriage, including the stages in which the bride and her dowry are prepared, but each community has developed its own additional local customs. A brief survey of special Sephardic songs known as "songs of the bride" (*cantigas di novia*) is sufficient to give us a graphic picture of a variety of different customs: there is a song to the mother-in-law on her way to meet the bride, one for displaying the dowry, another for the bride's ritual bath, a song of leave-taking, etc.

One of the customs was for the bride to bring the groom bedclothes. These were prepared during the time between the engagement and the wedding by the bride's friends and some of the girls of the family. In Salonika the process began with what was called "the day of laundering the wool." Moshe Attias has written the following description:

> Raw wool was bought at the market and a special place was set aside for laundering and drying it; when word was passed around among the neighbors that they are about to "wash the wool" it was understood as announcement of a wedding. The laundry day was always chosen during the summer prior to the wedding, because the sunny days are best for drying and bleaching the wool. . . . They place vats over an open fire in the yard and before long the women are sitting around them washing the wool. . . . The air is filled with exclamations, instructions, and light-hearted gossip. Now one of the players appears and jingling the miniature cymbals that surround the drum, she begins to sing. The rest of the women join in and the notes of wedding ballads are heard on all sides. Their merry tunes and familiar innuendoes elicit much laughter and increase the happiness and joy. (1961, p. 40)

This custom was observed by all the Sephardic communities in the Balkans where the occasion was celebrated in a ballad as follows:

> The white girl laundered much [white was the ideal of beauty]
> She washed, she hung.
> She rinsed with her tears
> With her sighs she hung.

The "player" referred to above is one of the professional singers called *tañaderas* (the drummers). This is a group of three women who are invited to sing and drum at all the ceremonies. They are well-versed not only in the musical repertoire, but in all the customs, and are actually the ones who conduct the ceremonies and supervise the details. Among other things, they head the various processions, carry the groom's gifts to the bride, sing while the trousseau is being displayed, accompany the bride's bathing and dressing. The musical style of eighteen Sephardic wedding songs in the Balkans, including that at the tañaderas, was thoroughly studied by Shoshana Weich-Shahaq (1979, p. 80).

Such groups of female musicians existed in other ethnic groups as well, and were called by various different names. In Yemen they were called *mughanniyāt* (poetesses or female singers), in Kurdistan, *muṭribāt* (female musicians), in Iraq, *daqqāqāt* (female drummers). In each case they conducted the ceremonies and sang, amusing the women and making them dance. The *daqqāqāt,* for instance, was comprised of four to five women who beat various drums (frame drum, kettle drums, a two-headed drum). The leader of the little band was noted for her fine voice and, being a talented performer, she was the soloist. While singing she accompanied herself on small kettle drums. The *daqqāqāt* would also perform at festivities of Muslim women. The texts of the songs in their repertory are included in Avishur (1987).

Among the ceremonies customarily held among the Sephardic Jews in the Balkans we should mention "Almoshama" night (night of the holiday). This night, always the last Saturday night before the wedding day, opens the marriage festivities. Widows, married and unmarried women, girls of the family, the bride's friends and female neighbors, come to her parental home to gladden her heart and raise her spirits on the eve of her departure from the family. Before the wedding the bride goes to the ritual bath, accompanied by the women of the family, female relatives, and friends who sing, beat the drums, and dance in her honor. The visitors pamper the girl, soap her, comb her hair, dry her body and perfume her, all to the accompaniment of song and music.

In Morocco the week of the wedding opens with the ceremonial "beginning of the seven" (seven days before the wedding) in which the groom, his sisters, and professional singers visit the bride's family and present them with trays bearing flour, ḥenna, soap, shoes, dried fruits, and jewelry. That same evening an amulet called "serira" is prepared, which the engaged couple are obliged to wear as a charm against evil spirits until the actual wedding takes place.

Ben-Ami (1975, p. 15) tells of another ceremony, called *azmomeg* (the exact derivation of this term is not known, as is the case with several other terms used in this chapter). The groom's mother brings a special tray of sugar, ḥenna, an egg, cloves, a mirror, and white cotton cloth, all covered by a kerchief. In the evening, after all the guests have arrived, one of the young people—not the future groom—breaks the egg over the bride's head, to the accompaniment of rhythmic sounds emitted by the women. After that, the singers put the ḥenna, the mirror and the cloves on the bride's head and cover it all with the cotton cloth. A custom similar to that of breaking the egg over the bride's head is followed by the Jews of Bida (a locality in South Yemen): a week before the wedding, on the evening of the day the match was decided upon—a date considered no less important than the wedding day itself—the groom brings a bottle of perfumed oil to the rabbi of the community. The rabbi then reads a special text and pours the liquid over the bride's head as a sign of the bond that has been forged by the engagement.

A widely popular and highly important custom in many communities is the ḥenna ceremony. The dried leaves of a certain bush are pulverized and a paste is made from them which is then rubbed on specified parts of the bride's body. The Yemenite custom starts with a colorful procession in which the bride is led out of the room where she has been dressed and lavishly adorned with jewels and trinkets. Veiled, she is led by two friends who are dressed and adorned exactly as she is in order to confuse the devil and thwart his attempts to harm the bride. Two singers lead the procession, singing appropriate songs to the accompaniment of a drum and *ṣaḥn.*[22] Someone in the crowd carries a wide tray called *mashara* on which are seeds, eggs, burning candles, and fragrant herbs. The women sing:

> This is the hour of compassion
> In which the demons retreat
> To the mountains of China [the farthest conceivable horizon]
> And God's blessing
> Descends over the earth.

After the procession the bride is seated in a place of honor where she remains motionless throughout the hours that pass until the ḥenna ceremony itself, vocalists helping to make the time pass pleasantly by singing and accompanying the dancers. As midnight approaches a few of the women prepare the ḥenna paste and place it on a tray decorated with leaves and burning candles. Each in turn carries the tray on her head as she dances and emits cascades of high tintinabulary sounds. Finally they spread the ḥenna on the bride's hands and feet and what is left is spirited away by the guests as a good luck omen. In Kurdistan they color the bride's hair with ḥenna, spreading it on her hands as well.

In Yemen, after the ḥenna, additional ceremonies were performed as the bride was dressed, bedecked with jewels, and her hair coiffed. With the women of Ḥabban (south Yemen) the bride is combed ceremoniously: first on the day on which she is given the jewels and then on the evening of the wedding. She is seated in the center of the room; the mother lifts the veil covering her daughter's face and says: "Behold, this is my daughter, engaged to so-and-so." The actual combing is a complicated and time-consuming operation as tradition requires the hair to be plaited into 150 braids. The Jews of Bida in Yemen have their own special custom: the father of the bride slaughters a goat, which he swings above her head seven times to protect her from evil. Only then may the combing ceremony begin.

Most of the customs and ceremonies touched upon above are accompanied by music made by women, and they attest to the importance of women's songs, above all in ceremonies connected with weddings. But this is only one theme and one aspect of the many different types of songs the women sing. Far removed from joyous events of a ritual, celebratory nature, we find other songs: those that befriend a woman, accompany her when she is alone, whether in trouble or in joy. The woman fortifies her spirit by singing to herself, and perhaps to her infant, who hears and absorbs the mother's confessions, longings, complaints, and dreams. This kind of singing presents a different, lyrical aspect, which is virtually not to be found in men's singing. It is the singing of a woman alone, of one who reveals her troubles, whether in a lullaby, a song of love or jealousy, in songs accompanying housework, while grinding with mortar and pestle or plucking a fowl, or when the husband or loved one has left for distant parts.

In his chapter on the folk song of the Ashkenazim, Idelsohn devotes a section to a description of the situation of the east European woman and sums it up by saying that all the special experiences of her life found expression in her singing.

"Thus, we find . . . laments of the young disappointed wife, of the young woman who had to stay with her mother-in-law. There are mother-songs, soldier-songs, grass-widow-songs, orphan songs, woman's-trade-songs, accusations against and curses upon the heretic husband. These songs are in a pathetic style and in a desperate sadness" (1929, p. 395).

It may be that the pathetic nature, the lyricism, the longing that to a great extent characterize the songs of a lonely woman singing to herself, endowed her with skill in the realm of songs of lamentation. Then again, this skill may also accrue from the symbolic connection between birth and death. Be that as it may, lamentations are a type of song exclusively sung by women. As in most other spheres, here too experts emerged—professionals who specialized in the esoterica of grieving and knew how to feed the flame of sorrow and weeping.

Distinctive Traits of Women's Singing

According to some, special women's songs exist because of the need to compensate somehow for the ban against the public participation of women in synagogue rituals. Women are even further circumscribed by the talmudic injunction to the effect that "hearing a woman's voice is indecent," which was interpreted as a prohibition against their singing in public. The doctrinal religious reasons for such prohibitions were intended to support conventional norms and concepts that define the woman's status and determine the kind of behavior expected of her. Yet they seem to have encouraged the emergence and crystallization of songs with unique values and characteristics, as women singing for other women became a way of skirting those prohibitions. In their songs the women can express their world, their experiences, and the Jewish and human values they uphold. Most of the time the women were quite isolated, closed within their households. The songs seem to have been a form of release through which they could express—even if only to themselves—those experiences and aspects of their lives that were special. With respect to professional musical groups, their fate was similar to that of musicians in most traditional societies: the services of artists are needed and therefore society tacitly condones their activities.

From the musical standpoint, are the women's songs different from those of the men? The composer Béla Bartók (1951), who studied the folk songs of Hungary, Romania and elsewhere, noted the uniqueness and archaic nature of the women's singing. He was of the opinion that an ancient strata of song was reproduced therein because traditional societies live in such a way that they come into almost no contact with their surrounding environment, to say nothing of foreign cultures. Furthermore, he explains, in traditional societies the woman is bound to the home and family and her opportunities for contact with the external world are far fewer than those of the men: pressures of making a living or the call to war sometimes took the man away from his home and exposed him to other people and unfamiliar traditions. Many ethnomusicologists were impressed by this theory; as an example we shall quote Gerson-Kiwi's article about the songs of Jewish women in Yemen:[23]

> For a long time the songs of women in folk-societies have attracted ethnomusicologists searching for archaic levels of musical expression. This is true, for example, in relation to the songs of women of the Oriental countries, particularly those within the sphere of Islamic culture. In this context we can include the Jewish women living in the Muslim countries, whose conditions of life are actually the same as those of the Muslim women. In the Jewish folk communities, just as in the Muslim ones, the social structure is generally molded around the male society, so that the women are prevented from participating in social, and particularly religious, ceremonies. As a result of this they have no part in study or education, which in these Oriental Jewish communities are primarily a function of the community's religious life. (1965)

The Characteristics of Women's Songs

The discussion of the songs women sing can best be summarized by enumerating their general and shared characeristics:

1. As Jewish women did not know how to read and write, their singing falls within the realm of the oral tradition and entirely lacks the background of a tradition of written songs that conform to metrical and aesthetic rules, which the men's songs possess. In the main, this is folk singing in the most authentic sense.

2. Consequently, these songs are not fixed in permanent form; gifted women can exhibit their creative ability by adding verses of their own or by rearranging material they include in their repertoires.

3. The women's songs—like those of the men—frequently reflect actual themes taken from everyday life in the community. Sometimes they even express opinions about public and political events.

4. The subject matter is highly variegated; some of the themes are functional, the song describing a specific event; others have generalized content. Some deal with public issues while others touch on the personal experiences of the individual. Most of the songs are centered on the world of the woman.

5. With only few exceptions, the women's songs are in the language spoken locally.

6. From the standpoint of performance, the songs are performed exclusively by women and for women. There is also a tradition of singing at home when alone (tending children or doing chores).

7. The songs are sung in public on occasions of a folk nature either by a group of women or by one individual with a good voice. There are also professional performances presented by female musicians who are specialists; these musicians often direct the various ceremonies and receive remuneration. Of course, in rural areas singing and dancing is usually—possibly exclusively—collective, and sometimes these places have no professional musicians. Ḥabban in South Yemen is such a place: there the women who dance accompany themselves with songs. The performers are divided into two groups that sing antiphonally.[24]

8. Professional performances are given by ensembles. The ensemble may consist of only two women—one who is the main singer and the other her assistant. It is the "diva" who decides which song will be sung, and she starts singing, while the second woman responds and often also plays the drums or an instrument other than the one played by the main singer. An ensemble can sometimes include up to five women. They are called "singers," to stress the musical and creative element, or "players" because they accompany themselves with rhythm instruments—various kinds of drums (primarily frame-drums) and, among the Yemenites, the *ṣaḥn* (a copper plate).

9. None of the groups of professional women musicians we know of use melodic instruments, but only rhythm instruments. Gerson-Kiwi feels that there is something archaic about this, which is conspicuously present in Yemenite women's singing.

10. The final point relates to Belá Bartók's hypothesis with respect to the archaic nature of the melodies sung by the women. This is an interesting point that some but not all of the repertoires substantiate.

8

Folk Creativity and Performance Practice

The many outstanding events and occasions that mark the lives of individuals and communities afford ample opportunity for men and women gifted in the performing arts to express their creativity, particularly when the society around them recognizes and appreciates their talent. Individuals, couples, and small ensembles appear in public as singers, instrumentalists, or dancers. With the exception of the few songs and dances in which all present are expected to take part, an important place in every ceremony or celebration is reserved for those who are recognized as gifted performers, be they amateurs or professionals. Some of the songs sung may be so closely related to liturgical *piyyuṭim* that the *payṭan* of the synagogue may perform them, even if the occasion is not, strictly speaking, a religious one. Other parts of the same ceremonies, actually the major parts, include songs and dances that are quite similar in style to local folk music. Those who perform them are often active in the musical life of the surrounding non-Jewish community.

With respect to the texts, unlike the liturgical *piyyuṭ* which is almost always a written work, few non-synagogal songs have written texts; many of them are created by individuals talented enough to set them to appropriate music and perform them. Not infrequently such talented musician-poets introduce some of their own songs into more traditional material. Moreover, as performers they may occasionally modify the traditional material. From many standpoints, a survey of the world of folk creativity affords the observer a fine opportunity to become acquainted with some characteristics of related music.

Traditional creativity that flourished in most Jewish communities abroad continues to find expression in several parts of Israel, although in more limited fashion. The folk poet still has a position of importance in his community, to which he is a source of pride and inspiration. Many who are not yet entirely comfortable with their relatively new status as Israelis would find life quite impossible without a medium through which to express their joy, but simultaneously, their uniqueness. Thousands of verses attest to this, as folk poets of all ethnic communities have reacted to the new experiences impinging on them. By its very nature, however, this poetic creativity is associated with certain conditions and with a congenial milieu, which may well disappear. Such folk poetry is recorded only in memory and therefore, almost by definition, leaves no tangible trace. Nevertheless, although the content may change, certain patterns generally survive. It is common knowledge that there are many now in Israel whose creative talent had been recognized by their traditional communities abroad; in coming to this country they were uprooted from their native surroundings and catapulted into the twentieth century with its technological innovations and the concomitant breakdown of time-honored social frameworks. In addition, they were confused and perplexed by the pressure to cope with trends that emerged in Israel's developing society, a disorientation that often impeded their integration.

Some theoreticians maintain that according to literary criteria, poems created by formally illiterate people cannot be considered poetry, and certainly cannot be considered as contributing to the cultural heritage of their author's particular community. Indeed, one cannot discuss such poetry from an aesthetic standpoint—but there is also no reason to do so. These poems, above all the ones that are accepted by the members of the community, are newly ripened fruit, although in actuality they are incarnations of a tradition many hundreds of years old. However, it should be noted, as G. Herzog says, "Folk song is part of folk culture, which is distinct from that of the cities and represents only certain facets of the culture of the nation" (1950, p. 1033). That being the case, interest in this oral poetry has greatly increased in recent years; a great deal has already been done to facilitate access to past and present traditional folk creativity and to advance knowledge about it. New means and methods of studying such living work and the techniques by which it is created have expanded the scope of research and brought about profound changes in our approach to it as creative art.[1]

Due to certain special characteristics of traditional creativity, and because one returns to it time and again, in a way it represents a reflection of the generations, with the new mirrored against the old. This is wholly integrated creativity in which text, music, and performance are the product of the mind and heart of one creator; hence it is the embodiment of uninterrupted cultural continuity. It continues to inject vitality into many customs, forms of thinking, and linguistic idioms, even after ordinary usage has discarded them, either because of radically changed conditions or pursuant to contact with foreign cultures. These more archaic cultural manifestations can be touchstones for understanding changes and permutations that have resulted from the conflux of different traditions.

How Is Creativity in Unwritten Songs Expressed?

Some generally known traditional songs are performed by all those present at a given event, while other songs, actually the majority, are performed by talented individuals, with the audience taking part in responses, refrains, or simple repetitious phrases. The talented individual performer may have earned the title of "poet" or "song writer" in his community, even if he does not exactly create texts or the accompanying music. The title may be bestowed because someone is recognized as potentially able to compose songs or to follow the dictates of his creative imagination and improvise freely while performing old, familiar works. Some of the changes introduced into traditional songs in the course of their performance occur because both texts and melodies are retained in memory; they have never been recorded in a rigid form that limits deviation. Changes and improvisations represent the point at which the performing vocal artist and creative poet meet.

Nevertheless, even the most creative folk poet does not produce something from nothing, nor does he invent something entirely new. Moreover, he does not want to; indeed, he refrains from markedly flouting previous practice. He must take his listeners into considerations; they want to hear familiar songs and he tries to comply with their desires and expectations. No performer in a traditional society can ignore the groups for whom he performs and whose approval he solicits. This element tends to restrict aspects of originality and innovative creativity. Moreover, one must remember that in societies based on centuries-old orally transmitted culture and traditions, the concepts "original" and "innovation" carry a negative charge. The ideal is to preserve the old and function in the spirit of tradition. From another standpoint, too, the creative individual must remain close to tradition. Since the work is given direction and form as it is being performed, there is not time for the rethinking and polishing done by the artist who records his work in writing. The moment a word or phrase leaves the singer's lips it irretrievably vanishes into thin air. Structure and sequence have immediately become immutable.

For that reason the folk poet draws his materials from tradition, from a repository of themes, phrases, idioms, and images which he adapts to a given situation. His talent is expressed in the masterful skill with which he compounds a new work from the old raw material. This process, often totally unpremeditated, is involved in poetic work and storytelling, but above all in musical improvisation and all types of musical creativity—folk, art, and traditional. We are thus led to conclude that one who creates oral culture is not only a creative artist, but also a custodian of tradition. In the course of time a selection occurs; inadvertently, some new songs are rejected while others are preserved—either because they commemorate a particularly impressive event or for some other sufficient reason. These are the songs that become permanently ensconced in the general folk repertoire.

The process briefly described above applies only in part to traditional music, yet it definitely applies to traditional art music.[2] This is because in the cultivated art the musician obeys normative compositional devices and has at his disposal melodic patterns and motifs that represent the various *maqamāt* (see chapter 5); when performing, he chooses from among them, arranging them in accordance with the dictates of the established norms and his ability and taste.

When a folk singer performs a simple song and announces it as his own, he is referring primarily to the text. The music, an uncomplicated theme repeated over and over again, is always taken from the reserve of traditional melodies. It is not too unusual to hear a man or woman sing the very same text to different music, or different texts to the same music. Indeed, by comparison with the constant addition of "new" texts to the total repertory of songs, the number of "new" melodies is very limited. Therefore, creativity is more conspicuous in textual material, but since there is no pressure to be innovative or original, the creative act may well express itself in the very adaptation of a given melody to a text with a different meter.

Furthermore, folk creativity is influenced by processes of acculturation that are more readily recognized in text than in music, as in most cases the latter maintains its distinctive traditional character. For example, consider songs relating to subjects such as unemployment or flights to the moon. The folk singer will almost always strive to affix his modern text to a tune taken from his community's traditional repertoire.

In light of what has been said above, it becomes clear that folk creativity produces an integrated work in which text, music, and performance are a single entity, the artistic expression of one person's spirit. Hence creating and performing are two aspects of a single interdependent act that reaches full expression only on some public occasion and in the presence of an audience that inspires the creative imagination of the poet-musician. Having a phenomenal memory, he is a kind of ambulatory archive in which are stored the songs of a given community; he also helps preserve them from extinction. Traditional texts, or texts that he himself composes, can be a source from which to learn about past happenings, about cultural values, about the community's reactions to current events. The poet-musician does not start with a blank page, but draws on an existing hoard of formulae, images, and patterns. He rearranges them and adapts the "new" work to tunes that are usually traditional; or as Herzog writes: "The body of folk song grows, rather, through a process of re-creation of materials already in existence" (1950).

The songs of the Jews contain some aspects with specific reference to Jewish communities and other aspects of a general nature that are shared with the surrounding society. This multihued collection includes epics, ballads telling of Jewish and non-Jewish heroes, reverential songs about saints, love songs, contentious songs, songs about animals, humorous songs, etc. Contemporary happenings such as things that occurred before leaving for Israel or while on the way, are also important themes. One example chosen from many is a poem written by Y.D., originally from Yemen, now in Israel. A folk poetess who created many poems describing the life of Yemenite

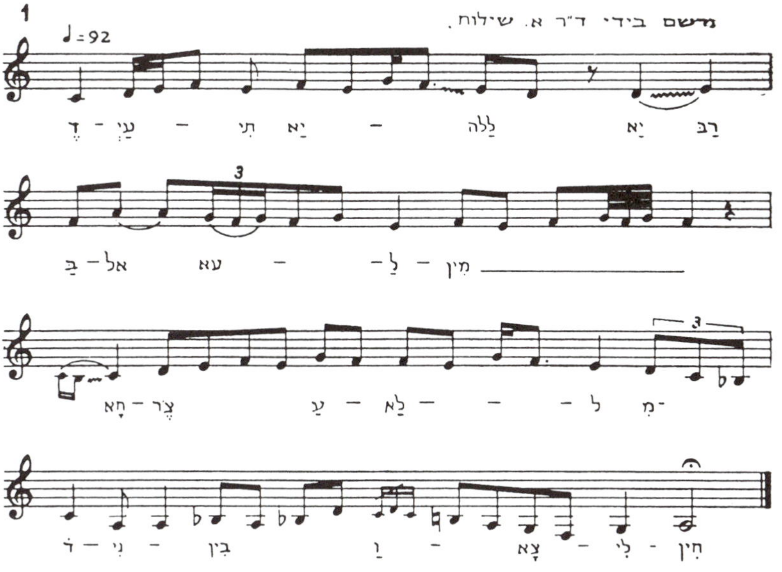

Fig. 27. Yemenite ʿaliyya song.

Jewry, she has given permanent poetic expression to the painful experiences that anteceded her emigration. Her descriptions of the riots and pogroms juxtaposed with the experience of going to live in Israel (*ʿaliyya*) make the *ʿaliyya* seem synonymous with redemption. She sings her Arabic-language text to a tune borrowed from the men's repertoire, the melody of "I thank my Lord," which she changes a bit so that it will fit her words (see figure 27). The poetess maintains that she created both words and music. It is indeed possible that she fit the words of the poem to the familiar tune unconsciously, or then again, the melody may represent a well-known song type.[3] A few of the poem's fifty-two lines are quoted below:[4]

I left Sanʿa through the Wadi
The denouncers following me like burning fire
I envied the bird that needs no provisions
I envied you, oh high mountains
In the dark of night none will alarm you I go on my way with the help of God and cry out
Farewell! Oh ever wakeful God
On embracer of the world, Oh tenant of the skies above
You who are more powerful than all others
No secret will be hidden from you, no eye turned aside
Remember your vow and bring your final promise closer

Spread your mercy and loving-kindness
Build your Sanctuary and save your people. . . .
I swear that I would not have voiced my great sorrow
Were it not to tell you about Yemen and its calamities.[5]

In his article "songs on Historical Events in Jewish Moroccan Poetry" J. Shetrit (1982) tells that he has found the manuscripts of more than one hundred poems in Hebrew and Judeo-Arabic that relate directly to various historic or social events from the twelfth century until today. Some of the happenings that earned poetic coverage: the cruel pogroms instigated by King Mula Yazid in the years 1790–92; the horrors of the famine in Meknes in 1780–81; the bombardment of Casablanca by French warships in 1907; events of the First and Second World Wars; the life and martyrdom of beautiful Suleika from the city of Fez who, despite torture, refused to convert to Islam. A song written in her memory was sung by Jewish girls in Morocco to a sad, touching melody, and there are other folk songs that tell of her captivating beauty and her death—the death of a heroine. Incidently, in 1952 an essay contest was held among Jew of Morocco on the subject of "Beautiful Sol" who met a martyr's death because she refused to become a Muslim and marry an aristocratic suitor (see Sol (1954) and also Attal (1973), who reports thirty-six items on her). Finally, even the arch-enemy Hitler merited a poem of thirty-six lines written after Moroccan Jewry was saved from the danger of conquest by the Nazis.

Concerning the existence of recorded folk poetry: it is possible to admit that a new poem that was heard and appreciated by an audience was probably written down, even though it fell within the category of folk songs usually learned and remembered by hearing. Whether it was recorded by the author or by someone else, the objective was to preserve and publicize a work that had been well received. The written version could then serve as a point of departure for others to study, memorize, and, intentionally or unintentionally, modify.[6]

The combined creation and performance of a song finds very varied forms of expression which are essentially common to Jewish musical traditions and the musical traditions of the surrounding non-Jewish societies. However, there is such a thing as a conspicuous Jewish stamp and we shall expand on it in the second part of this chapter. We shall also discuss a few ensembles that have specifically Jewish character.

The Yemenite *Dīwān*[7]

The *dīwān*—a collection of songs for weddings, circumcisions, the Sabbath, and holy days—contains the songs sung by the Yemenite men. Before the *dīwān* appeared, many of the songs for special occasions that were popular among the Jews of Yemen were those written by Spanish poets. In the course of time the poetic output of native Jewish Yemenites vastly increased and their work was included in the prayer books along with the classical Spanish *piyyuṭim.* As the number of poems increased, they were collected in a separate volume, known as the *dīwān,* a repository of all those poems that were originally written to be sung. This is a unique collection by virtue of its scope, the type of songs selected for inclusion, the occasions on which they are to be sung, and the fact that it belongs exclusively to the Jews of Yemen.

In chapter 5 we discussed special *piyyuṭim* of the Jews of Morocco and Syria that were meant only for the *baqqashot.* The *dīwān* is entirely different, as it includes all types of songs accepted by the Yemenite Jews. It is also unusual in that all the material it includes is meant to be sung and even to be accompanied by dancing. In addition, unlike other *dīwāns* or collections of Spanish songs that are widespread in the East, the Yemenite *dīwān* contains no instructions as to the melody to be used, or the way in which the song should be performed.

The earliest copy of Yemenite *dīwān* known to us is from three hundred years ago, from the time of Shalem Shabazi (1619–80), the greatest Yemenite Jewish poet. Indeed, many of his poems are included in the volume. He was apparently the first to introduce the custom of singing general, not only nuptial, songs at wedding ceremonies. The themes of dispersion and redemption—the main subjects of poems written by Yemenite Jewry for hundreds of years, and other general motifs as well—were introduced into wedding songs. From the musical standpoint this is not sacred song, but traditional folk singing. Although the *dīwān* does contain a number of *piyyuṭim* that are sung in the synagogue, most of its contents are intended for festive occasions, some of the songs even meant to accompany dancing.

In "Form and Melody in the Various Types of Yemenite Song," Yehuda Ratzabi notes that the songs in the *dīwān* are generally arranged in two categories: by the occasion they are intended for, and in accordance with their genres. It opens with hymns for the Sabbath and the departure of the Sabbath, these are followed by *nashīd* and *shirot* (two basic genres of Yemenite songs), and finally, wedding and circumcision songs. Ratzabi maintains that with the proliferation of poems and the compilation of the *dīwān,* it became clear that the songs fell into one of six classifications. We shall now briefly discuss these six genres.

Nashīd. The *nashīd* is built on classical Arabic principles for the *qasida.* Its many lines are divided into two metrically equivalent versets, the first called *delet* (door) and the second *soger* (lock). The same rhyme concludes each of the lines, which are based on one of the classical meters (see chapter 5). This is, therefore, a solemn work from the standpoint of theme, content, and performance; weighty in character, it is performed slowly and gravely. The *nashīd* is sung solemnly and antiphonally by the entire assemblage, divided into two groups; one group sings the *delet* and the other the *soger.* Its melody is placid, flowing, gracefully adorned, and is performed with heart-felt longing. Sanctity and solemnity, as we have said, mark its performance. Among other things, it serves as a sort of religious-symbolic introduction to the singing and dancing and is written entirely in Hebrew, the sacred language. The main function of the *nashīd* is to serve as a serious counterweight to the lighter parts of the program.[8]

Shirah. from the standpoint of its structure the *shirah* is similar to the strophic songs in the Spanish-Hebrew repertory (see chapter 5). In Yemen, strophic poetry was highly developed; it comprises most of the Jewish Yemenite songs. Thanks to several of its characteristics, the *shirah* is appropriate for cheerful singing and for accompanying dancing. The lines are brief, the rhymes variegated; the strophic verse—called in Yemenite tradition the *tawshīḥ* (see chapter 5, note 12)—serves as a kind of repeated refrain. The meter is simple, both mundane and sacred themes are included, and the songs are in Hebrew, Arabic, Aramaic, or two of those tongues combined. The singer accompanies the dancers by rhythmically beating on metal copper. The use of an oil can instead of a drum is usually explained by the prohibition against musical instruments that is associated with mourning for the destruction of the Temple. Occasionally the singer inconspicuously inserts words directed to the dancers, a passage not included in the original song, saying "Apple of my eye and heart, the refrain reaches out to you." This is apparently his way of signalling to the dancers that they are to execute the particular figures called for by the refrain.[9] Ratzabi (1968) points out that in the *shirah* the singer is not bound by the text as in the *nashīd;* he may permit himself to change the order of lines and even eliminate some entirely. He feels that the words are subordinate to the music and dancing and in effect only serve them, a manifestation that is widespread in folk singing throughout the Middle East. The *nashīd* and the *shirah* are both major elements in Yemenite singing, from the standpoint of their importance as well as from that of quantity: they number in the hundreds (some 95 percent of all songs).

Zaffah. An Arabic word that in the entire area indicates certain of the wedding ceremonies and, in the broadest sense, encompasses all the songs sung when the bride is brought to the home of the bridegroom on the wedding night, when the groom is taken to the bride's home, when the groom's head is shaved, and so forth. These are simple, functional folk tunes, brief melodies built on repeated musical phrases of limited range that have an archaic flavor. The public also takes part in their performance. The songs are in Hebrew (occasionally, although very rarely, one finds a song written in Arabic-Hebrew or Arabic). They are meant to extol and glorify the groom and open with appropriately formal phrases such as: "Bo le-shalom Ḥatan" (Welcome, bridegroom).

Ḥidduyah. This genre apparently has its source in a type of Arabic song known as the *Ḥidā'*,[10] which is also associated with weddings. The poet who conducts the wedding ceremony in the Arab village is called *Ḥaddāy*, which is derived from the same term. The *Ḥidduyah* is recited after seven blessings, while the groom's fingers are being covered with ḥenna and he is being accompanied home. The *Ḥidduyot* are short, simple songs that open with the words "Ashirah la-ahuv" (I shall sing to my beloved) or "Ahuv mehar hammor" (Beloved from the myrrh mountain). The *Ḥidduyot* are about the bride and groom, as in the following example:

I shall sing to my beloved, and arrange the song for him
I shall sing to the blessed one, and arrange the song for him
I shall sing to the hero, and arrange the song for him.
May this groom be blessed, his face aglow with splendor
May this groom be as Balshan ben Yair (Mordechai)
And his bride like his cousin Esther
Halleluyah, all is well, for He will be merciful forever.

Hallel. This is a short song in rhyming prose, in which invited guests bless the person who is the center of the celebration (be it a groom, a newly circumcised infant, a new homeowner), and it is also the benediction with which the host responds. The *hallel* is primarily in praise of God and it is recited after the singing. It is made up of short benedictions linked together in a single rhyme that opens and closes with "halleluyah." The *dīwān* gives the fixed formula for the *hallelot,* to which no new blessing may be introduced. This type of song, unique to the Jews of Yemen, is chanted.[11]

Qaṣīd. This is a poem with a strophic structure; it uses only colloquial Arabic and its content derives from the folk literature of the surroundings. Its connection with Jewry is extremely tenuous, nor is it necessarily about a wedding or any other specific event. The *qaṣīd* is actually an entertaining folk song that used the everyday language for the purpose of amusing an audience ignorant of literary Arabic. The subject may be an argument between the eye and the heart, between a bachelor and a married man, between coffee and tobacco, between one city and another. Some of the subjects are highly fantastic, such as, for example, a stolen cup. There is almost unlimited material here for folk creativity.

Repertoire of Ballads and Judeo-Spanish Songs

The repertoire of romances (ballads) and Judeo-Spanish (Ladino) songs is undoubtedly among the richest, oldest, and most complex of all Jewish musical literature. It has been in existence for hundreds of years and has successfully withstood the ravages of time; it overcame the uprooting in 1492 from Spain—its original source and natural environment—and even survived transplantation to new surroundings. This repertoire as we know it today is a mosaic of sacred and profane, Jewish and non-Jewish, old and new. The oldest and most basic component is the ballad, a lyrical epic that developed in Castille during the tenth, eleventh, and twelfth centuries. These were songs extolling the heroes of the Spanish aristocracy, glorious tales of knightly valor, courage, and honor. As time passes, the aristocratic circles allowed the ballads to fall into disuse and they were transformed into folk songs telling of love, jealousy, and faithlessness. As folk songs, they were built on sixteen-syllable lines subdivided into two parts of eight syllables each. The lines ended in an assonance, but despite the difference in consonants, a similarity of vowel sounds produces the effect of a corresponding sound. Each poem was divided into a series of successive lines ending in a similar sound and called *coplas* (stanzas); these were distinguished from one another by a change of assonants.

Samuel Armistead, one of the outstanding students of the Spanish ballads, has made the following comments with regard to the role played by the Judeo-Spanish heritage in the historic development of this poetic form: "Of all types of orally transmitted Spanish literature, the Romance establishes the most indisputably fruitful connection with the Spanish (Hispanic) past—the Iberian heritage of the Jews of Spain. Indeed, it is for this very reason that Western scholars, above all those making a special study of the Spanish language and culture, were the first to reveal particular interest in Spanish Jewry's repertoire of ballads. This repertoire offered a vital key to the corpus of ballads—the Romancero—of the Middle Ages and the 16th century, in that it solved mysteries and filled in lacunae" (1982).

Basing an approach to the study of the various aspects of Spanish Jewry's musical legacy on the assumption that this heritage crystallized primarily on Spanish soil and then moved with the Jews to wherever they settled after the expulsion in 1492, we can be reasonably certain that we are on firmer ground than when studying other Jewish traditions. Basically, this tradition has been vigorously perpetuated for almost five hundred years, a long period of survival that testifies to the unswerving devotion with which Sephardic Jewry nurtured it. This process seems to have been fostered by a universal phenomenon, one of those that characterize many of varied societies. Let us examine the nature of that phenomenon.

Music is generally recognized as the language of those emotions that are buried deep in the subconscious of an individual steeped in any given cultural tradition. Music not only accompanies and enhances major events in the lives of individuals, but is also closely associated with all aspects of community life. The person who participates in and enjoys the various events acquires the sense of security engendered by identifying with a group. As emblematic of cultural feelings, experiences, and values absorbed primarily in earliest childhood, music is a latent catalyst that at all times and all places stimulates the memory and precipitates recollections of remote events, thereby reminding people of their original roots. Music is always with us as a loyal companion, even when we distance ourselves physically from our source of origin or adopt new values as part of our assimilation into a new cultural milieu. The tunes that eddied around us in our childhood always reappear as if in a magic mirror, reminding us of sounds, sights, smells, and experiences of days gone by.

This pervasive human phenomenon is apparently behind the current compulsion people feel to seek their roots, although they may be separated from them by centuries of alienation. This desire for continuity modifies and regulates change and usually—though not always—succeeds in tempering radical upheavals. Its power may explain the remarkable survival of a musical heritage that had roots deep in the soil of Spain and was immersed in the emotional, cultural, and physcial atmosphere there. Those expelled from Spain and the rest of the Iberian peninsula carried this heritage with them proudly and lovingly wherever their wanderings took them; they nurtured it with endless devotion, it being the language of their emotions, the language that evoked childhood experiences and reminded them of tales of past splendor. Wherever they were, then, the exiles divided their longings between two homelands.

From our presentation of the material it might seem that the investigator is confronted with a relatively easy task. Ostensibly our discussion concerns a Jewish tradition conscientiously preserved for over five hundred years, admittedly uprooted from its creative source—but perhaps just because of that, it managed to survive for so long on alien soil. But beyond such a sweeping, almost romantic approach, an objective observer attempting to understand all the ramifications of the subject confronts many questions that evade unequivocal answers. At least as the situation appears today, there is a great diversity of opinions prevailing among scholars. For example:

1. Are the melodies of the sacred as well as the secular songs we hear sung today by the progeny of those exiled from Spain centuries ago, identical with those sung before processes of modernization set in and before tragic events occurred that brought about the destruction of old communities?

2. Assuming that changes have taken place, one is led to speculate on their nature. Have they been produced by the particular circumstances that have affected our generation, or are they part of an extended process that started long, long ago but is only now becoming apparent, in the wake of new circumstances. There is very little early documentary evidence about the repertoire of Spanish ballads. One precious source can be found in the song books compiled by Najjara and others, where the various *piyyuṭim* and poems are preceded by instructions concerning the tune to be adapted. Dealing repeatedly with this matter, Hanoch Avenary (1960, 1971, 1975) lists the first lines of dozens of Judeo-Spanish songs with accompanying tunes that the cantors and congregations of sixteenth- and seventeenth-century Jewish communities still knew fairly well. How revealing this *contrafacta* technique is for the musicologist has been recently clarified by J. Katz (1988).

The intensive collection and study of Romances by both Jewish and non-Jewish scholars (primarily Spanish) started in Israel and other places at the end of the nineteenth century. Gradually, thousands of texts and many hundreds of tunes were recorded, and studies were conducted in the spheres of language, literature, culture, folklore, and music. For twenty years now in the United States, Samuel Armistead and Joseph Silverman have been working in this field, collecting, analyzing, classifying, publishing, and preparing research reports. The American musicologist Israel Katz has been working with Armistead and Silverman, and the three scholars collaborated on the book *The Judeo-Spanish Romances of Tangier* (Armistead et al., 1977). This work analyzes the songs in accordance with their musical, linguistic, and literary characteristics, as well as from the standpoint of motif. The following year Samuel Armistead and Joseph Silverman's *The Judeo-Spanish Ballads from the Menendez Pidal*

Collection appeared as part of the same series. Pidal was one of the most important Spanish researchers and this book scientifically organizes his collection of 2,150 texts.

Among those who have collected texts and studied the various cultural aspects involved, special mention should be made of Moshe Attias's *The Spanish Romancero* (1961) and the *Cancionnero* (1972), which includes transcripts of some melodies. The *Cancionnero* is a collection of songs that are not ballads but *cantigas* (songs), a poetic folk form that flourished wherever Spanish Jews lived after the expulsion from Spain. These Judeo-Spanish folk songs developed in two directions: one branch includes sacred songs about the nation's Patriarchs, the holidays, the Torah with its doctrines and commandments, and Jewish moral values; the second branch has secular songs dealing with love and the human life cycle. P. Benichou's work also merits attention as it offers new perspectives in research on the Spanish ballad. The book stresses the folk creativity inherent in ballads belonging to the oral tradition, and shows how much a study of those ballads can teach us about the creative folk process.

As far as music is concerned, we now have whole collections, actually extensive anthologies, of Judeo-Spanish material in Western notation. Three of them were compiled by Leon Algazi (1958), Alberto Hemsi (1932–38); 1969–73), and Isaac Levy (1959) respectively. Hemsi, a talented composer, made new arrangements of some of the ballads he collected, and added accompaniments. Isaac Levy was one of the first to make his own arrangements of ballads, which he sang in public, accompanied by an orchestra or small ensemble.

Israel Katz, who studied the music of Judeo-Spanish songs, and was interested in the questions posed above regarding the fate of the original Spanish melodies, offered far-reaching conclusions in a lecture entitled "The Myth of the Sephardic Musical Legacy from Spain" (1973). As the title indicates, the author refutes the view held by most investigators that the Sephardic Jews in Israel and abroad have preserved the tunes of the Spanish ballads just as they were before the expulsion from Spain. Initially, Katz presented the theses promulgated by other scholars: one maintains that with the help of the melodies currently in use, Spanish researchers could reconstruct the tradition of the sixteenth century; the second, the approach of Edith Gerson-Kiwi (1964), maintains that the tunes heard today originate in the tradition that anteceded the expulsion from Spain, at least with respect to melodic patterns; and the third, that of Alberto Hemsi states that part of the repertoire—primarily the modal aspect—shows such a conspicuous Turkish influence that it cannot be ignored or denied. Hemsi however also suggests the possibility that Jewish tunes of Andalusia influenced the "primitive oriental music of the Turks" (1938, p. xiv).

In reference to Hemsi, one is confronted with two basic questions that in the opinion of this author must exercise anyone dealing with the subject:

What were the original tunes that accompanied the ballads of the Spanish Jews at the time of the expulsion and before? What happened to those tunes as they were transmitted orally over a period of four hundred years?

Katz maintains that even going back to the original source does not simplify the problem, because the Jews exiled from Spain were already a heterogeneous population: they came from various different Spanish centers, each of which had its own characteristic poetic style and tradition. Then, in addition to differences resulting from locale, one cannot ignore the differences between Christian and Muslim cultures: there is absolutely no firm evidence from which to draw conclusions about the musical tradition behind the development of the native Spanish *romancero* itself. Finally: musicological research has shown that as of the beginning of the eighteenth century, the musical repertoire of the Balkan and eastern Mediterranean Jewish communities gradually diverged from that of the Jews of Morocco, who maintained closer contact with the mother country, Spain. In effect, today one may speak of two distinct stylistic traditions.

In light of these premises, the author reaches the conclusion that even if the words, grammatical construction, and other linguistic attributes of the ballads faithfully reflect their original source, there is no guarantee that the melody does so as well. The Jews, widely scattered as they were after leaving Spain, seem to have absorbed new melodies from the different countries they moved to, and used them for the old ballads. Hence it seems very unlikely, if not entirely impossible, that the original melodies can be reconstructed by studying the way they are now performed by Sephardic Jews. Scholars differ as to the extent to which the contemporary melodies can be identified with the original ones. But traditionalists harbor no such doubts: having assiduously and lovingly passed the ballads down for over five hundred years, they are absolutely convinced that the original format has been retained. And indeed, such traditionalists resolutely pursued their objective, but what actually happened was that Spanish tradition—like all living traditions—was not impervious to revitatlization resulting from new elements brought into play by creative impulses. Far away from their source of origin, creative Jews were inevitably influenced by their new surroundings in the countries of exile. However it is quite probable that despite the changes, the contemporary musical repertoire of the ballads can be considered essentially a direct offspring of the *romanceros* created in Spain before the expulsion.

In light of this rather wary conclusion, which seems, however, to satisfy Katz, and taking the historic developments and circumstances into account, he drew a distinction between two major branches of what he called the repertoire of the Spanish ballad, one that developed in the eastern Mediterranean (the Ottoman Empire and the Balkans) and the other in the western Mediterranean (Morocco). Katz (1968) created a table that can serve to summarize this discussion, as it describes a number of stylistic characteristics or parameters that distinguish the two branches:

1. All ballads are sung monophonically without accompaniment. In those rare cases where accompaniment is present it will be harmonic for the Western tradition and heterophonic for the Eastern tradition.

2. The strophic form is paramount for all melodic stanzas, with the quatrain division predominating.

Table 1

Comparison of Eastern and Western Mediterranean Traditions

	Western	Eastern
1. Melodic stanza	Is modal (including major and minor) and diatonic in movement. Some ballads have distinct triadic and pentatonic characteristics.	Adheres to the class of melody types in the system of Turkish-Arabic *maqāmāt,* and is diatonic in movement.
2. Pitch	Subscribes to the Western concept of pitch.	Has a greater amount of microtonal intonation.
3. Tempo	Is even-flowing.	Varies from an underlying pulsating tactus to a parlando-rubato rendition.
4. Rhythm	Is fixed according to the rendition of the melodic scheme. Irregularities are caused by the addition or omission of syllables in the versification.	Varies within the phrase length.
5. Phrase Length	Is quite evenly distributed.	Varies according to the amount of vocal ornamentation.
6. Tessitura	Medium register.	Medium to high register.
7. Ornamentation	Slight degree of vocal ornamentation. This would correspond to our idea of neumatic ornamental style.	A great amount of vocal ornamentation especially at the end of phrases.
8. Tone quality	Typical of indigenous Spanish balladry.	Typical of Middle Eastern vocal practices

3. All melodic stanzas adhere to the principle of varied repetition.
4. The ambitus generally falls within the octave.
5. Dynamics are constant after the melodic stanza is established.
6. Tremolo is not part of the performer's practice.

Those parameters that differ in the western and eastern Mediterranean traditions can be compared in table 1.

To illustrate these comments we have included the musical transcriptions in figures 28 and 29. The first example, representing the western Mediterranean (Moroccan) tradition, is the ballad "Gerineldo," whose first three verses are transcribed with the melodic quatrain strophe AA'BC (R. Mendenez Pidal 1906, no. 101).

(- Girineldo, Girineldo, my fine knight,
Oh, who could have you for tonight
these three hours at my service!
- Since I am but your servant, m'lady,
you must perforce be mocking me.)

Fig. 28. The ballad "Gerineldo."

Fig. 29. The ballad "La Adultera."

The second Example is a brief selection consisting of the first two verses from the eastern Mediterranean ballad, "La Adultera," in a-a assonances. Notice the tripartite phrase structure, AA'B and the repetition of the second textual verse.

The Hasidic Niggun

The repertoire of the Hasidic *niggun,* a musical world in and of itself, is certainly on the borderline between sacred and secular. The Hasidic movement, which had its beginnings in the second half of the eighteenth century, created the type of vocal tune that has become known as the *niggun.* The *niggun* bestows beauty and dignity on the Hasid as he prays or joins his fellow Hasidim in public assemblage on sorrowful as well as joyful occasions. It is greatly expanded in the openings and closings of the traditional prayers on the Sabbath and holidays. It dominates gatherings intended to achieve *devequt*—ecstatic adhesion to God. The *niggun,* essentially, is the most important element of the Hasidic outlook. According to a Hasidic saying, "Silence is better than speech, but song is better than silence." The *niggun,* then, is more powerful than both speech and silence and helps the Hasid express his aspirations and longings. Worship of the Deity in joy and ecstasy is the foundation-stone of Hasidism, which endows the *niggun* with a central place in the movement: with its help the Hasid rises from one level to the next until he reaches the highest peak of enthusiasm—ecstatic *devequt.* This ascent is often supported by a single musical motif steadily rising in pitch. Thus music's role in hasidut is primarily its influence on the singer and dancer himself, rather than anything he may project to a passive audience. Since the *niggun* becomes a form of spontaneously expressed prayer, neither its structure nor performance can be subjected to aesthetic criteria. Its nature is unquestionably ritualistic, and it offers great latitude for individual improvisation.

The *niggun* is usually sung without words, and strives through the use of meaningless syllables interrupted by exclamations of pleasure or sorrow to express feelings that cannot be expressed in ordinary fashion. Depending upon circumstances, the singing can be slow, heartfelt, drawn out, and ornamentally embellished or wild and martially rhythmic. On occasion words are set to a well-known melody, in which new combination they are subordinate to the tune. Although the text may be highly significant both in its own right and because it marks a particular event, the choice of melody is almost always a result of chance rather than design; therefore certain adjustments are inevitably required. In many *niggunim,* the entire text may be merely one brief phrase repeated over and over again (see figure 30). The Hasidim permitted themselves to intersperse the text with words from the vocabulary of ordinary speech—Yiddish or even the language of the Gentiles.

The Hasidim draw distinctions among the major types of *niggunim.* The first and most important is the "rabbi's *niggun*" in which the secrets of the kabbalah are revealed. Almost all factions, dynasties, or "courts" of the Hasidic movement possess a repertoire of rabbi's *niggunim* either associated with a traditional text or entirely without words. A rabbi's *niggun* is solemnly sung on special occasions, usually as a recitative without a fixed pattern. It is performed by a good singer who is close to the rabbi. Known as *deveqah,* the rabbi's *niggun* is almost analagous to an anthem; it is the theme song, so to speak, of a given "court" or "dynasty."

Another type is the *devequt niggun* sung by the entire assemblage. Its function is to express the Hasid's devotion and inspire him to ecstasy.

The final type is the *stam niggun*—"just plain *niggun*—intended to be sung in unison by all present. This *niggun* usually has a musical meter, that is, a defined rhythm, to make it easier for the public to sing. Some are of an energetic, almost martial nature and are even called "marches." Indeed, researchers have traced themes of military marches running through them. Such *stam niggunim* are often used to

Fig. 30. Shiru lo zammeru lo, a Hasidic niggun.

accompany dancing, which Hasidim consider a sacred activity, as it encourages *devequt.*

Although each of the dynasties developed its own musical style and *niggunim,* all share the same purposes, essence, and principles. The best-known dynasties are Bretslav, Gur, Viznitz, Habad, Muzitz, and Karlin. Each have certain *niggunim* that are always sung on specific occasions and many others that have no permanent association with any particular event.

Lag ba-ʿOmer and the pilgrimage to Bar-Yohai's tomb in Meron should be mentioned as an outstanding example of a special event in Israel that draws crowds of Hasidim from various parts of the country; they leave their homes and all meet at Meron. Festivities begin in the evening with the lighting of campfires around the grave of Shimʿon Bar-Yoḥai. The following morning the special ceremony of *ḥalaqeh* (an Arabic word that means haircut) takes place—little three-year-old boys are given their first haircuts.[12] The use of the Arabic term is an indication of the same Oriental influence that is expressed in the adoption of Arabic and oriental Jewish melodies such as "ve-amartem ko leḥai" (see figure 31).

The musicologist André Hajdu (1971) has written an exhaustive monograph on the subject of the Meron *niggunim* and their sources.

It should be noted in addition that the Hasidim usually commemorate the date of death of the founders of their dynasty or special events connected with them. Such is the celebration of redemption of the Ḥabad Ḥasidim which falls on the nineteenth of the month of Kislev. On that day they celebrate the release from prison of the founder of the Ḥabad movement, R. Shneur Zalman of Ladi (1747–1873).

Fig. 31. Ve-amartem ko lehay, a Hasidic niggun.

Those who "composed" the Hasidic *niggunim* usually borrowed from a variety of sources, very rarely creating entirely original works. Sometimes the *niggun* was put together like the pieces of a jigsaw puzzle—fragmentary themes and motifs that rang in the ear were fitted together with original passages. Other times composers simply took over melodies from the folk traditions of their non-Jewish neighbors. This was looked upon as performing an almost holy mission since the borrowed melodies were thus purportedly elevated from corruption to sanctity. These alien tunes were always reworked until they acquired fitting stylistic attributes, a process of "Judification" or "Hasidization" that is based on creative principles inherent in folk music. The conclusion of Avenary's article about the *niggun,* in which he stresses primarily its spiritual and symbolic value, is appropriate at this point:

> At first glance, hasidic song may appear to be only a queer mixture of modern and old, of Hebrew and Gentile elements, of sacred and profane. Although it may sometimes seem to be "much ado about nothing," we must nevertheless give it credit for its ever renewed attempt to bring about an unusual concentration of the entire personality, and for aiming at a spiritual tension that is resolved in denial of self. All this is meant to be achieved, or at least promoted, by musical means. Hasidic song often starts from the trivial, but is ever directed toward the most uplifted exaltation. This "union of the upper and the lower world" is accomplished in the hearts of the singers, and may easily escape the casual observer's notice. (1979)

Jewish Musical Ensembles

All the examples of Jewish repertoires discussed until now have reinforced the claim that in traditional music, creativity and performance are two sides of one coin; at times one side is more apparent and at times the other. One can come closer to defining the aspect of creative performance through discussing those professional Jewish musicians who sometimes, either as individuals or as recognized groups, played for the non-Jewish world around them. In the course of this work we have had occasion to mention the use made by Jews of the music of their non-Jewish neighbors. It is now time to transfer the spotlight to the contribution of Jewish musicians to the surrounding non-Jewish society where they served as talented performers and creative artists in folk as well as art music.

With respect to art music, it may be assumed that as individual artists active in the musical life of their Oriental surroundings, their status was essentially no different from that of Jewish artists in the musical life of the West. Jewish musicians worked within the framework of the Great Tradition that crystallized in the Near and Middle East soon after the rise of Islam. They imbibed its basic values, served its objectives, and respected its structural patterns. They appeared in the conventional small groups and intimate frameworks accepted by Islamic society. Some of them became well known in the large musical centers such as Iraq, Egypt, Morocco, Persia, and Bukhara. Artists who performed as individuals and not as members of Jewish ensembles usually maintained their contact with Jewish community activities, particularly on festive occasions of a general or family nature. Although they were generally not prevented from participating actively in the singing of *piyyuṭim* in synagogues, some people nevertheless disapproved such participation, fearing that the musician might exhibit inappropriate behavior due to insufficient knowledge of prescribed religious conduct. Needless to say, this matter was not always dealt with as delicately as one might have hoped. In both the East and West throughout the years, there have been functioning ensembles of either exclusively Jewish or primarily Jewish musicians; we shall discuss some of them at greater length below.

Jewish Musical Ensembles in Iraq

Jewish musicians in Iraq were among the mainstays of those who perpetuated old musical styles, just as they were the moving spirits behind innovations that began to crystallize in the third decade of the twentieth century. The quintessentially classical style in which Jewish musicians excelled until the mass exodus to Israel in 1949 was the Iraqi maqām, as confirmed by the testimony even of non-Jewish experts (see for example Ḥassan 1980, p. 109; Warkov 1987).[13]

The Iraqi *maqām* is sophisticated, highly structured musical form wherein the performance of both vocal and instrumental parts are strictly defined by traditional norms. In the past it was performed in private homes to an aristocratic audience of intitiates. Between the two world wars the custom evolved of giving performances in selected cafés before audiences of a more popular folk character. In both cases it was an intimate, understanding audience of critical listeners who often articulated their reactions, expressing approval and encouragement.

Set in one of the basic melodic modes with a fixed accompanying rhythmic mode,[14] the Iraqi *maqām* is an intricate composition with many interwoven parts—vocal and instrumental, ready-made pieces and improvisations, texts in classical Arabic as well as in dialect and other languages: Persian, Turkish, Kurmangi (the language spoken in Kurdistan), and even Hebrew. It also contains sets of expressions, short phrases,[15] and vocal devices that give each *maqām* its special imprimature.

The conventional form begins with an instrumental introduction, then a soloist performs the *taḥrīr,* wherein he develops the *maqām*'s theme in a low register; following that is the part called *miyāna* in which the ensemble develops the high register, the higher octave, and then proceeds to the part called the *taslīm,* in which the *maqám* is gradually brought back to its point of departure. Now a second singer accompanied by the instrumental ensemble sings the *pasta*—a light folk song intended to relieve the tension that has prevailed for some time. The ensemble responsible for performing the main *maqām* is called *tchalgī Baghdād,* and it consists of four musicians who play the following instruments: *santur* (board zither mounted by seventy-two strings, struck by two wooden sticks); *joza* ("coconut"- a 3- or 4-stringed spike fiddle of coconut shell); *dumbak* (a clay drum); *daff* (frame drum surrounded by small cymbals); a main singer called *qāri'l-maqām* (*maqām* reader); and a second singer known as the *pastajī* (performs the *pasta*).

Certain elements of this style penetrated the singing of the Hebrew laudatory *piyyuṭim,* influencing those who specialized in their performance. These specialists were called *abū-shevaḥot* (father of the praises), and they gave polished artistic presentations both in and outside of the synagogue.

At the beginning of the twentieth century in major Middle Eastern centers, particularly Egypt and Iraq, a style developed that was later known as the "mainstream of Middle Eastern music"; a term representing a new concept in ethnomusicology, used to designate the dominant tendency, sort of halfway between popular and classical music. This style combines elements of the Great Middle Eastern classical Tradition with some new elements that infiltrated as a result of contact with popular and classical Western music.

Among some of the important Jewish instrumentalists and singers of the nineteenth and twentieth centuries who were active in general musical life, we can name Bidon, who played the *kamān* (a string instrument, something like a *kamanche*), the singers Salmān Mūshī, Reuven Michael, Rejuan and Shmūlī, the *santūr* players Ṣaliḥ Raḥmon Perno and his son, and members of the Bason family. Coming closer to our own times, there is the famous *ʿūd* player ʿEzra Aharon, who moved to Palestine in 1933, after having participated in the demonstrations given by the Iraqi ensemble at the First Congress of Arabic Music (Cairo, 1932).[16] Incidentally, other Jewish musicians were also part of this official ensemble. In addition, we should mention the Kuwaiti brothers (violin and *ʿūd*), who after many fruitful years in Kuwait acquired a reputation in Baghdad and were included among the founders of the Iraqi radio's ensemble that was inaugurated in 1936. The Jews Joseph Zaʿrur (*qānūn*), Yaʿakov Morad (*nāy*—flute), and Salāḥ Tāku (cello) were also part of this ensemble.

One of the Jewish ensembles that became well-known during the 1940s was made up of students attending a Jewish school for the blind. After their arrival in Israel in the early fifties, musicians from this ensemble and the one associated with the Iraqi Radio became the nucleus of the section of the Israel Broadcasting Authority Orchestra that is used for Arabic broadcasts.

Many tales have been told about the importance as well as distinctiveness of the

Jewish musicians, some centering on their own occasional inability to appear because they had to fulfill the doctrinal obligations of their religion. An article published in a local Jewish journal in the year 1884 tells the story of a respected Muslim who invited the ensemble of the *Kol Yisrael Ḥaverim* (Alliance Israelite) school to play for a wedding celebration in his house. But as luck would have it, the event was scheduled for the seventh night of the Passover holiday. Because of the sanctity of the holiday, the ensemble refused to appear and the host, a very influential man, caught the members of the group and locked them up on the roof. A local rabbi tried to intercede, but to no avail; the Ḥakham Bashi (official chief rabbi) took action with the Muslim government, which promised to free them, but reneged on the promise. Finally, the sound of their screams reached the ears of the governor (the *wālī*), and he ordered their release.

Instrumental Ensembles in Morocco

Ben-Ami enumerates eleven reknowned Jewish ensembles that functioned in the Moroccan cities of Mogador, Marakesh, Fez, Safi, and Mazagin. According to Ben-Ami, the most famous of them was Shmuel Ben Radan's group in Marakesh. It was called "The Double Four Ensemble" because it included twice the usual number of players. Ensembles were ordinarily made up of four instrumentalists: The *ʿūd* (lute) player, the *rabāb* or *kamancha* (fiddle) player, and two drummers. This particular group had three *ʿūd* players, three fiddles (a *rabāb* and two *kamanchas*), and two drummers. Ben-Ami describes the ensemble's appearance at weddings:

"Not only did the musicians' playing add to the pleasure: they also filled the role of entertainers. They would amuse the crowd with jokes and anecdotes that were very well received. The gestures and miming were even more important than the contents" (1975, pp. 224–25).

Some of the ensembles were itinerant and willingly traveled outside of their local areas. They always dressed in festive attire and sat on a special couch. Synagogue *payṭanim* also appeared with some ensembles if they were expected to perform prayers and *baqqashot*. Thus the sacred and secular would sometimes intermingle. These ensembles also performed for non-Jewish circles, and their artistry gained them high esteem with the Sultans. Ben-Ami writes about this:

"It is customary to say that each Sultan had his Jewish musician. It is known, for example, that ʿAbd el-ʿAziz, who ruled from 1894 to 1908, was particularly fond of Jewish musicians. . . . When Sultan Muhamad ibn Yusuf the Fifth (ruled from 1927 to 1961), father of the present Sultan el-Hasan the Second, rose to the throne, he visited Mogador where he was received by a group of Jewish musicians" (p. 224).

The presence of Jewish ensembles in the royal courts and the Sultans' affection for them is the subject of a story told by Jews and called "Singers of Sorrow." The story tells that on the Ninth of Av, of all times, the Sultan very much wanted to enjoy the singing and playing of a Jewish ensemble that usually appeared in his court. He issued an order calling upon them to come to him. Painful as it was, the musicians could not refuse, and played the lamentations appropriate for the Ninth of Av. The Sultan found the sad songs powerfully expressive and was interested in learning more about them and their source, whereupon the Jews told him that on this day it was forbidden to make music and be happy, as this was the date on which the Temple had been destroyed. From that day on they were known as "Singers of Sorrow" (D. Noy, 1967).

Instrumental Ensembles in Iran

In a study of Jewish musical life in the city of Shirāz, Iran, Lawrence Loeb (1972) has stressed the important role of Jewish musicians there, both as instrumentalists and as instrument makers. In the first part of his article the author reveals some surprising facts. For example, in Shirāz until 1950 the term *muṭrib* (musician) was synonymous with a professional Jewish musician. In 1903 there were sixty such professional musicians there, all of them Jewish. To grasp the full significance of this number, one need only compare it with the number of Jewish musicians in Tehran, the capital, where it swung between thirty and forty. The art of making music belonged to certain families; these families would also choose names such as *Shirahcon* (from the Hebrew *shirah,* which means song or singing), *Qānūnī* (Qānūn player), Nightingale player.

It was customary to form ensembles of from six to nine musicians, at least one of whom was a singer. Their major instruments were the *ṭār* (a long-necked lute), the *kamancha* (violin) and *zarb* (goblet drum). Among Jewish musicians it was very rare to find one who played the *santūr* (board zither), essentially an instrument for solo performances.

On the whole these musicians lived harsh, dangerous lives. They had to appear in parades, accompany caravans, and play for governmental officials under difficult conditions. At the beginning of the century the profession was considered degraded and contemptuous, though it promised a good income. For despite society's reservations about musicians and their way of life, they were needed to supply highly desirable entertainment under a variety of circumstances. In Jewish society too the musician was held in low esteem. In Loeb's opinion, this was caused by, among other things, the fact that music was an insecure and uncertain source of livelihood; it was work that had to be done at night, it had no fixed routine, and because of it the musician had to neglect his family, eat ritually impure foods, desecrate the Sabbath, and join the dancers.

At the end of his article Loeb touches on a very important problem—the mutual influence of Jewish and non-Jewish music in Iran. He posits the challenging hypothesis that acculturative influences flow not only from the culturally dominant society to the society that is dominated, but in the opposite direction as well. After offering a number of general examples he supports his hypothesis with a description of the situation in which professional Jewish musicians, steeped in their distinctive local Jewish tradition, either consciously or unconsciously transmitted melodies from that tradition to the music of the non-Jews. To demonstrate this Loeb tells the following story, reminiscent in many ways of the story about the sorrowful singers:

> Isaac, one of the great musicians during the reign of Sultan Nasser el Din (1848–1896), was called to play for the Shah who was in a dour mood. It happened to be Yom Kippur but Isaac had to obey the Shah's order; he played the *ṭar* and sang *piyyuṭim* he had heard that day in the synagogue. When the Shah inquired about the source of these moving songs, Isaac answered that they are the holiest of all prayers sung by the Jews, whom he had had to leave at the Shah's behest. The ruler immediately let him return to the synagogue, showering him with expressions of gratitude and gifts of gold coins.

The closing sentence of Loeb's articles notes that some fifty years before, Idelsohn had developed a theory showing the influence of Middle Eastern music on Jewish music; he concludes by saying, "the time has now come for us to begin to reverse our focus."

An article by the well-known ethnomusicologist Bruno Nettl and myself on the subject of classical Persian music in Israel referred to the role played by Jewish musicians:

> It may be assumed that in other places where Jews were concentrated at the end of the 19th and during the 20th century, such as the areas around Isphahan and Hamadan, a similar situation governed mutual influences prevailing among Jews and Muslims. Not very much is known about the role of the Jews in the musical life of the large cities, particularly Teheran. . . . On the whole it seems that in modern Teheran the Jews continued to be conspicuous in traditional popular musical life. They play at weddings and entertain population sectors that have undergone a process of urbanization, but not the fanatic Muslin strata (1978, p. 147).

We had been convinced that there were musical Jewish families in Persia, and also that the activity of the Jewish musicians centered on folk and semi-classical levels much more than on purely classical music. Actually, they were well-versed in a variety of repertoires: local, folk, and semi-classical, and seem to have had a strong influence on musical life in the provincial regions.

Both articles discussed the central problem of what caused Jewish music to emerge and flourish and eventually to fill a relatively important role in the musical life of the non-Jewish surroundings. The latter article maintained that the special role played by the Jewish musicians in Iran was undoubtedly a result of the Muslim position vis-à-vis religious minorities as well as vis-à-vis music. Before 1925, when the Pahlavi family rose to power in Iran, the Shiite view of the depravity of all nonbelievers dominated the country and the Jews suffered persecution, oppression, and discrimination. However, because for religious reasons Islam viewed the musical profession as reprehensible, the path was cleared for talented Jews to prove their worth as professional musicians in Muslim society. To a great extent, the same explanation holds true with respect to other traditions we have described above, indeed, to all traditions in which professional Jewish musicians excelled throughout the Muslim world. However, when we come to consider the situation prevailing in modern times, things appear to be more complicated in everything pertaining to new styles and the various kinds of amateur music-making in Iran.

The European Klezmer

As long ago as the fifteenth century there were already organized Jewish musical groups wandering from place to place in Europe, performing among both Jews and Christians. As we shall see below, parallels can be drawn between these *klezmers* of the West and the Jewish musicians of the East, different though the scope and content of the European klezmer may have been. One of the most fundamental differences lay in the fact that Europe had a tradition of written music that almost in its entirety fell within the sphere of art music. Alongside this, there were divergent shades of folk music, most of which belonged to an oral tradition.

The various types of music also sprang from different sources. Oriental art music, despite diverse regional styles, had its source in the Great Tradition, while the instrumental music, from the standpoint of both style and place, was nurtured at other wellsprings. In Idelsohn's opinion, "The music which the Klezmers used to perform was of Jewish as well as of non-Jewish origin—music of all the various styles, according to the demand of their audiences, from elegiac tunes to frivolous dances" (1929, p. 460).

Badḥanim (merry-makers) often appeared with the klezmers. The eastern European *badḥan* had a defined role with an attendant musical element. It was his responsibility to hearten the young bridal couple by singing amusing songs to a special tune, he conducted the prescribed dance ceremony, and so on. In describing a Hasidic marriage, Yaʿacov Mazor writes:

"From the musical standpoint one can divide the *badḥanim* into two types. Those who prefer to sing in free recitative style in tones similar to various kinds of cantillated readings of lamentations, belong to the first type. Those of the second type choose to adapt the verses to known tunes with defined meter and rhythm, tunes that fall into one of two groups: either traditional *badḥanim* tunes, or *niggunim* of various kinds—joyous ones, dance tunes and well-known melodies" (1978, p. 72).

For descriptions of the European klezmers that for hundreds of years were to be found all over central and eastern Europe, we have many documents available, including even musical notations. A number of old klezmer melodies were written down at the beginning of the eighteenth century in the collection *Simhath ha-nefesh.*[17]

The cellist Yehoachin Stuchevsky, himself a scion of a klezmer family, studied the klezmers and published a comprehensive monograph about them which contains historical elements, biographies of famous klezmer players, musical examples, etc. In the first part, which includes a historical survey, Stuchevsky tells of Jewish klezmer guilds and renowned bands. One well-known guild, that used the violin as its emblem, worked in Prague:

> The Jewish musicians in the city would work hard for years to uphold the tradition—and not for the sake of reward. . . .
>
> In the 1680s it was customary to celebrate the *qabbalat Shabbat* in the Meisel synagogue with instrumental music and the "sweet singing" of Shlomo Zinger, who was accompanied by musical instruments (organ and harps).
>
> Many Jewish musicians in Prague were known by name and took part in the city's general celebrations. In Hungary in the first half of the nineteenth century an outstanding musician was Mordecele Rosenthal. (In actual fact, he was Marcus Rozsafoldgi, known to have been among the originators of Hungarian national music.) One of the oldest guilds in Poland was active in Lvov in the first half of the seventeenth century. In a contract drawn up in 1629 between Christian and Jewish players, the Christian guild permitted members of the Jewish guild to play at weddings and feasts of Christians and the Jewish guild was granted the right to invite Christian players to substitute for Jews on the Sabbath and holidays. (1959)

The instruments used by the Jewish klezmers were the violin and the *Hackbrett* or *cimbalom.*[18] A well-known klezmer player whose name became familiar to the outside world was Michael Yosef Gozikov, who was born in 1806 and died at a young age in Aachen, Germany in 1837. An offspring of a klezmer family, he began his musical career as a flautist, but ill health soon forced him to give up the flute. He built himself an instruments similar to the *Hackbrett,* but instead of strings he used wood-shavings and thus produced a kind of xylophone that was given the name of "straw violin." He played it with such virtuosity that he became something of a legend in his lifetime. In his chapter on famous klezmers, Stuchevsky included many names, among them Stampanio—who was immortalized in Shalom Aleichem's famous novel.

The klezmer's economic and social status—like that of Jewish musicians in the Orient—was quite insecure. Stutchevsky comments on this as follows:

"The social standing of the klezmer was not particularly good. . . . Lack of permanent employment, the absence of a permanent residence, having no property or material possessions, flouting religion and exhibiting no signs of normally accepted humble demeanor, all combined to establish the inferior social status of the klezmer."

In his opinion, music as such was not quite like a professional matter for the klezmers. Generally speaking, they had no musical training and were not learned in musical theory. Concepts such as the technique of composition, the theory of harmony, figured bass, form and style, were foreign to them and lacked all meaning. But as against this, they were endowed with spirited musical imaginations and an excellent ear; they could absorb and assimilate, and had a highly developed sense of rhythm.

9

The Dance

In Jewry, dance is directly associated with music and is therefore an important aspect of the various events that have been discussed in previous chapters. Some of the same fundamental problems we dealt with at length in connection with music reappear when discussing dance. Here too the lengthy contact with foreign cultures in the Diaspora confronts us with questions of identity and multiplicity of styles; here too there have been conflicting views as to the permissibility of this form of expression in all its aspects. There is a plethora of literary texts at the disposal of the scholar, but there is an almost total absence of the kind of descriptive material that would enable us to reconstruct actual dance figures and steps. It should also be stressed at the outset that unlike Jewish music, the Jewish dance has not yet been the subject of comprehensive, systematic study.

Dance in Ancient Israel

In the Bible, Mishnah, and Talmud, dance is referred to in various contexts, but none of these references contain descriptions of how the dances actually moved. Bathja Bayer, in summarizing a discussion of dance in the Bible, remarks that one picture or statue is better testimony than a thousand words.[1] Recently a few newly discovered iconographic findings show dancing figures found at Megido, the Negev, and other sites in Israel. Meager as this quantity of evidence is when compared with the abundance and variety that has been found in Egypt, it nevertheless gives some idea of the dance in biblical times. Outside of such tangible evidence, there are many biblical descriptions of occasions that inspired dancing. One such example is Judg. 21:21, where a festival is described during which it was customary to dance in the vineyards. The approbation implied by the text leads some to believe that the reference is to an ancient religious holiday, as the description tells of the "daughters of Shiloh" who leave the city to dance at "a feast of the Lord from year to year." Others believe it was the celebration of the vines on the fifteenth of Av. B. Bayer (1978) does not agree that this is the holiday referred to, even though the Bible associates the celebration with the vineyards. S. D. Goitein (1958, pp. 252–53) describes these dances, done only by women, as "their sacred dances," while some modern scholars believe that the reference is to ritualistic dances connected with fertility rites, although the Bible offers no indication at all that this is so.

Group dances performed by women held a place of particular importance in the Bible. Dancing to the accompaniment of drums is associated with celebrations of military victories and welcoming home heroes who have routed an enemy. The women's role was to receive and extol the fighters. Miriam and the women burst into song and dance accompanied by drums to mark the miraculous parting of the Red Sea that saved the people of Israel from the pursuing Egyptian army (Exod. 15:20); Jephtah's daughter dances out to meet her father returning from victorious battles (Judg. 11:34), and the women of Israel come out to dance before Saul and David upon their return from fighting the Philistines (1 Sam. 18:6).

Another religious but popular event that inspired the king and his subjects to dance was the bringing of the Ark of the Covenant up to Jerusalem (2 Sam. chap. 6). Bayer suggests that this celebration may be a vestigial remnant of customs followed by nomadic tribes when they were transferring a sacred object from one camp to another. A slightly different version of the same event appears in 1 Chron. 15:23–29, the major difference being the participation of "professional" musicians (that is, the Levites) in the Chronicles description. As if to stress the formal and aristocratic nature of the event, this version tells us that David was "clothed with a robe of fine linen," whereas according to 2 Samuel, he wore a cloth vest. More instruments accompany the procession and the dances in 2 Samuel than in 1 Chronicles, which may have something to do with the more popular, folk character ascribed to the event in 2 Samuel. Finally, in Chronicles the verb "dance" is used, whereas in 2 Samuel it is not, the Hebrew original using the descriptive verbs "leaping" and "twirling," but not explicitly "dance." This is an appropriate point at which to note that, on the whole, Bible scholars agree that divergent descriptions of the same event usually derive from the different outlooks and intentions of the various authors of the biblical books (or chapters).

In the Song of Songs we find the rather obscure verse:

"Return, return, that we look upon thee.
What will ye see in the Shulammite?
As it were a dance of two companies. (7:1)

This verse seems to have been taken from a traditional wedding dance. The mention of "a dance of two companies" may imply two groups of dancers, a type of dancing that can still be seen at Bedouin festivities in the Middle East.

Detailed descriptions have been handed down to us from the period of the Mishnah, from which we learn that there was folk dancing at religious celebrations. An example is the folk festival of *beit ha-Sho'evah* (the water-drawing festival) about which the *Sukkah* tractate tells us, "He who has not seen the festival of water-drawing, has never in his life seen a festival" (*Sukkah* 5:1).[2]

The Tel Qasilah excavations revealed two objects showing dance scenes from which social implications can be derived. One is a ritual pedestal depicting a number of dancing figures; the other is a bronze plate with a line of seven dancers. From the dancers' positions and the way they are holding hands in both scenes, they seem to be part of a group performing a circle dance (Mazar 1983; Gressman 1927).

With respect to the social significance of the dance it should be noted that there is a school of though that assumes a connection between the artistic and cultural patterns that have formed while a society is in its early stages, and the social and political structure, as well as technological and economic level, of that society. Developments frequently occur in technological, social, and other spheres that bring about changes in artistic and cultural patterns. Social patterns and dance patterns are often connected, a connection reflected in the shape and size of group formations, the degree of individual freedom of expression, and the attitude toward improvisation as against maintenance of fixed forms. Interrelationships in general society can determine the interrelationships among the dancers: one dancer may head the group or there may be full social equality among all the dancers.[3]

Dance in the Jewish Diaspora

When the Jews were sent into exile the dancing associated with the normal activities of a nation in its own country ceased; there was no longer reason to celebrate nature holidays or military victories by dancing. Nevertheless, some vestige of the women's dances may have remained in the female singers and drummers who accompany the joyful dancing of women in many of the ethnic groups, particularly in the Jewish communities of the Middle East. Dance in the Diaspora seems mainly connected with events of a personal nature, particularly with weddings. And yet, it is not entirely absent from celebrations or gatherings of a lighter, purely entertaining character.

Dance has a vital function in the Jewish community on two important holidays: on Purim and Simḥat Torah.[4] To these one may add the *hillulot*—jubilees—and particuarly Lag Ba-ʿOmer and the pilgrimage to the grave of Shimʿon Bar-Yoḥai that goes back to the sixteenth century (see chapter 7).

In European Jewry of the Middle Ages, dancing for pleasure was an end in itself. According to Friedhaber (1984) in thirteenth-century German-speaking countries most of the large communities already had special establishments used as dance halls and called either *Tanzhaus* (dance hall) or *Spielhaus* (playhouse). In Spain, writes Eliahu Ashtor (1960), the children played with miniature wooden horses called *kurrāj*. These toys resembled the pirates' wooden battle horses that were favorites among the adults. Girl dancers were particularly fond of the horses and would decorate themselves by hanging the models on their bosoms when they appeared at parties. Indeed, the dance of the wooden horse was known throughout much of the world.[5]

Later, during the Renaissance, when dance was raised to the level of an art and began to fill the basic role in cultural life, Jews in Italy not only sent their children to study dancing, but also ran dancing schools. The growing participation of Jews in the cultural life of their surroundings prompted the Church to issue orders forbidding them to run schools for dance or to give dancing lessons. This did not stop them, however, and we know of several famous Jewish dancing teachers who were attached to the courts of princes in different parts of Italy. The most famous of them was Gulielmo Ebreo (in other words, Benjamin the Jew) from Pesaro who taught at the court of the king of Naples and in the Medici courts in Florence. His book on the art of the dance was widely read. Dancing became so integral a part of Jewish life that teachers of Hebrew were also expected to teach dancing. Friedhaber (1988, pp. 67–77) discusses the highly developed role that the dance played in Jewish society of the Duchy of Mantua in the seventeenth and eighteenth centuries.

In Spain before the expulsion as well as in other places in the East (in the palaces of the Ottoman Sultans Ibrahim the First and Muhamad), Jewish groups of violinists and dancers appeared regularly. Jews danced not only within the traditional framework of the Jewish community, but also with the Gentiles, some of them even teaching their non-Jewish neighbors the art. Jewish "entertainers" traveled around Germany dancing and performing acrobatic tricks at weddings. These and other activities, such as men and women dancing together, and the moral issued involved in dancing on the Sabbath with or without instrumental accompaniment, evoked hostile reactions on the part of the rabbinate.

Rabbinical Attitude toward Dance

There are many discussions in the rabbinical legal and moral literature and the responsa about dancing as an expression of joy and gladness. Opinions range from luke warm compromise to withholding approval to outright hostility. Unlike the music that accompanies prayers and *piyyuṭim,* the dance is not a fundamental element in worship; its only possible role, therefore, is on occasions when joy pervails, although even then there were clear limits. R. Abraham, son of Maimonides (1135–1205), claimed that women who imitate the dances of the Gentiles and even dance before men, indulge in the kind of deplorable behavior that places them among those completely excluded from the world to come. The rabbi expressly refers to the custom that was widespread among the Jews of Egypt eight hundred years before which required a specially costumed bride to perform a solo dance holding a sword.[6] R. Abraham forbids the custom itself—on the grounds that it imitates the Gentiles—and also the bride's dancing before men. Germany's rabbis issued judgments sharply condemning the practice of men and women dancing together at festivities. Only husband and wife, sister and brother, or father and daughter were permitted to dance as couples.

Despite the official prohibition, however, the custom evolved of doing "*mitsvah* dancing" at weddings: distinguished members of the community dance with the bride, holding the edges of a kerchief to avoid all physical contact between the dancers. Of course, the most severe prohibition was proclaimed against dancing for amusement—in other words, dancing for its own sake, entirely dissociated from any special public or private event.

In Spain it was acceptable even on the Sabbath for young people to dance together, accompanied by musical instruments, but in his responsum, R. Shlomo Ben Aderet (1270–1343) warns that they are thereby overstepping all moral bounds.

During the seventeenth century in the countries of the West it was quite usual to send the children for dancing lessons as part of Western education and culture. R. Elhanan Henly Kirchhain (1727, p. 26)[7] condemns this custom, advising people who capriciously permit their children to study at dancing schools that they could live just as well without this pleasure, while the money could be used for doing good.

There is another interesting prohibition that we find in the responsa of one of the Greek rabbis of the seventeenth century, Rabbi Aharon Bar Ḥayim Abraham hacohen Peraḥiah (1627–89). He banned the presence of non-Jewish musicians at Jewish wedding ceremonies, to ensure that they would not witness the women dancing in their fine dresses and ornaments. Like all the famous rabbis of Salonika, he forbade the hiring of Gentile musicians, at the same time forbidding the women to dance in their presence. Incidentally, the participation of non-Jewish instrumentalists at Jewish weddings was fairly usual in other places as well.

Selected Dance Traditions

The traditions of the Hasidim, the Jews of Yemen, and Kurdistan Jewry are among the most prominent traditional cultures that have attributed and still do attribute dynamic importance to dance in daily life as well as in the festive life of the community. We shall concentrate mainly on these three traditions, although there are other groups such as the Moroccans, Georgians, Lybians, and Ethiopians, in which spontaneous and folk collective dancing is important. Then there are still others where dancing is done almost exclusively by organized groups.

Hasidic Dancing

From the very beginning of Hasidism, the movement has considered the dance a fundamental element, an instrument for inducing religious ecstasy. The maxims and proverbs of the Hasidim extol the vital role of the dance as an integral part of worship. A saying attributed to the Ba'al Shem Tov (see chapter 7, note 10) maintains that "With the Hasidim, dance is prayer." The ecstasy that finds expression in the spontaneous dances of *devequt*—devoted adherence to the Almighty—is a realization of what is written in the Book of Psalms (35:10): "All my bones shall say: 'Lord, who is like unto Thee,/Who deliverest the poor from him that is too strong for him,/ Yea, the poor and the needy from him that spoileth him?' "

The dance helps the Hasid rise above the mundane, that is, on the one hand detach himself from material things and on the other, elevate himself toward the spiritual. The Baʿal Shem Tov explains the basic form of the Hasidic dance, which is circle-dancing, as follows: "because in a circle there is neither front nor back, beginning nor end, each person is a link in the chain and all are equal" (Daniel 1952, p. 163). As conceived by Rabbi Nachman of Bretslav (see chapter 7, note 11), dancing is an integral part of worship and prayer, and has its appointed place even during the High Holidays. Mass circle dances enhance various occasions in and outside of the synagogue. On Simhat Torah, for instance, it is a *mitsvah* for old people, children, and even chance passers-by to join the circle of singers and dancers each time the Torah scroll is carried around the synagogue.

In addition to circle dances, the Hasidim developed dances done in pairs as well as almost acrobatic solo dancing that requires intense concentration and maximum muscular control. While executing such solos, the dancer will sometimes place a bottle on his head or balance a stick on his forehead that ends in a pyramid of bottles; he may even dance with a burning torch in his mouth.

Among the important and well-known wedding dances are the *Sher* and the *Sherele,* both cheerful square dances for four couples. Then there is the *Broigez-tantz,* (mad-dance), a dance-game performed by couples who first pretend to be angry with one another and then make peace. Actually, this is a combination of two dances—the *broigez* and the *sholem.* Friedhaber (1984) gives lengthy descriptions of the basic patterns and sources of these dances:

> These dances were usually performed by a single couple, with the rest of the crowd forming a circle around them. The steps and figures were often freely improvised but remained in character so that the two themes the dance expresses were easily recognized. When the "broigez" theme was danced, the dancers' movements were teasing and aggressive, they refused to dance together and avoided one another. And when the motif was "peacemaking" the steps and movements suddenly became soft and languishing, the couple gradually coming together to dance in unison, with the bystanders often joining in."

In discussing Jewish wedding dances, the dance-game of *broigez* and *sholem* has been described by some investigators as traditional and very old, but they offer no evidence to support the contention. With respect to the various "*mitsvah* dances" the texts quite credibly date them as having been popular toward the end of the fourteenth and beginning of the fifteenth centuries (1365–1427). This is based on evidence brought by the "Maharil" (R. Yehuda Low of sixteenth-century Prague) who already mentions them in his book on customs, *Minhagot.* But we have no date at all for the dance-game; in fact, no discussions or references in the literature indicate a date earlier than the nineteenth century.

Other Hasidic wedding dances involve the women who dance with a special braided loaf and salt, symbols of hope for a good and prosperous life, and the dance of the beggars with the bride—inseparably bound up with the character of the wedding (this was the source of inspiration for a scene in the play *The Dibbuk*).[8] Another popular dance at weddings is the "*mitsvah* dance" already mentioned, in which the closest male relatives of the bride are expected to dance with her, without touching her. This led to the custom of the bride and her female relatives dancing with a kerchief in their hands.

Yemenite Jewry's Dance

Dancing was very important to Jews born in Yemen. In addition to the stylistic diversity characteristic of rural and urban settlements in various areas, there are basic differences between the dances of the women and the men. Separation of the sexes is rigidly observed, the women dancing with one another, the men only with other men. The women may watch the men's dances, but they do not take part in them,[9] a situation directly opposite to what we know about the relation between the sexes in Kurdish dances (see below).

In an article by Gurit Kadman (1952) on the influence of Yemenite traditional dances on the new Israeli folk dances, she unequivocally and emphatically distinguishes between the dances of the men and those of the women. In her view, the men's dances have a religious function, even if they are performed on secular occasions. To support this claim she points to the fact that the dancers, or the singers who accompany them, start by praising the Lord. She goes on to state that the men's dances are incomparably more interesting, variegated, creative, authentic, and less influenced by the non-Jewish environment than those of the women, whose dances she describes as refined, quiet, reserved, and lacking in ardor.

In this article, written at about the time of the "Magic Carpet" enterprise (which brought most of Yemen's Jews to Israel at the beginning of the 1950s), the author very likely refers to the dances of the Jews of Ṣanʿa. In later lectures she herself discussed the stylistic differences in the dancing of urban Jews and those who lived in outlying villages, where daily contact with the non-Jewish world was unavoidably closer. This contact influenced the character and even the steps of the dances. The Jews of Ṣanʿa themselves distinguished between two basic styles: one—tempestuous, unrestrained, and described as "going wild"—is disparaged, a pejorative attitude that may stem from the feeling that these frenzied dances are in a way an imitation of the behavior of non-Jews. The second style is reserved and conservative; it is considered refined dancing and is generally esteemed. This more delicate, stylized dance is done in relatively small rooms, in urban centers.

Dancing usually took place during ceremonies and celebrations at which the invited guests filled the rooms to capacity. It was customary to place a special platform in the middle of the room on which the best dancers appeared in pairs, threes, or small groups, the dancers being replaced from time to time. Their dancing was a combination of certain fixed basic figures and many improvisations; in the course of time the most talented dancers added new elements to the basic patterns.

Fundamentally, the men's dances were composed of steps and figures executed in a very small area. Vertical is the dominant line—with agile, springy bending of the knees, sometimes crouching almost to the floor. The movement of the back is soft and supple, its undulations even reaching the head, which in turn responds by moving freely on loose shoulders. The very expressive hands are used for an infinite variety of delicate gestures that change from dance to dance and in accordance with the number of dancers performing, while permitting each dancer a certain freedom of movement.

Like the men's dances, those of the women are performed by good dancers on a small platform specially placed for this purpose, with the dancers changing from time to time. They accompany themselves with responsorial singing in which they are joined by singers sitting alongside the platform who, holding small metal castanets, beat drums or copper plates. A popular group dance starts with the dancers advancing in a zigzagging line, the leader moving from front to back and back to front until the whole group is arranged in two almost parallel lines joined at one end to form a "U." The women's dances are less variegated, more restrained.

The Yemenite sense of humor finds expression in entertaining dances and games. Despite the generally restrained nature of the dancing, dancers sometimes propel themselves into a state of ecstasy.

In conclusion, one may say that two elements are common to the dancing of the men and the women in Yemen:

1. The dance is always accompanied by singing, rhythm instruments, or hand-clapping, but no melodic instruments are used.[10] As might be expected, while the words of the women's songs are from the oral tradition sung in an Arabic dialect and dealing with secular subjects concerning the woman's life, feelings, and experiences, the men's songs are taken from the *Dīwān,* the anthology referred to above. The language used may be Hebrew, Aramaic, Arabic, or any two of these combined. The subject matter is mainly longing for Zion and redemption.

2. Except for certain women's dances, the singing and rhythmic accompaniment are executed by two poet-singers, male or female.

Dances of Kurdistani Jews

The dances of Jews from Kurdistan are distinguished from those of all other Jewish ethnic groups in that the men and women dance together. Such an intermingling of the sexes, to say nothing of the physical proximity, is hard to conceive of in a society whose dance patterns evolved within a Muslim religious and cultural framework. On the other hand, it may be that non-Jewish Kurdish tribes also waived the Islamic stricture enforcing separation of the sexes, and the Jews followed suit.

We have interesting eyewitness testimony on this matter. R. Yehiel Fishel (Yaʿari 1942, p. 49), an envoy from the Holy Land, in describing his visit to Mosul (Iraqi Kurdistan) in 1860, writes: "to the point where if a Jew holds some kind of celebration, the non-Jews also come to share his happiness. And men and women, boys and young virgins, dance together, and among them may be a Gentile and even the wife of the Chief Rabbi." In addition to this important testimony written more than a century ago, a comparison of the dances of the Jews and those of their non-Jewish neighbors indicates their great similarity. Indeed, at times the figures, the steps, the way they hold one another, the style and temperament of the dance, and even the mingling of the sexes, are exactly the same as among the non-Jews. Nevertheless, religious leaders sometimes expressed disapproval of men and women dancing together.

The dances are accompanied by songs in Kurmandji, the language spoken by the Kurds, not in Aramaic, which is the special dialect of the Jews of that region. Two instruments are also used to accompany the dances: the *zurna,* a nasal-sounding wind instrument similar to the oboe, and the *dola,* a large double-headed drum that is beaten on both sides with one thick and one thin stick. The same songs, dances, and instruments are popular in the non-Jewish communities as well.

Most Kurdish dances are based on open or closed circles, with couples or soloists taking turns in the center where they improvise figures and steps, but always within a conventional framework. Some of the men brandish short swords as they dance, a vestige of the marital heroism of the non-Jewish Kurd. When their hands are free, the women wave colorful kerchiefs as they dance. They hold hands in a variety of ways, sometimes crowded closely together in a tight line and sometimes further apart in more open lines, raising and lowering their hands and suddenly changing grips as the direction of the dance changes. The figures vary from the shortest unit of six steps to lengthy, intricate units that contain as many as fifteen steps. These figures are repeated as long as the given dance goes on—and there is nothing to prevent the same dance from going on almost endlessly.

The Dance in Modern Israel

In the countries of the Diaspora the Jewish ethnic dance developed in close association with the dance current in the surrounding non-Jewish community, but in Israel a new situation arose: in one form or another the ethnic traditions continued to exist while alongside them a new Israeli folk dance evolved. At certain stages it was inspired by the forms of the ethnic dances and influenced by their make-up and content, very much like the Israeli folk song—at least in this context.

At the time of the first waves of immigration the names of the dances introduced by the pioneers testify to their eastern European origin: *hora, krakoviak, polka, kazachok*. Even the group dances that fell into the general category of "rondo" bore the obvious stamp of countries overseas. During the twenties the first signs of a new Israeli dance began to emerge. Three major aspects typified this process:

1. Several women, some from the world of the art dance abroad, and some who were born in Israel, took the initiative. Six of them in particular played a decisive role, four having come to the country during the twenties: Gurit Kadman, winner of the Israel Prize for dance, came from Germany in 1920. During her sixty-five years of activity she contributed to creating and molding the Israeli dance, took part in educating generations of dancers, and helped preserve the dance heritage of ethnic groups. Cheska Rosenthal came to the country in 1921 and settled in Kibbutz Gan-Shmuel. She came from a rural district in Poland where she had learned the dances of the farmers and in Israel she was instrumental in renewing the ceremony of bringing the First Fruits. Leah Bergstein came here in 1925 as a professional dancer, joined a group of shepherds at Kibbutz Beit Alpha and organized sheep-shearing festivals and shepherds' dances. Rivka Sturman, who came in 1929 and settled in Kibbutz Ein Harod, came from the field of artistic dancing, and is considered one of the outstanding creators of the Israeli folk dance. Two Israeli-born dancers are Yardena Cohen and Sara Levi-Tanai. Cohen settled in Haifa and sought inspiration for her dances in the melodies of the Oriental Jews and the Arabs; Levi-Tanai, winner of the Israel Prize for educational dance, is a talented choreographer who imbibed the music and dances of her fellow Yemenites and eventually established the "Inbal" dance group.

2. All those active in the field were connected with the festivals celebrated by the labor settlements. Their members were the sole audience and active initiators when it came to creating and performing.

3. The main themes were the holidays: reconstructing nature festivals following the biblical pattern—the spring festival, sheep-shearing, the First Fruits, the harvest, etc. (It is well to bear in mind that the so-called biblical dance is the product of its modern creator's imagination.)

The prime aspiration of those who came with the first waves of immigrants was to become agricultural workers, and they felt a need for songs and dances that would reflect a nation living and working on its own land. People who had creative ability in the fields of music and dance assumed the task of consciously creating an Israeli folk art.

Using oriental elements they absorbed from natives in the region (Bedouin, Arabs, Druzes, and Tcherkesses) and Jewish material they had brought with them, combined with Western principles they had absorbed in their countries of origin (including what they had learned in schools abroad), they created something of an artificial synthesis that was meant to fulfill the needs of an Israeli folk repertoire. Thus songs and dances were created to be performed at festivals, most of them relating to the annual agricultural cycle. In the course of time some of the works became part of a more or less permanent repertoire, while others were forgotten. In many cases almost no recollection remained of the names of the original creators, and transformations typical of folk art began to take place. As an Israeli song and dance crystallized, elements of ethnic Jewish material were included as well.

Although the formative period of Israeli dance is close to us in time—it is actually still going on—we have very little written material on the subject. From the texts available, we have chosen to quote a short passage from Yardena Cohen's *With Drum and Dance,* in which she describes the festival of bringing in the first fruits at Kibbutz Ein Hashofet in the mountains of Ephraim.

> The first celebration of the harvest festival in the mountains of Ephraim was modest. But it was something novel, almost revolutionary, for the members and the area. I sought a means of expressing the beautiful surroundings through an original dance with appropriate costumes, performed in the wide open fields.
>
> Evening after evening I worked in the school room at Kibbutz Ein Hashofet with a group of girls, trying to train them to execute movements that were entirely new for them. "This is a new language," I told them, "We must become accustomed to expressing feelings and experiences in it, just as we are training our ancient language to pass our lips. . . ." Three dances were created then, two pastoral and one—a "hymn of praise," a ceremonial dance giving thanks for the first fruits. A choir accompanied the dancers and children released white doves in honor of the "Temple of the First Fruits." This was an attempt to bring the membership out of the immediate kibbutz area with its farm buildings and dining room, to open fields. I wanted to show the members that "the stage" for the festival can be the recently harvested field of stubble and the flowering hillsides, that seats for the audience are the ground in the shade of wagons laden with first fruits. At that time this was something of a daring innovation, but it was all pervaded by an ingratiating simplicity and rural innocence.
>
> Kibbutz Ein Hashofet was the first to break new ground and its neighbor, Kibbutz Daliah, followed. (1963, p. 47)

Indeed, Kibbutz Daliah eventually became a most important center for the development of Israeli dance. The year 1944 deserves special mention in the history of Israeli dance. That year, as the Second World War was coming to an end, Kibbutz Daliah held the first folk-dance assembly in which two hundred dancers took part. Friedhaber discusses three interesting manifestations that came to the fore at this gathering:

> The first manifestation was the three dances "The Haystack," "Water, Water," and "Bring Us Wine" all of which had the same basic step—the hop and transfer of weight accomplished while crossing one leg over the other. This step later assumed a most important place in the development of Israeli folk dances, becoming a major component of many dances created later. The second manifestation was the dance created by Sara Levi-Tanai, and the use she made of basic figures of the dances of her Yemenite community; in the course of time one of these, known as the "Yemenite figure," acquired a special place in many Israeli folk dances. (1984, pp. 155–56)

The third manifestation Friedhaber found remarkable was the group of dancers of Yemenite origin—the first appearance of an ethnic dance group.

The second gathering at Daliah, in 1947, marked the great development that had taken place in the past three years. By this time four hundred dancers from towns as well as rural communities took part, and there was an audience of twenty-five thousand. The third gathering was held in 1951 and began to show the influence of the mass immigration. This was a turning-point with respect to traditional dances, with greater emphasis placed on the participation of ethnic groups. Eight hundred dancers appeared before an audience of sixty thousand; they performed Israeli dances, dances of Jewish ethnic groups, and of national minorities living in Israel. In the years that followed, the Israeli dances became more closely attached to the traditional ethnic dances, while concomitantly the traditional dances were subjected to processes of increasingly rapid change, not unlike processes that were taking place in Israeli music.

Ethnic Dance in Israel Today

Since the establishment of the state, just as during the years before statehood, ethnic dances have continued to exist in Israel as part of traditional ceremonies marking joyful events in the life of the individual (circumcision, engagement, marriage) or general seasonal events (Simḥat Torah, pilgrimages to graves of saints, as well as holidays that are now being renewed such as the seherane and the mimuna—see chapter 7). It should be noted at once that only in rare and isolated instances can one speak of continuity with only insignificant changes. Obviously, in the new circumstances changes were inevitable in customs, ceremonials, dress, and of course, in music and dance as well. Natural spontaneity gave way to a kind of artificial reconstruction. The ceremonies themselves were shortened—very often, the young people dance modern Israeli dances, disco, and pop alongside the traditional dances. Traditional dress had almost completely disappeared from the scene and has been replaced by imitations—not always successful ones. Nevertheless, here and there one still finds clear traces of traditions that anteceded immigration to Israel. At the same time people with initiative are constantly organizing and developing new frameworks within which ethnic groups can perform selected dances from their tradition. Such performances are the outcome of various different endeavors, two types of which are prominent:

1. Some performances are the result of initiative and organization coming from outside of the ethnic group, generally an institutional element interested in presenting traditional work to an audience.[11] They may devote a performance entirely to one ethnic tradition or may include several different traditions. For example, the Cultural Committee of the Histadrut established a unit to encourage ethnic dancing and it arranges special evenings devoted to the theme. Similar activities are fostered by the Youth Folk-Culture Center in Jerusalem. The performances are usually open to

the general public, which may be either an Israeli or foreign audience (in the frame of international conferences held either in Israel or elsewhere).

2. Initiative and organization may emanate from an internal ethnic element. In such cases the major objective is to encourage the young people of the particular community to nurture, preserve, and identify with their ancestral tradition, while publicly displaying its hidden wealth so that it will not be forgotten. Most of such performances, particularly when they try to remain close to the tradition, are held before an audience composed primarily of members of the specific ethnic groups responsible for the arrangements.

Even when a special effort is made to remain faithful to the tradition, the very act of staging the dances in stylized fashion entails an element of choreographic reconstruction. The degree of reconstruction varies: there are those who try to adhere to the original source, while others create an art dance based on the concepts, patterns, steps, and other elements stemming from the tradition. This is so, for example, with the Jewish Georgian dance groups in Israel. One can see stylized choreographic arrangements based on dance elements taken from their traditional repertoire. Performances are built around extremely skillful soloists whose energetic movement and acrobatic leaps are breathtaking, while men and women in the background move separately, and with the utmost restraint. This tendency to arrange folk dance elements in interesting and impressive choreographic forms, together with remarkable performances of solo dancers, is most prevalent in the eastern European countries today. The patterns of this approach were established by the greatest Russian choreographer, Moiseyev, who succeeded despite intricate choreographic arrangements in preserving the unique character of the ethnic dance. Jewish choreographers who came to Israel from Georgia brought this approach with them and they apply it skillfully in their performances of the Georgian dances.

This process reaches the acme of perfection in the Inbal Dance Theatre. In 1950 the Oriental Dance Group appeared in the framework of a theater for new immigrants, under the direction of Sara Levi-Tanai. They presented a program including songs and dances from the tradition of the Yemenite Jews. This was the nucleus of the Inbal dance group that has made a wonderful mark on the process that started with the reconstruction of the fine Yemenite dance tradition. They attained the level of delicacy inherent in artistic dancing, but remained faithful to the traditional steps and figures brought by Yemenite immigrants. Their work has had a profound influence on the Israeli dance. Inbal strove to adapt new dance styles and with their help to develop, as the founder of the group has said: "a special dance language based on the Yemenite pattern." This objective has not always been easy to achieve.[12]

10

Looking Backward and Forward

The point at which we embarked on our ambitious across-the-board exploration of a multiplicity of musical traditions coincided with a dramatic moment in the history of those traditions. It was the moment when they were moved en masse to the new State of Israel from the Diaspora where, for many centuries, they had been in contact with foreign cultures. Contemplating the picture at that crucial starting-point, we found an intricate web of musical idioms and styles that we have described metaphorically as a musical Tower of Babel. It immediately confronted us with certain bewildering questions: Is it conceivable that these diverse, disparate elements possess some common core? What marks their Jewish identity? In other words, what distinguishes them from the indigenous musical cultures by which they were surrounded for so many years?

Scholars seeking pertinent answers to these vital questions have all been hampered by the absence of musical evidence. Indeed, as the various traditions have been transmitted orally, they have left no concrete traces from which the investigator can reconstruct their past essence with any measure of certitude. Therefore, in trying to retrieve the chain of past musical events, it would be well to address oneself to evidence and clues found in various extant literary sources, while making extremely cautious use of contemporary musical examples drawn from the traditions as we know them today. Deriving conclusions from the contemporary musical scene confronts scholars with many problems that we will touch on below. At this point, however, the issue is relevant to the extent that this was the very material Idelsohn used to support many of his theses concerning the antiquity and Jewishness of our musical traditions. As we have stated (see chapter 1), searching for a melodic archetype with ancient Jewish roots beneath the countless layers of accumulated tradition, he found it in the basic musical motifs of the various biblical cantillations (see his comparative table in figure 2).

An important tier in Idelsohn's theory of what endows a tradition with Jewish identity is the fundamental hypothesis that Oriental Jewry's traditions, being very old, necessarily perpetuate ancient forms and stylistic elements. This assumption stems from, among other things, the reverence with which those traditions related to the ancestral heritage, and the fact that the musical legacy of the Oriental Jewish communities remained constantly associated with the same geographical area. Following this line of thought, he further confirmed his own theory through the similarity he found when comparing Jewish Oriental tunes—mainly Yemenite—with the Gregorian chant. As he could not conceive of the possibility that mutal borrowing had occurred, Idelsohn came to the logical conclusion that both emanate from the same source, that is, the music of ancient, pre-exilic Israel. Despite the great merit and attractiveness of Idelsohn's contribution, it cannot be blindly accepted in its entirety. As he found, there is indeed a similarity in the cantillation archetype and the Gregorian chant, but it is limited to notated general melodic patterns; it does not take into account distinguishing traits as they emerge in performance practice. In this connection, the eminent scholar C. Sachs writes: "The manner of singing, its timbre, force and specific animation are often more suggestive and essential than the melodies; cultural and anthropological traits depend on the ways things are done rather than on the things themselves" (1943, p. 23).

Considering Idelsohn's observations in the light of the above statement we may add that it is usually easier to perceive similarities than to discover subtle but important differences, especially in closely affiliated styles. Here the emic/etic dichotomy[1] can be quasi-determinant. It is not unusual to find that what appears as a significant and distinctive mark from an emic standpoint, from an etic standpoint may seem to be no more than a meaningless variation. Ideally, therefore, the scholar should explore both views as he proceeds in his investigation.

Another fundamental assumption found in Idelsohn's work, and in subsequent studies as well, bases itself on the stability of Oriental musical traditions and their supposed resistance to change. Now that Israel exists and has brought all the traditions together under a single roof, as it were, we are in a position to cast much sharper light on this assumption, and verify or refute its validity. In Idelsohn's time, prevailing conditions were such as to permit the relatively enduring use of old forms, with little need for receptivity to change. In pre-state days it was the early immigrants to this country who absorbed newer arrivals from their former countries of origin, and this perpetuated old cultural forms. The confrontation of different traditions with the new reality was of a generally smooth nature; if the new arrivals so desired, they could integrate into the milieu familiar to them from the "old country."[2]

After 1948, however, the phenomenon of mass immigration to the State of Israel changed the entire process of absorption of newcomers. The state—with its predominantly European orientation—considered itself responsible for absorbing immigrants and for creating a unified people and culture. During the first years of statehood the overwhelming majority of new arrivals were from Oriental countries. They were abruptly exposed not only to a new and complex existential situation, but to a pervasive Western culture that they were expected to adopt as their own. Thus, newly uprooted from their natural surroundings, they were confused by the entirely strange environment where Western concepts held exclusive sway, particularly in the sphere of the arts. In addition, they experienced a painful emotional conflict due to the state of belligerence that prevailed between Israel and the surrounding Arab countries, some of which had only recently been home to them. They had to seek ways of reconciling their national identification with their emotional attachment to the culture of Arab countries that were the enemies of their new country. The fact that they were expected to re-emerge as "Israelis," which meant that they had to be "integrated" into an alien Western culture, only complicated matters. Moreover, it was frequently denied that they had anything that might be called a culture of their own. Their status in the country they had come from was that of a minority community; but in the creative arts many individuals had been completely integrated and in some cases they even dominated their particular creative field. In the new situation, their civil status was changed, but they had become a cultural minority, as the culture they brought with them was not legitimized by the establishment.

Under such pressure, exacerbated by well-orchestrated endeavors to modernize the newcomers and encourage them to abandon their traditions, they were not very likely to attempt to resist change. The question is: what forms did the changes take? Did the newcomers submissively resign themselves to dropping their traditions or were they inspired by their deep reverence for their ancestral heritage to continue to perpetuate it, if almost surreptitiously? This thorny question, as we shall see below, has no single, simple answer; under the impact of new conditions, a wide variety of stylistic and other changes took place.

To return to Idelsohn, doing justice to his approach, we assume that he did not deny the fact that change of some sort occurred; he simply focused on what seemed to him the unbroken chain of old traditional concepts, and concentrated only on what he viewed as "authentic." Any change, therefore, was considered a corruption of almost consecrated norms, hence insignificant and unworthy of attention.[3] His approach to tradition was that of an archeologist: interested only in what it could reveal to him about the past. In this he was essentially very much in sympathy with the way his informant viewed change.

Before embarking on an exploration of the manifold transformations the different musical traditions have undergone in Israel and the various directions these changes have taken, it should be noted that the highly complex phenomenon of musical change is universal. As such it has given rise in modern scholarship to a plethora of interpretations and approaches, some of which should be briefly reviewed here as they are of particular interest and relevance for our purposes.

Continuity and Change

A great many publications dealing with theoretical or particular cases of musical change appear under this dichotomous label—to the point where it has become almost a cliché. Nevertheless, it remains indispensable as a term of reference; change in all its variations and nuances can and should be assessed only against a given or assumed continuity. The relationship between continuity and change, the criteria by which the line demarcating them should be determined, and even the definition of the nature of change as a whole remain subject to the views and interpretations of the individual investigator. At one extreme one finds those who until quite recently considered change to be an unwelcome disturbance or alteration of the "original, authentic" tradition. The opposite pole is made up of scholars who maintain that change is a normal phenomenon that characterizes all or most traditional music the world over, and therefore all recent folk creations and permutations should be considered and explored. The following survey of views can give an idea of some of the approaches to this complex matter.

In dealing with the phenomenon of change, Alan Merriam says: "Change is a constant in human experience . . . no culture escapes the dynamics of change over time. But culture is also stable. . . . The threads of continuity run through every culture, and thus change must always be considered against a background of stability" (1964, pp. 303–4). Merriam also adopts the distinction between change that originates from inside the culture itself and change imposed on a culture by outside elements. The former is usually associated with "innovation" and is embedded in the concept of cultural variability; the latter is associated with processes of acculturation. Merriam reflects the anthropological approach which assumes that all societies experience the same changes. Fourteen years later, J. Blacking, dissatisfied with the available theories of musical change, urges scholars "to distinguish musical change analytically from other kinds of change, and (to distinguish) radical change from variation and innovation within a flexible system" (1978, pp. 1–3). Hence, by considering variation and innovation as normal phenomena in any musical system, Blacking advocates applying the concept of change only to "significant changes that are peculiar to musical systems." To further clarify his meaning he adds: "Musical change should signify a change of heart as well as mind, since music is a metaphorical expression of feeling." Bruno Nettl, who has devoted considerable thought to the problem of musical change, wrote in an early publication: "Change is an everpresent component in musical life" (1964, pp. 230–38), which largely concords with Merriam's view. Referring generally to the same idea, later Nettl reached a more subtle definition: "The continuity of change," and used it as the title for a whole chapter dealing with musical change (1983, chapt. 13). In this chapter he proposes a classification of four types or levels of change. The first, of which there are very few examples, substitutes one musical system for another—in other words, there is a complete change with absolutely no continuity. The second, "radical change," refers to a new musical system the form of which can nevertheless still be traced to an old one; this type of change can be easily illustrated. The third type relates to innovation as a manifestation of the element of change that is probably inherent to every musical system. Elaborating on this Nettl maintains: "Most societies expect of their artists a minimum of innovation, and some demand a great deal . . . even in societies that do not value innovation as greatly, a certain amount of change is needed to keep the system from stagnating and to contribute to its vitality." This is what brings him to conclude: "Change is the norm, hence the continuity of change in our title." The fourth type discusses "allowable variation"; this is distinguished from the "innovation" of the third type by "lack of direction."

The absence of a single accepted theory of the highly complex phenomenon of change pertains not only to attempts to measure it and define its nature; it involves the search for patterns and regularities and the basic questions of why, how, and under what conditions music changes. Rather than risk redundancy by engaging in a discussion of the multifarious arguments that have been put forward in answer to these questions, it may suffice to bear in mind J. Blacking's recent contribution: "Musical change, like all aspects of cultural change, is neither subject to laws nor the inevitable consequence of happenings. Musical changes are not caused by culture contact, population movements . . . they are the results of decisions made by individuals about music" (1986).

To further confound the issue, we should finally ask, who is to determine change—of whatever nature—in a musical system? Should it be an objective outsider or the people who practice the music being evaluated? This brings to the fore the full significance of the emic/etic dichotomy. Most available studies seem to be one-sided, falling into the snare of subjectivity, as suggested by Blacking's statement that "All evaluations of musical change tell us more about the class and interests of the evaluators than about the nature of musical change" (1978, p. 4). We will not be far from the truth if we extend the implications further and assume that most, if not all, the known evaluators represent the etic perception of change. Incidentally, this assumption finds confirmation in the conclusion of the above-cited chapter by Nettl: "I once asked my teacher of Persian music how long a particular practice had been extant. 'We have always done that,' he replied. 'Always?' I asked, 'You mean for the last 200 years, for example?' 'Of course not,' he replied, 'nobody knows what was going on 200 years ago.' I had not penetrated his sense of change, of history. So far, ethnomusicologists have concentrated on their own perception of musical change, learning little about the perception of musical continuity and change in the various societies of the world. This too remains one of the most significant tasks" (1983, p. 186).

A Convergence of Divergent Outlooks

The above piquant story that concludes Nettl's thorough analysis of the phenomenon of change is a typical manifestation of a particular emic perception of change that would seem to be culture-bound and not merely an isolated curious instance. In the framework of the struggle between "Ancients and Moderns" during the Golden Age of Arabic music in the ninth century, the greatest musician of that era Isḥāq al-Mawṣilī (d. 850), refuted his opponents who disapproved of his academic and classicist approach by saying: "May we be empowered to transmit what we have learned as it has been taught to us."[4] This reverence for the ancestral legacy, with its implied rejection of change and innovation, may suggest that a similar perception of change motivates representatives of Jewish musical traditions who have escaped—or avoided—the impact of modernity.

One may reasonably assume that such an approach to the phenomenon of change finds its expression in the words of Ecclesiastes: "What has been is what will be, and what has been done is what will be done and there is nothing new under the sun" (9:1). Considering its possible theological implication, this concept means enhancement of the immutability and perpetuity of the divine pre-established perfect order of the world. Since the perfection of divine creation encapsulates in latent form everything that ever has been or will be, what appears to the noninitiative as novelty is an illusion, as it is always present, although often in abeyance. Thus change is an imperceptible part of continuity and it is incumbent on man to bring those manifold hidden parts to light, in the endeavor to approximate perfection.

This approach to change may also be applied to certain inherent behavior and characteristics that are considered predestined, not modifiable, as they are incorporated in the divine conception of the universe and its various components. It is in this spirit that one can interpret the metaphorical verse in Jeremiah (13:23) "Can the black man change his skin, or the leopard his spots?" Of course, this has not been the only approach to change, nor has it prevented an occasional seeking after novelty and change for their own sake.

Nevertheless, the perception of change as a reflection of continuity has been prevalent and therefore should be taken into consideration when evaluating changes undergone by various groups of ethnic newcomers as a result of their confrontation with the new reality in Israel. This approach reveals itself at the level of motivations and visions that stimulated both the veteran settlers of Western background and the newcomers of Oriental origin.

The Quest for National Identity and Style

The mass transfer of the different ethnic traditions found Israeli society at the height of a long struggle over the nature of the new culture that would and should appropriately reflect the rebirth of the Jewish nation in its ancient land. Under pressure of circumstances, the central aspiration to create one unified people from many heterogeneous elements gained momentum. In this process of search for appropriate identity, music played an important role. The first generations of European pioneers were haunted by the necessity to change rapidly and radically, by the urgent desire to eradicate the stereotypic image of the Diaspora Jew. The new culture they and the following generations sought was entirely secular. By contrast, the majority of the masses of Near Eastern immigrants were largely imbued with a religious and messianic spirit. They were therefore reluctant to change in the ways the establishment expected of them, that is, to re-emerge as Israelis, which would have implied abandoning their original culture. Their target was the exaltation of Judaic values: the shining light of redemption, the promotion of the sanctity of life. They were not moved by the universalistic and socialistic renewal sought by the enthusiastic pioneers who had come to the country before them.

In the attempts to create a national style in music from the 1920s on, one finds many and varied tendencies; they range from a call for total adherence to the great musical achievements of the West with emphasis on the universalistic aspect of the new national aspirations, to the urge to adopt the Orient as a source of inspiration. But at quite an early stage we already witness the establishment of a *fait accompli* that had a decisive effect on future development. In the twenties, when the first Hebrew town, Tel Aviv, was no more than a tiny, sandy site, several Western-style musical institutions came into being. These included conservatories, choirs, instrumental ensembles, and even an opera.[5]

Those who nurtured this tendency maintained that Jewish particularism and uniqueness would come to the fore via the rendition of musical masterpieces in Hebrew and through selection of works based on biblical and other texts related to the Jewish people and its history. Thus, oratorios by Handel, Haydn, and Mendelssohn, or operas such as *Samson and Delilah* by Saint-Saëns, were considered perfectly apt and consequently found ample place in the repertoire.

Advocates of this view believed that the distinctive mark of identity in the new Hebrew music should not necessarily be concerned with modifying the norms and aesthetics of Western music. This ideology continued to inspire the first generation of composers in the land of Israel to such an extent that the utopian ideal was to see the advent of a Jewish Glinka.[6] Those who advocated the development of a characteristic national music were hardly ready to accept the use of east European Jewish folk songs as a mark of distinctiveness; for them it symbolized the Diaspora. They believed that the new national style should be characterized by a music of the region more in harmony with the physical and human landscape. The most far-reaching theses in this respect maintained that Jews are Oriental and Oriental tunes are close to their heart. Despite Western education and European enlightenment, on a subconscious level Jews are children of the Orient. According to M. Ravina, "The foundations of Oriental music are the foundations of the Jews' music. . . . The rhythm, one of the essential elements in music that the West has neglected to develop, occupies a prominent place in Oriental music. . . . Oriental music is closer to the general designation of music; it is more genuine, it attaches greater importance to the human voice than to musical instruments, it is concrete, natural." (M. Ravina, 1927). In 1930 a musician and theoretician named Sandberg published articles advocating writing in microtones and avoiding, as much as possible, performances of Western music.[7]

Despite this unequivocal song of praise to Oriental music, it should be remembered that for most if not all of those seeking the charmed Orient, its meaning and essence have remained vague. Interestingly, the numerous composers of folk and art music who at that time sincerely addressed themselves to Oriental musical material made no direct contact with it, although they could have done so quite easily.

Be that as it may, the ardent desire and sustained efforts to find an adequate synthetic expression for the new reality has stimulated the emergence of a shared novel song genre, based on the shared language of the *yishuv.*[8] The resultant product extensively adopted Jewish Oriental and Arab tunes and rhythms, and combined them with predominant style. In writing original tunes, composers often avoided major and minor scales and connotations of conventional harmony. Instead, they made ample use of medieval musical modes such as the Dorian, Phrygian, and Mixolydian,[9] even using the Oriental Ḥidjāz mode that offers a similarity to the *ahavah rabbah* mode found frequently in Ashkenazic ritual prayers and Hasidic music; this endowed their work with a certain affinity to old Mediterranean music. Distinct repeated melodic patterns became associated with each mode, the melody usually moving within a small orbit around a pivotal note, its progression generally diatonic, with few jumps. Rhythmically, these songs employ various kinds of syncopation and asymmetric meters. Biblical sources separated from their traditional connotations were frequently used as the basis for texts. Jewish traditional festivals inspired appropriate individual songs as well as large song units initiated by the kibbutzim with a view to reviving certain ancient agricultural celebrations, which we referred to in more detail in chapter 9.

The songs were usually communal, i.e., meant for group singing and not only to be performed for a listening audience. The Oriental flavor of the compositions was further accentuated by the vocal performance typical of numerous artists of Oriental Jewish origin. Nevertheless, the composers, who were predominantly of European origin and had received a Western musical education, were not trying to create a new type of Oriental song but rather a new Israeli folk music deriving from what they looked upon as the nation's ancient roots. The new folk songs reached back to the sources, but molded them in modern form. It was precisely this combination that appealed to the composers as an expression of the ideal of "integrating the Diaspora" that inspired them; the official "melting pot" ideology was thus supported.

Oriental Musicians' Part in Elaborating the New Style

The most illustrious mediator between Israeli and traditional ethnic society during the 1930s was the Yemenite singer Bracha Zephira. Orphaned at the age of three and having been educated primarily in Western institutions and environment, she later became the transmitter of traditional tunes to local composers who, under her supervision, arranged many pieces for her. As a gifted performer she, as well as other Oriental artists, promoted arrangements of traditional music, bringing them to wide audiences. They were gradually recognized as folklore messengers. It should be noted that exotic Yemenite singing has always been highly acclaimed; it also has come to symbolize the magical, genuine, and exotic Orient, perhaps representing the "other." That is why Zephira's deviations from the so-called authentic style aroused critical reservations. So it transpired that after all the enthusiastic public ovations, the reaction of the Israeli establishment led some critics to reproach Bracha Zephira, motivating her to turn away from the sources and offer substitutes in line with the taste of the largest segment of Israel's society. Some time later, when she had left the limelight of the stage, she confessed in a sad retrospective that "despite the fact that the composers approached the traditional song with respect and love, they produced Oriental songs dressed in heavy, complicated attire—that is to say, Western music endowed with a whiff of Oriental exoticism" (Zephira 1978, pp. 21–26).

Ostensibly an enthusiastic champion of the synthetical style she helped create, Bracha Zephira went so far as to coin the expression "suffering-pot," in contradistinction to the melting pot ideology. She wrote: "For the individual who returned from exile with a tradition and mentality of his own, the process of adjustment sometimes consisted of a suffering-pot."

Another Yemenite artist who contributed a great deal to the development of Israeli song and dance is the Israel Prize laureate, Sara Levi-Tanai. She became widely known as the founder and director of the Yemenite dance group Inbal that came into being in 1949. With a group of naturally gifted, sparkling Yemenite dancers she mounted programs of authentic Yemenite dances in a slightly stylized version, together with new Israeli shepherd dances, and enjoyed immediate success and an enthusiastic following. But as soon as she turned to a sophisticated form of art dance based on traditional Yemenite steps and themes, she encountered strong resistance. Her public did not want Inbal to become another modern dance group.

The general Israeli public wanted Bracha Zephira and Sara Levi-Tanai to uphold the image of spontaneity and authenticity. In a way the staged Yemenite heritage represents for many a kind of restoration of a lost paradise in an age of materialism and technology, while symbolizing the desired link with the remote past of ancient Israel. Interestingly, none of this held true for other ethnic communities. The Yemenites were viewed as exceptional, which helped propagate an image of them as a versatile, artistically gifted people, whose tradition significantly enriched the emergent Israeli culture. For many non-Oriental Jews the Yemenites came to symbolize Oriental Jewish culture in general. (For further details see Shiloah 1986.)

The Emergence of Ethnicity

These two women and a few other artists like them, however, were exceptional in that they created a bridge between two periods: that of the pre-state Jewish community in Palestine and that of the community in the early days of statehood. The bulk of their contemporaries, although also carriers of ethnic traditions, remained passive; they continued to cultivate their own heritage, but parallel to the dominant trend. What occurred following the mass immigration after the state arose, is a different story. Traditional music continued to be vital, especially in the realm of religious practice and to a certain extent on occasions of family and community rejoicing. Yet, although some of the traditional forms survived with little, if any, alteration under the impact of the new environment, considerable change took place in many forms of Oriental music. This latter development gained special momentum as a result of growing dissatisfaction with the official melting pot ideology and the desire for cultural equality. By the 1970s this had generated the emergence of ethnicity.

Young artists born in Israel or brought to it as infants, seeking ways to free themselves of feelings of harassment and discomfort, found expression in music that reflected their views about the nature and character that should be embodied by the national style. Some went so far as to emphasize and sharpen the Oriental element of the synthetic style elaborated by the veterans of the pre-state period. The thrust of the most extreme Oriental composers was in the direction of adopting the model of Oriental music's concepts and norms. The most outspoken protagonist of this tendency is Shlomo Bar, a gifted musician who in 1949 was brought from Morocco to Israel at the age of four and grew up in a *maʿabarah* (transit-camp). Being naturally talented, despite his lack of formal musical education, he adopted the language of music to express his feelings and ongoing experiences. He chose the drum to accompany his singing because he considered the rhythmic beat as a life-giving elixir, a vitalizing source of energy and inspiration. Inspiration and improvisation gradually became the cornerstone of his conception of what is "Oriental" in music. He saw it as distinguished by spontaneity and freshness, as against the rational, logical, and intricate forms of expression that determine Western musical art. In time, this concept of the Oriental reached far beyond the limits of Middle Eastern musical styles, embracing, among other things, Indian music. He saw his approach as corresponding perfectly to the new reality, and firmly believed that Israeli culture should move eastward.

In 1978 Bar founded his performing group *Ha-breirah ha-ṭivʿit*—The Natural Choice—a name he considered most appropriate in light of cultural and ecological conditions. The group comprised musicians from the United States, Israel, and India. Under his direction and inspiration they performed in a fusion style, combining Israeli songs with an Oriental flavor, Jewish Moroccan melodies set to modern Hebrew poetry, interlaced with Indian music and some Western elements.

Another trend characterized by a strong penchant for Oriental music became prominent in the late seventies and early eighties. Motivated by similar aspirations to achieve separate but equal status for the Oriental culture in Israel, numerous composers and performers of Oriental background, descending mainly from folk strongholds (e.g., Yemenites, Kurds) have elaborated a new style that combines traditional Jewish elements with popular Greek and Arabic music. Groups of amateurs without any formal musical training, composed of a star singer and a small group of self-taught instrumentalists who play the buzuki, electric guitar, *ʿūd,* drums, and synthesizer, usually perform to enthusiastic audiences at weddings and other family celebrations. They came to be known as the "singers of cassettes." They acquired this appellation, which for some has rather derogatory connotations, because their songs were distributed on cassettes rather than records. The cassettes were produced by enterprising promoters and sold mainly by merchants in the vicinity of the Central Bus Depot in Tel Aviv. However, their wide audience, which gradually included increasing numbers of Arabs, demonstrated unconditional admiration by making these cassettes by far the best sellers of any recorded music in Israel. This was the crucial point of a development that led from the earlier ideal of a uniform national culture to a proclivity for legitimate cultural pluralization within Israel's Jewish population.

It was against this general background that the sociologist Erik Cohen and I undertook to explore the manifold transformations undergone by the Oriental musical traditions. Our attempt to define and conceptualize the diversity and multidirectionality of the new forms of change was based on a broad programmatic approach, the purpose of which was to analyze musicologically significant processes of change in terms of sociologically significant variables. The findings were summarized in a suggested typology of stylistic dynamics based on four variables, two of a more musicological and two of a more sociological character, a typology that is a substantial part of our joint study, "The Dynamics of Change in Jewish Oriental Ethnic Music in Israel" (Shiloah and Cohen 1982, 1983, 1985). This study was followed by another joint article in which we analyzed the principal substantive trends of change (Cohen and Shiloah, 1985). The preceding historical survey clearly indicates the intricacies involved in the problem of change in musical styles under the impact of external forces. The following typology of stylistic dynamics is an attempt to systematize the existing variety.

Directions of Change in Ethnic Music: A Typology of Stylistic Dynamics[10]

The models for stylistic change in ethnic art and music current in the literature are based at least tacitly on the premise of unidirectionality, if not unilinearity, of change. This is in principle true even of the most sophisticated approaches in the field. Thus, Graburn (1976) bases his typology on the concept of "acculturation," and despite his important distinction between arts produced for an internal and an external public, his typology is essentially unidirectional in conception. Nettl's (1978, p. 127) approach, couched in terms of "tradition," "modernization," and "Westernization," seems to be based on a similar premise; interestingly, the very richness of concrete stylistic transformations that he lists raises questions as to the sufficiency of these three simple terms to account for the variety. Moreover, any assumption of unidirectionality or unilinearity suffers from a major theoretical drawback: it precludes the conceptualization of various types of stylistic dynamics emerging under different circumstances. Our typology of stylistic dynamics encompasses four variables:

1. Perpetuation vs. innovation in musical production or performance. The variable relates to the extent to which musicians merely reproduce already existing stylistic elements or introduce novel ones.

2. Orthogenesis vs. heterogenesis of the process of musical change. This variable is adopted from the work of Redfield and Singer (1969) and refers to the extent to which ethnic musical styles are replicated, or further developed and elaborated, under the new conditions (orthogenesis), or combined with extraneous elements to create new, original musical styles (heterogenesis).

3. Internal vs. external audience. This variable, adopted from Graburn (1976), relates to the intended audience of the work; the internal audience is the audience of the musician's own ethnic group, while the external audience ranges from other Jewish Oriental groups to the general Israeli, Jewish, or world public.

4. Spontaneous vs. sponsored musical production. This variable relates to the source of the initiative for new musical production, and is of much importance in Israel, where ethnic cultural events often do not occur wholly spontaneously, but are in various ways sponsored by a variety of outsiders or public and national institutions.

A complete cross-classification of all these variables would be cumbersome and is in fact unnecessary. We have found that a nine-fold classification, as presented in table 2, does justice to the important developments in ethnic music that came to our attention, and we shall discuss each type in detail.

1. *Traditional:* continuation of preimmigration musical forms. This type includes the bulk of liturgical music, which is still regularly performed in ethnic synagogues and festivities, as well as some paraliturgical and secular musical pieces, such as functional songs and dances related to major family rituals: birth, circumcision, bar mitsvah, wedding ceremonies, and death (dirges are still commonly used); songs related to the yearly festivals, like Purim and the Passover seder family feast; and the home hymns (*zemirot*) sung at Sabbatical repasts, cradle and epic songs, romances, pilgrimage songs, and so on.

In the first period after immigration, under the impact of the exhilaration of arriving in the Promised Land and of the more prosaic hardships experienced there, some novel themes appeared in the secular music of the purely traditional type. A major example are the *aliyah* (immigration) songs (Shiloah 1970), which were created spontaneously and informally performed for an internal audience, particularly among Yemenite, Iraqi, and Moroccan immigrants. The creation by gifted folk poet-singers of such "new" songs is characteristic of most musical cultures of the Near Eastern region. These poet-singers express the feelings and complaints of the community concerning current affairs by creating a new text that they associate with an old tune. Jewish poet-singers used to compose such songs in the Diaspora and continued to do so upon immigration to Israel. Their works cover diverse topics, sometimes

Table 2

A Typology of Stylistic Dynamics in Jewish Oriental Music in Israel

	Spontaneous; Internal Audience	Spontaneous-sponsored External Audience	Sponsored; External Audience
Perpetuation; Orthogenetic	(1) Traditional	(2) Conserved	(3) Museumized
Innovation; Ortho/hetero genetic	(4) Neotraditional	(5) Transitional	(6) Pseudoethnic
Innovation; Heterogenetic	(7) Popular	(8) Ethnic fine	(9) Fine

expressing the enthusiasm of the immigrants and sometimes their protest, particularly against alleged discrimination and injustices perpetrated against them. Since no musical innovations are introduced in such songs, we have classified them as traditional; moreover, even if new literary motifs are introduced, these too are expressed in stereotyped traditional forms. The scope of musical production in the purely traditional style diminished soon after immigration and various innovations appeared even in the spontaneous ethnic music.

2. *Conserved:* deliberate preservation of traditional, preimmigration musical styles, edited and adapted for a new, external audience. Though members of the ethnic group may be interested in the dissemination of their music, the editing and adaptation is usually done by outsiders, professional musicians with a Western musical education.

Examples of such music are traditional tunes with certain characteristics removed or modified in order to facilitate their performance by outsiders, who are unable to perform them in their original form. The modifications range from simplification to stylization; microtonality, a large part of traditional ornamentation, rhythmic freedom complexity, as well as inherited vocal intonations, nasal and gutteral emissions and pronunciations are neglected. The long individual improvisations are shortened and heterophony in group singing is changed into monophony. This process starts by the intentional simplifications in transcriptions of traditional tunes into Western notation to make them accessible to outsiders (see, for example, Adaqi and Sharvit 1981), and culminates in performances of these tunes from the simplified notated version. The Center for the Integration of the Jewish Oriental Heritage[11] aims to propagate the musical heritage of the communities by helping to adapt it to a modern Western audience, while preserving its distinctiveness. In this sense the work of E. Avitzur, a modern composer sponsored by the center, could be seen as performing a conservational function. However, from another perspective, his are also original compositions, and will be discussed under the rubric of fine arts (type 9).

Simplification and stylization along similar lines also characterize the staging of traditional dances. While in museumization (type 3) the emphasis is on the strict preservation of the "authentic," conservation changes the original somewhat, as it strives to make it acceptable to a wider audience.

3. *Museumized:* traditional, preimmigration music, collected and preserved in its "authentic" form by ethnographically trained outsiders, in the interest of scientific and artistic documentation of ethnic arts and performed primarily for selected external audiences.

The movement to safeguard the authentic traditions before they disappear or change goes back to A. Z. Idelsohn, who came from eastern Europe to Jerusalem in 1905. However, the movement received its major impetus in the wake of mass immigration after the creation of the State of Israel. Traditional music and dances were collected by Edith Gerson-Kiwi, Gurit Kadman, and other ethnographers. Major collections were stored in several archives, including a national archive affiliated with the National and University Library in Jerusalem. These thousands of documents now serve as material for research, musical education, and occasionally for the preparation of records edited by scholars. Composers use the archives in order to acquaint themselves with the disappearing "original" traditions, and sometimes use the melodies they like in their own compositions. Scholars like Gerson-Kiwi have also organized special concerts devoted to the performance of "authentic" music and dance, for example, in the framework of international musicological congresses. Such performances took place at the East-West Encounter in Music (1963), the International Congress of Jewish Music (1978) and the International Days of Contemporary Music (1980). Gurit Kadman, who devoted herself to the collection of traditional dances, has initiated their revival in "authentic" forms, performed by members of the various ethnic communities.

4. *Neotraditional:* innovative continuation of traditional musical styles, occurring spontaneously within the ethnic group, but absorbing some outside influences; the synthesis is to a degree heterogenetic. Thus, many immigrant groups, which prior to immigration had their own little musical traditions, adopted the so-called Jerusalemite-Sephardic style. This style, in turn, developed at an earlier stage within the old, established Sephardic community of Jerusalem and incorporated elements from throughout the Ottoman Empire. This style, enriched by additional Middle Eastern elements derived from the immigrants' traditions, now dominates the synagogal music of Oriental communities such as the Iranian, Bokharian, Moroccan, and Yemenite. It provides the basis for an emergent "pan-Sephardic" style in Israel, toward which most of the generation of Israeli-born Oriental cantors are inclined. A striking example is a young Yemenite who sings in perfect "pan-Sephardic" style.

In addition to such homogenization, there is also a tendency toward various forms of syncretism in liturgical music, one of its most interesting forms being the penetration of elements of Ashkenazic *ḥazzanut* into the synagogal music of some Oriental communities. A good example is a recorded collection of traditional Moroccan hymns sung by a famous Moroccan cantor, H. Luk. Here, the original style still predominates, but the cantor has purposely introduced Western instruments and stylistic elements borrowed from Near Eastern music and from Ashkenazic *ḥazzanut*. Thus, even in liturgical music, the music most resistant to change, some processes of heterogenization can be observed.

5. *Transitional:* this category, embracing the bulk of contemporary ethnic musical production, consists of music which, while still in many respects essentially orthogenetic, introduces so many extraneous elements that it becomes progressively heterogenetic. While directed primarily to an external Oriental or general public, its production and performance is typically the result of a combination of spontaneous initiative within an ethnic group and sponsorship by institutions or individuals from the outside. Traditional tunes, melodic patterns, and ways of performance are fused into new popular songs, which are usually set to a Western accompaniment. Some top performers in this style, particularly singers such as Bracha Zephira (at an early stage of her career), Joe Ammar, and Yigal Ben-Ḥaim, enjoy a wide popularity both within their group of origin and among the general public. Others, such as Shoshana Dammari and Esther Gamlieli achieved an international reputation, and were among the principal popularizers of what is seen abroad as "typical" Israeli music.

The transitional style is widely disseminated through records and radio and television programs. Owing to the sponsorship of public and national institutions, special events for music in this style have been initiated. The principal one is the yearly Festival of Songs in the Oriental Style. Due to borrowing and amalgamation of elements from various traditions, the differences between the "transitional" music of different ethnic groups tend to be gradually obliterated as a mainstream popular Oriental style emerges in Israel. Also, musicians from one ethnic community learned to perform the transitional music of the others and thus to diversify their programs. At the major ethnic festival of the Moroccan *mimuna* (Ben-Ami 1975) a wide variety of transitional pieces are performed, in addition to some museumized ones, by musicians from various ethnic groups. A great deal of music in the transitional style is purely commercial, making money for producers and performers through popular concerts and the sale of records. Through the growing penetration of outsiders this style tends to be transformed into "pseudoethnic" music (type 6).

6. *Pseudoethnic:* the artistic transmutation of ethnic musical forms by producers and performers from outside the ethnic group for an external audience. While the works are presented as ethnic music, their form has undergone such far-reaching changes to Western stylistic patterns that, properly speaking, they no longer belong to the realm of ethnic music. This indeed is what happened to many of the songs, composed by Jews of Western origin or rearranged, harmonized, and orchestrated by them at recent Festivals of Songs in the Oriental Style. This development was vehemently criticized by Ben-Moshe, who in a review of a particular festival that appeared in *Ba-ma'arakhah* (the bulletin of the Sephardic and Oriental Jews), argued that "the 'style' of the festival had no connection whatever with the Oriental Jewry;

even arrangers and performers were Western Jews" (Ben-Moshe 1981, p. 24). The "ethnic" label on music of this type refers, at most, to superficial imitations of traditional elements incorporated in the new songs. The outsider composers, arrangers, and performers are most anxious to meet the standards of the commercialized "light" music currently popular on the market, rather than render traditional ethnic musical patterns. Pieces in the "pseudoethnic" style are similar to other light music in their use of big orchestras and overwhelming sonorities, and in addition are fraught with stereotypic Oriental elements such as Spanish rhythms and harmonies. Many so-called Israeli songs using adapted Oriental musical elements exemplify a version of the pseudoethnic style still more remote from the original.

7. *Popular:* the spontaneous production or performance by members of one ethnic group of music adopted from other musical traditions—Oriental, Mediterranean, or even Western—for an internal ethnic audience. Contrary to all previous types, this music is alien in its origin to the traditions of the ethnic group and hence purely heterogenetic. A striking example is the wide adoption of modern popular Greek music by different Oriental Jewish communities. At big family rejoicings, Greek music performed by Jewish Oriental musicians is very popular. Indian popular music also enjoys wide currency. Insofar as the musicians introduce no changes into such music, it is in fact perpetuative, rather than innovative, despite its heterogenesis.

8. *Ethnic fine:* this category includes the works of ethnic artists who, while making use of the musical heritage of their own group, fuse this with elements taken from other, including Western, musical traditions to produce works of an essentially innovative, heterogenic character. While often spontaneously initiated, the musical production of such artists is later frequently sponsored or helped by outsiders. A major characteristic of this type is the effort of the ethnic musicians to "aestheticize" folk music and elevate the traditional style to the rank of concert hall "fine art." These musicians, such as Bracha Zephira and Isaac Levy, who are animated by a desire to enhance the prestige of their own tradition, have frequently had recourse to outsiders—composers and performers—to transpose traditional tunes into new, concert-hall forms. However, in the long run, some of the products of this collaboration became more and more sophisticated and led finally to fine art compositions, with only some Oriental flavor left (type 9).

A similar process occurred in Oriental folk dancing; this is best exemplified by the Inbal dance company. Initiated by Sara Levi-Tanai and originally based on Yemenite folk dances, the company soon employed choreographers of Western origin. Gradually it introduced musical elements from other Oriental traditions, and even some Ashkenazic ones. The sequences of the dances were presented in a "dramatic framework" (Manor 1975). Inbal thus moved consistently away from folklore and into the realm of art. The recent appearance, as mentioned in chapter 10, of The Natural Choice (*Ha-breirah ha-tivʿit*) ensemble, under the leadership of a Jew of Moroccan origin, Shlomo Bar, introduced another interesting variation into this type. The leader, who serves as a singer, drummer, and flautist in the ensemble, joined with an American guitarist, an Indian Jewish violinist, and an Israeli-born Jew of Bokharian origin as contrabassist, to create an amalgamated, completely new style, dominated by his powerful personality. The composer seeks to integrate widely different musical traditions, and yet endow his work with a pervasive Oriental spirit. It thus represents a balance of stylistic plurality and stylistic fusion.

9. *Fine:* this type includes modern Western music produced by composers of mostly Western origin, who have formal musical training and who utilize ethnic thematic elements in their works.

The sponsored introduction of Jewish Oriental musical elements into works by composers of Western origin underwent a more complicated process: the composers of popular Israeli folk songs borrowed exclusively from the "little traditions." Composers of serious music initially also borrowed from the same source, but later turned increasingly to the Great Tradition. The latter is exemplified by attempts to introduce into art music the *maqām* and other patterns of the great Near Eastern tradition.

Epilogue

The events with which we closed the last chapter of this work are near in point of time to those with which we chose to open our study. Both the opening and closing mark milestones along a route that encompasses many centuries and many places. Traversing this route is like following an imaginary path in a story rife with upheavals and rich in tangled situations. Obviously, the musical tale we have elaborated, with its various and sundry links, is not a tendentious reconstruction of events and does not offer ready-made solutions to the problems raised; it rather mirrors a given reality as objectively as possible. That reality is the life lived by an ancient people exiled from its land who, for two thousand years of dispersion, tried to preserve its cultural values, while oscillating incessantly between tortured suffering and hopes of spiritual and physical redemption.

A discussion of the way the musical heritage is entwined in this complex web, and how that heritage was affected, brings the observer face to face with a problematic situation. On the one hand we know that music is the language of emotions rooted deep in the individual's subconscious; it expresses his hidden experiences, experiences that are changed with symbolic messages shared by him and the members of his group. Participating in those common experiences and sharing those messages endows the individual with the sense of security gained from identification with the group. From this point of departure, which views music as symbolizing feelings, impressions, and cultural values buried deep in the sense of group security, it would be correct to assume that in practice, the musical heritage of the people of Israel was not destined to change basically. Confirmation or denial of this vitally important assumption confronts one with the objective difficulty we have already discussed in our introduction—the dearth of musical documentation on which to base definitive argumentation.

Furthermore, one must relate to two central factors that undoubtedly affected the degree of stability or of change undergone by the various traditions. The first factor involves the ideological position of official authorities on the subject of music. This position, as has been explained at length in the foregoing pages, swings from total negation of music as a stabilizing, elevating element in ritual, to disapproving reticence that nevertheless compromises under pressure of the situation as it exists. The denial of music might have been decisive, were it not for the significant counterweight established by the perception of the mystics. And yet, paradoxically, the negative stand of the keepers of traditional law indirectly contributed to the stabilization of the various traditions, for it served as a barrier of sorts to excessive incursion of alien music into the essence of the ritual, saving it from radical change. The second very influential factor involves the constant, long-range exposure of the various traditions to local musical cultures that surrounded them. There is no doubt that there was an affinity with the alien musical cultures they were in contact with; in this context it is sufficient to mention the struggle of the rabbinical authorities to counteract it. To what extent this obvious affinity undermined the stability of musical traditions or had the contrary effect, that is, strengthened their foundations and imbued them with vitality that prevented their ossification, cannot be definitively assessed.

At the beginning of this Epilogue I used the word "story" to characterize my particular comprehensive way of looking at the musical tradition of the people of Israel, a way that combines pictures of reality as it exists with scenes that appear on the stage of history. I conclude these remarks in the spirit of the theatrical epilogue and appeal to the reader's generosity, asking him to forgive me for the absence of conclusive answers to some of the many questions raised. The only excuse I can offer is that there still are not, and perhaps cannot be, unequivocal answers.

Notes

Chapter 1: Identity and Character of Jewish Music

1. The *qānūn* is a trapezoidal zither; its twenty-four strings are plucked with a plectrum attached to the index finger of each hand. Little moveable bridges placed under the ends of the strings allow their tuning to be modified by the player.

2. The Great Tradition designates the "high and sophisticated" musical art style developed in Near Eastern music after the advent of Islam, constituting a skillful fusion of selected elements from previous Near-Eastern Great Musical Traditions with elements from Arab folk song. It was widely adopted by those cultures including the Judaic, that came under Islamic influence.

3. The *psanterin* is one of six musical instruments comprising the ensemble that gives the signal to worship the golden image set up by Nebuchadnezzar; it is referred to four times in Daniel—3:5,7,10,15.

4. The *santūr* is another type of zither. It has seventy-two strings grouped in fours, supported by eighteen moveable bridges in two rows of nine, dividing the whole into three registers. Two sticks are used to strike the strings.

5. The Inbal Dance Troupe was established in 1950 by Sara Levi-Tanai; its members were Yemenite dancers and singers and its first program consisted exclusively of Yemenite folklore. In the process of crystallizing its own special dance language, the group gradually adopted modern dance techniques. See chapters 9 and 10 for further details.

6. The term used in eastern Europe, derived from the Hebrew word for instrument (*klizemer*), designates a professional folk musician. See chapter 8 for material about the klezmers and their music.

7. This information is based on an interview with him held in April 1979.

8. Mark Slobin (1984) describes the origin of the new klezmers in the United States.

9. *Yuval: Studies of Jewish Music* 5 (1986), is dedicated to the memory of Abraham Zvi Idelsohn. The first section includes documentary material about his life and work.

10. At that time a number of well-known scholars—Erich von Hornbostel, Otto Abraham, and Carl Stumpf—working in Germany and Austria, founded a new scientific discipline called

"comparative musicology." Two record archives were established then in Vienna (1899) and Berlin (1905); both helped Idelsohn with the recordings he made in this country.

11. In the introduction to volume 9 Idelsohn writes: "For the first time in the editing of folk song, a collection presents the songs classified according to musical characteristics and so arranged as to make these characteristics apparent (scale, various predominant characteristics within the scale)."

12. The *maqām* system will be treated briefly in chapter 5, in the section, "Creativity in the Singing of *Piyyuṭim.*"

13. For further details see Schleifer (1986).

14. From 1855 to 1906 Parisot spent time in monastaries in France and Spain. He published studies on Oriental Christian church music. With respect to Jewish music, outside of the chapter in the book referred to here, Parisot wrote an important entry for the *Vigouroux Biblican Dictionary* (1902), "The Recitative of Oriental Jewry."

15. Parisot probably refers to the type called direct Psalmody. Unlike the responsorial Psalmody which is the alternation between soloist and choir, and antiphonal Psalmody which is the alternation of two choirs, this type has no alternation, and is simply straightforward. This is a type of musical declamation that antecedes the Gregorian chant.

16. According to Parisot the medieval Christian church followed the Greco-Roman melodic pattern: the series of eight scales—also known as "harmonies"—that were the core of musical theory in ancient Greece and Rome.

17. The Mozarabs, from the Arab *musta'rab,* were Christians who lived under Muslim rule in Spain and adopted an Arab-Spanish (Andalusian) way of life. They were allowed to continue to cultivate their unique rite and music, the Mozarabic, whose formation antedated the Muslim conquest. Until the eleventh century their liturgical singing developed separately from the Gregorian system.

18. In this connection see Herzog and Hajdu (1967).

19. The Gregorian Responsorium is a Gregorian chant for one voice that usually follows readings of the New Testament. When the text is not a direct biblical quotation, it is taken from a sermon by a religious authority. The Responsorium, of varying length and complexity, has a fixed melodic pattern.

20. The Ambrosian liturgy was the basis of the Gregorian chant. Some of its tunes were attributed to Ambrose of Milan, one of the fourth-century church fathers. The Eastern influence was manifested in the many embellishments that adorned this music.

21. Lachmann's study was based on recordings made in 1929 in one of the two congregations of Djerba, the congregation known as the "small neighborhood." In his opinion it was less exposed to external influences than the one known as the "large neighborhood." For a comparison between Lachmann's study on the "small neighborhood" or village, and a recent study on the "large neighborhood," see R. Davis (1984–85) and (1986).

Chapter 2: Problems of Methodology in the Study of Jewish Music

1. Within the frame of West European Jewry's emancipation movement at the beginning of the nineteenth century, various reformist streams evolved as a result of hopes of joining and imitating progressive modern society, and adopting its art music. Hence large choirs with organ accompaniment became the stock-in-trade of progressive cantors, among whom Shlomo Sulzer, Shmuel Naumburg, and Louis Levandowsky were outstanding. See also end of chapter 3.

2. All of these composed music commissioned by Temple Emanuel in New York.

3. This applies particularly to the Jewish communities in developed urban centers where art music flourished. Of course, to some extent there, too—and particularly in smaller, more remote communities—there was a conspicuous folkloristic element in their musical traditions.

4. See chapters 8 and 9.

5. This pertains primarily to the theoretical discussions of a mathematically speculative nature. On the conceptual level one frequently finds original approaches and ideas.

6. Judith Cohen (1974) gives a lengthy portrayal of Jubal as reflected in the Christian texts of the Middle Ages.

7. It should be noted here that the names of musical instruments and related terms that appear in the Bible have always presented difficulties for translators because they involved thorough knowledge of the musical subjects of the period as well as of archeological findings and cultural conditions in neighboring countries. We have therefore chosen to cite the original terms alongside the translations—which are not always accurate. Specifically, the first two instruments are types of lyres; see Bayer (1968). Drum is a general appellation that includes various types of drums; according to the Septuagint the *menaʿneʿim* are cymbals and according to the Vulgate, *sistra,* although the references may be to clay rattles. *Tsiltselim* and *metsiltaim* signify the same instrument, the first indicating three or more, and the second a pair. The sixteen instruments mentioned in the Bible are all described by Bayer (1963).

8. Additional details appear in chapter 7 and 8.

9. See chapter 6.

10. In the introduction to the publication of the scroll on the war of the Sons of Light against the Sons of Darkness, Yigal Yadin (1962) devoted all of chapter 5 (pp. 87–112) to a detailed description of the varied usages and musical terms associated with the *haṭsoṭsra* and *shofar* (trumpets and rams' horns).

11. Two articles by David Flusser (1958 and 1968) give excellent background material touching on the group's contacts with the first Christians, and their social messages.

12. This material was published by Neubauer (1895).

13. Older evidence of the participation of a choir in prayers can be found in Fleischer (1974) and in *maqamah* 24 of *Taḥkemoni* by Yehuda Al-Ḥarizi (see chapter 3).

14. The Italian composer Christiano Giuseppe Lidarti wrote several compositions for the Portuguese congregation in Amsterdam. Shortly before that, the composer Abraham Caceres, a member of the Amsterdam congregation, also composed cantatas to the words of the prayer "The soul of all that live and breathe" (Adler 1966).

15. The author uses the term "ʿArab" (an Arabic-speaking country) rather than Morocco as a rhetorical flourish. The book is included in the works of Romanelli edited by H. Schirmann (1969).

16. See, for example, Jean Tharaud (1921).

17. It should be noted that, although mentioned by Delacroix, the *ʿūd* is missing from this trio; in its place is an extra drummer who sometimes claps his hands.

18. Although Dumas describes this as the form of payment used by strangers who happen to be present during the dancing, this was actually the way all observers, including the local people, paid the dancers. It should be noted, however, that this passage refers to two types of dancers: the women of the family who dance spontaneously and the professional dancers who perform more elegant, stylized movements.

19. Al-Kindī was called the Philosopher of the Arabs because of his southern Arabian lineage. He wrote at least 265 works dealing with various branches of knowledge, including thirteen treatises on the art of music. Only six of these are still extant.

20. The section on music is included in Adler (1975).

21. Yehuda ben Shaul ibn Tibbon was born in 1120 in Granada and died in 1190 in Marseille, France. He was a physician and well-known translator from Arabic to Hebrew—the first of a distinguished line of Tibbons who were physicians and translators. He translated the above work of Saʿadia Gaon, *Ḥovot ha-levavot* of Ibn Paquda, as well as the *Book of the Khazari* that is under discussion here.

22. The sections on music were published with a commentary by Shiloah (1966).

23. This technique will be clarified later in this chapter.

24. Baron Rodolphe d'Erlanger (1935) published this entire work in French translation, with comments. The material on "empty" and "full" appears in volume 2, pp. 66–77.

25. For a description of this work and its Latin translations, see Shiloah (1979).

26. "The Epistle on Music" by the Brothers of Purity has been published in French and English translations with commentaries—Shiloah (1964/66; 1978). The introduction to the English translation includes information about its writing and theories.

27. The four humors are blood, yellow bile, black bile, and phlegm.

28. The four strings of the classical Arab *ʿūd* are called, in descending order: *al-zīr* (high), *al-mathna* (second), *al-mathlath* (third), *al-bamm* (low). The names of the first and fourth strings are Persian while those of the second and third are Arabic. When a fifth string was added above *al-zīr,* it was called *al-ḥād* (highest). The strings of the modern *ʿūd* have other names.

29. The section on music was published by Adler (1975: 166–68).

30. This well-known distich is included in his sixth *maḥberet,* line 341. The *maḥbarot,* conceived after the model of al-Ḥarizi's *Taḥkemoni,* are Immanuel's best known literary work.

31. This Arabic-language book written in Hebrew characters is still extant in manuscript. It deals primarily with a discussion of the Hebrew metaphor. The chapter on music with an English translation and commentaries was published by Shiloah (1982).

32. See Adler (1975).

33. For general background material see Simonson (1962).

34. This homiletic discussion was tranlated into German by Herzl Shmueli (1953).

35. See note 6 above.

36. The talmudic legend about the *kinnor* that plays of its own accord at midnight appears frequently in the literature of the kabbalah (see chapter 6).

Chapter 3: Music and Religion

1. This song became famous in its day because of a trial held in the United States in which the Israeli composer Issachar Meron and the American composer Julius Grossman both claimed to have written the music. The American court ruled that the first two parts of the melody were composed by Meron while the third part was by Grossman. Credits appeared accordingly in printed editions of the song.

2. The song is by the French singer of Egyptian origin, Dalida.

3. Under the influence of esoteric doctrines, this type of allegoric interpretation was widespread. See chapter 4.

4. At the time of the Second Temple the rabbinical sages already expressed opposition to the infiltration into Israel's houses of worship by Greek songs, which they considered pagan music. See the discussion later in this chapter.

5. *Maqāmah* (plural: *maqāmāt*) is an Arab literary form consisting of short narrative passages in rhyming prose. Two characters usually appear in the tale: the generally passive narrator and the active, aggressive hero. Two Arab writers, al-Hamadānī (d. 1007) and al-Ḥarīrī (1054–1122), introduced a defined structure to this type of literary work. The *maqāmāt* of al-Ḥarīrī were translated by Yehuda al-Ḥarizi, who used them as a model for his book *Taḥkemoni.*

6. Up to this point al-Ḥarizi was harshly critical of the cantor's ignorance and his confused rendition of the prayers. From here on the poet attacks the quality of the original songs the cantor wrote and included in the services.

7. See note 12 of chapter 2.

8. A rabbi who lived in Germany in the 17th century, he was well educated in scientific fields. His book *Ḥavvat Ya'ir* includes responses in matters of traditional law.

9. The material that follows is from a discussion broadcast over "Kol Yisrael" in 1968,

about cantors and their function. Y. L. Ne'eman, author of important books on the biblical accents and *Ḥazzanut* (cantorial works), represented Ashkenazic *Ḥazzanut*.

10. *Coplas* is the name given to a sequence of poetic lines. Early in the eighteenth century rabbis encouraged the use of this form for creating poems in Ladino on religious themes. They thereby hoped to raise the spirits of the oppressed masses of Jewry in the Ottoman Empire.

11. For more about the *maqām*, see chapter 5. In some Sephardic synagogues the Sabbath and holiday prayers are said in the special *maqām* appropriate for each occasion.

12. As in note 9.

13. The work is anonymous. The inside cover bore the legend: "Composed and published with the help of God by men learned in the Torah in the holy city of Jerusalem." The author hiding behind the phrase "men learned in the Torah" belongs to extreme ultra-orthodox circles. Some of the traditional legal judgments cited in the book were indeed written by rabbis of the ultra-orthodox sect in Jerusalem.

14. A rabbi who officiated in Frankfurt on the Main, he was adamantly opposed to adopting alien tunes for the prayers. His book *Yosef Omets* includes customs—primarily of Frankfurt—and regulations for every day of the year, encompassing matters of ethnics and behavior.

15. The reference is to the celebration called *melavveh malkah* (Accompanying the queen), the festive singing that accompanies the departure of the Sabbath, which is likened to a queen; she is welcomed with song upon her arrival on Friday night, and accompanied by song when she departs on Saturday night. This celebration is particularly popular among the Hasidic movements.

16. It is interesting to note here that in a question the Jews of Gabes (Tunis) put to Rabbi Hai Gaon, the same passage from Hosea appears as the title for the anonymous work we have discussed. About the answer, see below.

17. In the main the book is a collection of *piyyuṭim* by the author and other writers. These *piyyuṭim* were intended to be sung in the course of the *baqqashot*. For a discussion of the latter, see chapters 5 and 6.

18. The *Great Midrash* constitutes one of the commentaries on the Pentateuch.

19. See J. G. Frazer, (1919, vol. 3, pp. 446–80; Shiloah 1979b).

20. The appearance of non-Jewish musicians at joyous Jewish events was quite usual in many congregations, particularly those in urban centers. On the other hand, when a community was blessed with its own talented people, Jewish musicians would appear at the celebrations of their non-Jewish neighbors.

21. The text is published in Adler (1975).

22. The Turkish city Izmir, birthplace of Shabbatai Zvi and his Sabbatean movement, where there was a Jewish community from the seventeenth century on.

23. The new style that developed after 1830, the date of the establishment of the Hellenic state (modern Greece) is expressed by the first appearance of harmonization of the traditional homophonic hymns, and by the composition of multivoiced works similar in style to Russian multivoiced church music.

24. See Adler (1966).

25. See Adler (1975).

26. Maimonides refers here to the talmudic saying: "Qol be'ishshah ʿervah" (Hearing a woman's voice is indecent) (Babylonian Talmud, *Sotah* 48a).

Chapter 4: Cantillation

1. The first is called *shaliayḥ tsibbur* (representative of the public) or cantor, the second "lector" or "reader." They also fulfill the function of translators, rendering the biblical text into Aramaic—at one time the colloquial language. In the synagogue of antiquity, the text was read and

explained by members of the congregation; today, too, laymen can sometimes be heard reading the Bible, but because it was not certain that enough qualified individuals would be found, a permanent "reader" was appointed to fulfill the function.

2. See chapter 5.

3. In Plainsong the term is used for a group of notes set to a single syllable. It is also frequently used in the sense of *fioritura*.

4. The reading of the Ten Commandments is considered most solemn and important. In congregations influenced by the art music of the Near East, this solemnity was expressed not only in extensive embellishment but also in intentional modulation, that is, changing from one *maqām* to another. A particular *maqām* was adapted to each Commandment, giving special consideration to its ethos.

5. This is a relatively simple example in which a brief melodic phrase is repeated unchanged. As to the Yanina community, see Shiloah (1972).

6. See note 21 of chapter 2.

7. Apparently based on words of the rabbinical sages (tractate Gittin ch. 71, p. 1): "From what they said, and not what they wrote." In any event, this passage is intended to underscore the power of oral transmission in the culture of medieval Jewry.

8. The signs (diacritical points) and graphic symbols designating the cantillation in the text of the printed Hebrew Bible are the product of the School of Massoretes (Traditionalists) that flourished in Tiberias (Palestine) between the seventh and ninth centuries C.E. Aharon Ben-Asher (first half of the tenth century) was the massoretic authority whose critical annotations on the biblical text became the basis for all subsequent editions.

9. For hundreds of years the *Keter* (Aleppo Codex) was in one of the synagogues in Aleppo. In 1948 it was partially burned during anti-Jewish pogroms in the city, but about two-thirds was salvaged and brought to the National University Library in Jerusalem.

10. The Leningrad Manuscript is the oldest extant copy of the entire Bible. It is generally considered as the edition most representative of the system created by Aharon Ben-Asher.

11. In ancient days the widespread custom was to read the Bible to the accompaniment of pre-established, known gestures that showed the reader which accent was indicated or guided the learner who was practising correctly accented reading. The use of hand signals is still customary today in certain communities (Yemen, Tunis, Morocco, Germany). In this connection see Asher Laufer (1973).

12. To stress the hierarchic sequence of the disjunctives in some places, a system was used of naming them in descending order of importance: emperors, kings, princes, adjutants. All composers were called servants.

13. As will be explained below, from the compositional standpoint the system used for the three books Job, Proverbs, and Pslams—known as "EMET," an acronym created by the first letters of their Hebrew names—is different from that used for the remaining twenty-one books of the Bible.

14. *Zarqah* is the name of one of the accents.

15. In the same work Avenary (pp. 12–13) reprints an earlier recording of notes that he discovered in 1973, one that had been previously unknown to researchers. Recorded between the years 1411 and 1505, it appears in a Hebrew manuscript, Münich 42, fol. 1–2.

16. See figure 2.

17. See note 13.

18. In a footnote Idelsohn adds that "the system of accents for chanting was employed also for the Mishnah and Talmud, accentuated parts of which are retained in Ms. in several libraries." Evidence of this practice is to be found in Profiat Duran's *Maʿaseh Ephod* (The work of the Ephod [1403]). See Adler (1975, p. 129).

Chapter 5: The *Piyyuṭ* as a Factor in the Development of Synagogal Music

1. E. Fleischer (1974) discusses institutionalized choirs of proficient singers that accompanied the cantor in the rendition of early forms of Palestinian *piyyuṭim*.

2. In this context *seliḥah* is a poetic genre indicating a *piyyuṭ* expressing penitence and asking forgiveness for sins. The plural form *seliḥot* is used for a special order of services on fast days and during the penitential season. The *seliḥot* include different types of *piyyuṭim* called *tokheḥah*, *ʿaqedah*, *teḥinnah*, and *baqqashah*.

3. The lamentation is one of the earliest forms of *piyyuṭ* in Israel. Many lamentations were written during the Middle Ages in Europe and countries of the East; some were about the terrors of the Crusades and other forms of oppression, others mourned the death of an individual or commemorated days of national mourning. This type was developed by the classical writers of *piyyuṭim;* many lamentations were also written by Italian and German *payṭanim*.

4. The special Sabbaths were called: *Shabbat Shirah* (Sabbath of Song—on which the reading of the Pentateuch includes the Song of the Sea); *Shabbat Zakhor* before Purim (when it is said: "Zakhor [remember] that which Amalek [archetypical enemy of Israel] did unto thee"); *Shabbat Gadol* (Great Sabbath) before Passover; and *Shabbat Shuvah* (Penitential Sabbath) during the ten days of penitence at the beginning of the New Year.

5. With reference to the kabbalistic center in Safed during the sixteenth century and its influence on the signing of *baqqashot*, see chapter 6.

6. An alphabetic acrostic that appears as far back as the Book of Psalms; Psalm 119 includes a number of verses for each letter of the alphabet. On commemorating a dead person it is customary to read the verses that form an acrostic of the deceased's name.

7. Donash ben-Labrat, linguist, poet, and musician, born in Fez (Morocco) c. 920. After moving to Baghdad he studied with Saʿadia Gaon and served as cantor and *payṭan*. In the sixth decade of the tenth century he arrived in Cordoba (Spain) where he became famous for a bold innovation: he introduced the use of the Arab quantitative meters in Hebrew poetry.

8. The term *yated* (plural *yetedot*) (peg) is derived from the Arabic *watad*. Like other prosodic Arabic terms, *yated* is borrowed from words describing parts of the tent in which the nomad lived. The rules of prosody were formulated systematically by the grammarian Khalīl ibn Aḥmad (d. 791) who used as his model the classical Arabic poetry that anteceded the emergence of Islam. The idea came to him as a result of watching a smith who beat an anvil rhythmically with his hammer, which brings to mind the story linking the invention of the science of music to Pythagoras. See chapter 2, notes 6, 34.

9. There are sixteen classical Arabic meters, not all of which could have been adapted to the Hebrew language. Actually, out of the eleven that were adapted, only a few were used.

10. Salomon ben Yehudah ibn Gabirol, (known in Latin as Avicebron) born c. 1021 in Malaga (Spain), died c. 1060 in Valencia. One of the greatest Hebrew poets and the first to introduce strophic forms into liturgical Hebrew poetry. As an important Neoplatonic philosopher, he exercised an influence on the kabbalists.

11. This name was given by the scholarly investigator of Hebrew poetry, Haim Brody.

12. From the time of its initial appearance in the tenth century, the *muwashshaḥ* was used for vocal music with a defined structure. It was widespread in North Africa and the Near East and until recently was a favorite musical form. See E. Gerson-Kiwi (1975) and Lois al-Faruqi (1975). In parallel to the *muwashshaḥ* developed another genre of strophic song the *Zadjal*. Mainly of folk inspiration, the *Zadjal* was written in the vernacular dialect and knew a considerable popularity.

13. Expert Arab singers preferred to open a strophic song with a line called *maṭla*—a guiding or orientational verse. This custom found its way into folk singing, and most strophic songs start with a *maṭlaʿ*. In rural songs of this region, the opening refrain is called *ṭalʿa*. The Spanish

muwashshaḥ also had an "exit"—the *kharja*. For the *kharja* the singers usually chose a refrain in colloquial Arabic or, on occasion, in ancient Spanish.

14. These *piyyuṭim* are among the Sabbath hymns recited at mealtime.

15. At the time of Shmuel Hannagid (993–1055), secular strophic songs were already being written in Hebrew.

16. In chapter 8 we expand on the tenet of creative traditional music.

17. This is closely related to the widespread technique of *contrafacta* which means the adaptation of known song melodies to new *piyyuṭim*. Instructions regarding the incipits (titles of pre-existing songs) to be used already appear in Spanish anthologies, particularly in those published after the early sixteenth century. See Katz (1988).

18. For additional details about the life and work of Najjara, see Yahalom (1982).

19. The traveler Romanelli, chapter 2 above, in his description of the musicians in Tangier (Morocco) referred to this technique.

20. In various anthologies there is a special section for introductions, which usually are also identified with the special *maqām* to which it is customary to sing each of them.

21. A more extensive discussion of the concept of the *maqām* and its historical development is included in Shiloah (1981).

22. Mi-Sinai tunes means tunes received by Moses on Mt. Sinai. *Sefer Hasidim*, par. 302, interprets the phrase in Exod. 19:19 "and God answered him by a voice" as: God taught Moses the biblical modes. In point of fact, the biblical modes originated in the Rhineland from the eleventh to fifteenth centuries.

Chapter 6: Music in the World of the Mystic

1. For futher details, see later paragraphs, "The *Baqqashot*" and "Influence of Kabalistic Mystical Theories on songs."

2. The philosopher and homiletic commentator, Rabbi Isaac ʿArama was the rabbi of the Zamora and Qalʿat Ayud communities (Spain). His homiletic preachings are an important source of information about the history of the Jews of Spain before the expulsion. Philosophically, he belonged to the anti-Aristotelian school of thought. He died in Naples, Italy.

3. The author lived in Guadalajara (Spain), like Moses de Leon, the author of the Zohar (Book of splendor). For the latter, see the discussion later in this chapter.

4. Ibn al-ʿArabī lived in Spain until 1194, after which he traveled to North Africa, Egypt, Iraq, and Turkey; he died in Damascus. Due to his major work, *The Meccan Revelation*, he was considered the greatest of all mystics. For further details see Shiloah (1979, pp. 151–54).

5. The *Hekhalot* literature is associated with traditions that have been preserved in talmudic and midrashic works, but it contains additional material as well. This literature has always been closely associated with Aramaic and Hebrew theurgic literature, particularly of more ancient times and of the Gaonic period. For additional details see G. Scholem (1967, pp. 40–79) and J. Dan (1978).

6. Attributing works to the tannaim is one of the pseudepigraphic devices employed by many medieval writers.

7. In cults of some Sufi orders *fanā'* is also seen as corresponding to a telescopic process of surrender of being by which the mystic submerges his being in his *shaykh*, *imām*, Ali, Muhammed, or God.

8. The text of this brief tract was published in S. I. Baer's *ʿAvodat Yisrael* (1868, pp. 547–52), the standard prayer book for Ashkenazic communities in Germany.

9. All languages are related to the holy tongue, or as Scholem writes, "Every language issues from a corruption of the aboriginal language—Hebrew—and they all remain related to it" (1967, p. 134).

10. Scholem's fourth lecture (1967, pp. 119–55) is entirely devoted to the doctrines and followers of this important figure. See also M. Idel (1982).

11. See chapter 2, note 7.

12. The text is included in Adler (1975, p. 36).

13. This statement is from the anonymous treatise *Sha῾rei Tsedeq.*

14. This is a quotation from the anonymous treatise *Sod ha-shalshelet* (Secret of the shalshelet [the name of one of the biblical accents]). See Idel (1982, p. 161).

15. *Dhikr* (Remembrance of God) is the name given to the ritual practiced by all Sufi orders. In most cases the act of collective remembrance is combined with *samā'*—listening to poetry and music as a means of intensifying the devotee's feelings of love for God.

16. Certain Western art music of the seventeenth century seems to have tried to imitate the idea and a number of musical works were composed for several choirs dispersed around the church.

17. The *Keter* is not known in Ashkenazic Jewry. In the Vitry prayer book associated with practices followed in France, the *Keter* is called *Qedushah-Rabba* (Magnum-Qedushah). The idea of the *Keter*—sung by the "hosts of Angels above" together with the people of Israel "below," thereby crowning the Almighty, blessed be He—is a distinctly mystical conception.

18. J. Dan (1980) explores the active powers influencing the world by reference to a thirteenth-century treatise, *On the Left Emanation* by Isaac ben Jacob ha-Cohen of Spain.

19. Based on the Song of Songs (2:6). In Morocco the *baqqashot* open with this *piyyuṭ* (see below).

20. All the ideas in the last section as well as those on the shofar in the next section have been gleaned from the Zohar. They all appear together in Shiloah (1977).

21. A general discussion about the shofar appears in chapter 3. The next section focuses on the kabbalistic symbols associated with the shofar.

22. The shofar is made of the horn of a ram or goat. The original horn, which is blown through a small aperature in its narrow end, is not fundamentally changed. The *shofar* can produce very few sounds, the three basic ones being: *teqi῾ah*—a long sound which usually ends on a slightly raised note; a note of embellishment is sometimes also added at the beginning. *Shevarim* are three short sharp *teqi῾ot* that sound like sighs. The *teru῾ah* in Ashkenazic tradition consists of many short, rather staccato units, while in the tradition of Oriental communities the *teru῾ah* is a long, wavering trill on a single note.

23. The reference is to Rabbi Shimon Bar-Yoḥai, a famous tanna, student of Rabbi Aqiba, who lived in the middle of the second century. He was among those who actively opposed Rome and its culture and therefore had to go into hiding for thirteen years. From the thirteenth century on, the kabbalists attributed the Zohar to him.

24. In the description of the resurrection of the dead in Muslim literature, the trumpet replaces the shofar; in Christian music it is the tuba.

25. The last words contain a parallel with Theophany, for the revelation of the deity there too was accompanied by loud sounds, lightning, and a heavy cloud.

26. The two manuscripts are from Germany; one can be found at present in the Hungarian Academy of Sciences in Budapest and the other in the Cambridge University library.

27. See note 2.

28. See note 18.

29. A popular tradition of the Middle Ages attributed to Pythagoras the ability to hear the music of the spheres, which ordinary mortals cannot hear. The Brotherhood of Purity, for example (see Shiloah, 1978, p. 38), believed, apparently due to traditions they absorbed through Byzantine culture, that Pythagoras, "thanks to the purity of the substance of his soul and the sagacity of his heart, heard the music produced by the rotation of the spheres and the heavenly bodies."

30. Philosopher, kabbalist, and astrologist, about whom little is known. He was born in

Spain and migrated to Italy after writing *Midrash ha-Ḥokhmah*. In 1245 he became an astrologist at the court of King Frederick the Second in Lombardy. *Midrash ha-Ḥokhmah* was never printed. The passage referred to is included in the manuscript.

31. The appellation "ha-Ari" which means the lion, entered popular usage at the end of the 16th century. Before reaching France, the Ari sojourned in Egypt, where he already began to devote himself to esoteric studies.

32. He was twenty-two years old when he began to deal with the kabbalah in accordance with the system of R. Moshe Cordovero. He was also drawn to the other esoteric sciences and for more than two years engaged in alchemy. After the death of the Ari he moved to Jerusalem where he officiated as a rabbi and head of a rabbinical academy. He died and was buried in Damascus where he spent the final years of his life.

33. Shlomo Alqabetz was born in 1508 apparently in Salonika, Greece; he was a kabbalist, preacher, and *payṭan*. He died in Safed in 1584.

34. The notebook is now in the National University Library, Jerusalem.

35. See chapter 5, note 4.

36. A Jewish traveler of the nineteenth century, Israel Yosef chose to be known as Benjamin the Second, as he hoped to emulate the famous Jewish medieval traveler Benjamin of Tudela. He was born in Romania in 1818; from the age of twenty-six until his death in 1864, he traveled through the countries of the Near and Far East and America. He published his impressions in a book called *The Travels of Israel*.

37. An article by P. Fenton (1975) includes a comprehensive survey of the *baqqashot* of the East and West.

38. *Mafṭirim* is derived from *mafṭir*—one who concludes; the three or more concluding verses of the weekly Sabbath Torah portion are called *mafṭirim*. The term was adopted as the name of a famous group of Turkish singers of religious music.

39. Affected by modern influences, the *baqqashot* borrowed a concept from the world of sports—the derby. Indeed, during the *baqqashot* days, two Jerusalem synagogues hold a "derby," competing over the singing of *baqqashot* songs.

40. R. Shalem Shabazi was the central figure in establishing the *diwān* of the Yemenite Jews, which is exclusively devoted to poetry (see chapter 8). His poems occupy the largest part of the various *diwāns* that were published from the seventeenth century on. Starting with the end of the seventeenth century the printers of *diwāns* usually attribute them to Shabazi, although the work of other poets may be included as well. See Y. Tovi and Shalom (1988).

41. This is one of a group of songs sung while accompanying the groom from place to place, as part of the marriage ceremonies. It is a short song with a fairly simple structure and tune.

Chapter 7: Non-Synagogal Music—Between Sacred and Secular

1. See chapter 2, note 1.

2. In a few Near Eastern congregations it is customary to read the words of widsom and morality of the Mishnaic tractate *Avot* in a solemn, ornate tune on the six Sabbaths between Passover and Shavuoth, after the morning or afternoon prayer. The cantors and other people with good voices, including children, participate in the singing.

3. In the previous chapter we mentioned a notebook with particular musical interest that belonged to Isaac Offenbach, the father of the famous opera composer.

4. Influenced by processes of modernization, it is becoming increasingly accepted practice among traditional groups to write down the songs and even publish them.

5. For the participation of Jewish musicians in the musical activities of surrounding communities, see L. D. Loeb (1972); Nettl and Shiloah (1978); Shiloah (1983).

6. See chapter 3, note 20.

7. B. Nettl (1973, pp. 53–54) considers the cumulative song to be a "special type of humorous song found in many countries." He defines it as a song "in which each stanza, while presenting something new, also incorporates elements from the previous stanzas."

8. The texts were written by Kirchhain, who set his own poems to music. The collection was printed by a Jewish press in Fürth (Germany).

9. Chapter 5 includes a brief explanation of the classical Arab *qaṣīda*. The Moroccan *qaṣīda* preserves the quantitative meter of the classical *qaṣīda*, but also evolved its own characteristic qualities, to some extent under the influence of the surrounding Berbers. The text is in colloquial Arabic (the Maghrib dialect) and the structure is like a folk song, with a refrain. The subject matter was more varied, touching on the lives of the individual and the group. See Amzalag (1984).

10. Rabbi Israel ben Eliezer Baʿal Shem Tov (1698 or 1700 to 1760) is the founder of the Hasidic movement. According to the Hasidic tradition, at the age of 36 he was revealed as a teacher and guide. His doctrine stressed *devequt* (devoted adherence to the Almighty), the importance of devout individual worship, and the striving for perfection of each person.

11. Rabbi Nahman is the founder of Bretslav Hasidut. He was born in 1772 and died in Uman (Russia) in 1810. His grave there has always been the site of pilgrimages by his disciples. He promulgated a doctrine of spiritual messianism and belief in the predestined birth of the Messiah from among his offspring.

12. See chapter 5, note 23.

13. According to the tradition, Rabbi Meir Baʿal Han-nes is outstanding as a wise and just man (*ḥakham* and *tsaddiq*) who lived in the second century C.E. and was buried in Tiberias. Every year festivities are held at his grave, in the nature of a prelude to the joyous jubilee held for R. Shimʿon Bar-Yoḥai four days later, on the thirty-third day of the *ʿOmer*.

14. This is the name of a comprehensive codex of prescribed, traditional rules and regulations. The *Shulḥan ʿArukh* was written with the intention of acquainting the masses with the rules of behavior in simple form, eliminating all controversial differences of opinion that might have existed. It became the definitive arbiter with respect to the observance of traditional law in all parts of the Jewish Diaspora.

15. The *genizah* is a secret hiding place, a disposal site for preserving books in Hebrew that have gone out of use. The genizah in the Ezra Synagogue in Old Cairo that was discovered in 1896–97 included some two hundred thousand pages; they are now in the Cambridge library and other large libraries in various places. The material is of utmost importance as a source of information about the Jews.

16. He is the Ezra who, with the help of Cyrus, king of Persia, led the exiles back to their land to build the Second Temple.

17. Mordekhai is the hero of the Scroll of Esther.

18. During Christian pilgrimages to holy sites throughout the world it is also customary to sing songs about stations along the way.

19. For more about the songs of the *ziyāra* (pilgrimages) among the Jews of Babylonia, see Avishur (1982).

20. The types of *shirot* will be described in the next chapter.

21. A. Merriam (1964, p. 194) includes songs of insult among the various topical songs, but our songs of curses do not belong in this category; they are rather a special type of humorous songs the aim of which seems to confirm Merriam's statement that "in song the individual or the group can apparently express deep-seated feelings not permissibly verbalized in other contexts" (p. 190).

22. *Ṣaḥn* is the name of a copper plate on which the singer beats the rhythm with a ring.

23. Five years before Gerson-Kiwi, Johanna Spector (1960) published a study of the same subject, that is, the wedding songs of the Jewish women of Ṣanʿa. For the art of singing among Moroccan women see Yedida Stillman (1980).

24. The women of Ḥabban customarily tied slender chains to their hair which shook as their heads moved, creating a thin, metallic sound.

Chapter 8: Folk Creativity and Performance Practice

1. Although dealing in particular with Yugoslav epic poetry, in this respect Lord's (1965) had been a highly influential book. The musical component in this folk creativity is treated in a general manner in Brailoiu (1959); Herzog (1950); Nettl (1983, chap. 14); and for the Middle East, Shiloah (1974).

2. It is true that folkloristic music and art music in the East are both transmitted orally, with all that implies; from this standpoint, they largely behave in similar fashion. But urban art music is subject to defined theoretical rules, various social and aesthetic norms, and in large measure it differentiates among the artist, the amateur, and the ordinary listener.

3. Most of the songs sung by the men are in Hebrew while those of the women are all in Arabic dialect. The women generally avoided adapting the men's *piyyuṭ* tunes to their Arabic-language songs.

4. The song in its entirety is included in Shiloah (1970), which contains a comprehensive discussion on the emergence and development of the songs of the various ethnic groups.

5. The last stanza hints at the prohibition forbidding a woman to sing in public.

6. Herzog writes: "Even when folk singers are literate they rarely use writing for their songs. . . . Writing down the words in song-books is a relatively recent practice" (1950, p. 1033).

7. *Dīwān* is an Arabic word which in this context means anthology of poems or songs.

8. The Arabic term *nashīd* usually designates the loud and solemn recitation of poetry. It also means reciprocal singing, that is to say one group of people sings for another group. Hence, the *nashīd* is a group song and cannot be performed in solo.

9. For details about the Yemenite dance see chapter 9.

10. The *Ḥidā'* is one of the oldest types of Arabic song. It is mentioned in pre-Islamic poetry as the "song of camels." In the rural folk song of today, it is used as a general appellation for songs for weddings and other festive occasions.

11. For further details about the musical aspects of this type, see Sharvit and Ephrayim (1984).

12. This custom, unique to orthodox Ashkenazim, is followed when a son reaches the age of three; it is explained as fulfilling a vow not to cut a boy's hair until he is three. The ceremony is held in the presence of the *tsaddiq* who is the child's patron. It may be a symbolic rite of passage stressing the child's masculinity, as until then he has lived together with the girls, under his mother's protection. From now on he attends the Ḥeder and begins to engage in biblical studies.

13. In his book the Iraqi composer Jalāl al-Ḥanafī (1964) enumerated 188 famous musicians, 15 percent of them Jews.

14. The rhythmic component is important for the definition and character of any given Iraqi *maqām*.

15. These special words and expressions have no connection with the texts of the songs—a large part of them are not even in Arabic; they serve to identify various kinds of *maqāmāt*.

16. This important congress was held under the auspices of the Egyptian King Fuad the First, with the participation of the greatest European scholars of traditional music such as Bartók, Sachs, Lachmann, Farmer, and others. Artists representing all the Arab musical centers also participated.

17. See chapter 7, note 8.

18. The *Hackbrett* and *cimbalom* are respectively the German and Hungarian names for dulcimer—a trapeze-shaped instrument whose strings are set in vibration by small hand-held hammers. The instrument resembles the Near Eastern *santūr* described in chapter 1, note 4.

Chapter 9: The Dance

1. Taken from an unpublished lecture delivered by Bathja Bayer at an international seminar on dance in the Bible, held in Jerusalem in August 1978.

2. In the same Mishnaic chapter *Sukkah,* there is a description of a dance with torches; the most important personalities in Jewry took part in it. The Babylonian Talmud refers as follows to the same Mishnah: "It is told of Rabban Shimon ben Gamliel that when he celebrated *Simḥat Beit ha-Sho'evah* [the water-drawing festival] he would take eight flaming torches and toss each one high in the air, and the one never touched the other."

3. This universal concept, integrating the dance with reference to an extensive series of socio-cultural relationships, is the focal point of two works: C. Sachs (1963) and Royce (1977).

4. On both of these holidays people are obligated to be happy and to actively demonstrate this happiness, which they usually do by dancing. The rabbinical authorities have placed no ban on dancing that is an expression of religious ecstasy.

5. For information about the *kurrāj* dances of the Arabs during the Middle Ages, and their similarity to dances practiced by other cultures, see Shiloah (1962).

6. This source, like those that follow in this context, is included in Friedhaber (1984, pp. 27–39).

7. This appears in the book by Kirchhain, *Simhath ha-nefesh,* which includes both the words and notes of Jewish songs, as mentioned in chapter 7, note 8.

8. *The Dibbuk* is the famous play by S. Ansky (1863–1920). It was first performed in Russia and produced by Vachtangov. It has since become a permanent part of the Habima Theater's repertoire.

9. In recent years in Israel, influenced by the new way of life, development of the dance has been based on both new and traditional steps.

10. The Jews of Yemen explain their abstention from the use of musical instruments as associated with mourning for the destruction of the Temple; this is discussed more fully in chapter 3. However, the Jewish position undoubtedly received further support from the fact that the surrounding Muslim society also refrained—for religious reasons—from playing instruments.

11. In chapter 10 we shall expand on the role of external elements in initiating some of the processes of change that occurred within the ethnic groups.

12. For more on Inbal see chapter 10.

Chapter 10: Looking Backward and Forward

1. The emic/etic dichotomy is borrowed from linguistics where the terms characterize opposing approaches to the study of linguistic data. According to Crystal (1987): "An 'etic' approach is one where the physical patterns of language are described with a minimum of reference to their function within the language system. An 'emic' approach, by contrast, takes full account of functional relationships, setting up a closed system of abstract constructive units, on the basis of a description." In ethnomusicology, "emic" is used to depict the viewpoint of a member of the society being studied; "etic" represents the viewpoint of the analyst.

2. Before the establishment of the State of Israel, immigrants arrived in the country either individually or in small groups. Their social absorption was generally achieved through the efforts of people from similar backgrounds who to a great extent had continued to perpetuate the traditional patterns of life of their countries of origin. At that time there was no social pressure in the direction of change.

3. According to this conception, the term "authentic" was associated with original, traditional, and ancient. Those who upheld this image believed that tradition reflects something static, something that maintains its own unchanging identity. In their view it was only exposure to modern life that caused changes to occur, and these changes were looked upon as a "corruption."

4. Isḥāq al-Mawṣilī on his part accused the "modernists" of his day of blurring the simple, clear lines of classical music by loading it with excessive adornment.

5. The first musical school was established in Tel Aviv in 1909, when the total population of the city was five thousand souls. Extensive musical activity began after 1926, the year in which the well-known conductor of the Petersburg Opera House, Mark Golinkin, formed the pioneering Tel Aviv opera.

6. Michael Ivanovitz Glinka (1804–57) was considered the creator of the national Russian opera and founder of the modern school of Russian music.

7. J. Hirshberg (1980, p. 5), commenting on this information, says: "Sandberg's extreme approach led to no viable musical results, but traces of similar ideas continued to appear in critical and journalistic writings in later years."

8. Before the State of Israel was established, the *yishuv*—short for "Jewish Yishuv"—signified the resident Jewish national population and its institutions.

9. Ancient musical modes were used for the purpose of endowing the music of the land of Israel with a special character; it was hoped that this would be achieved by avoiding the use of conventional harmonies.

10. This part of the article is quoted here in full.

11. The Center for the Integration of the Oriental Jewish Heritage in Culture and Education was established in 1978 as a unit attached to the Ministry of Education with the aim to lend support to institutions and individuals for the preservation, study, and promulgation of the distinct heritage of various communities.

Bibliography

Abadi, Mordechay. 1873. *Miqra Qodesh.* Aleppo: Eliahu Ḥay (Hebrew).

Adaqi, Yehiel, and Uri Sharvit. 1981. *A Treasury of Jewish Yemenite Chants.* Jerusalem: The Israeli Institute for Sacred Music (Hebrew and English).

Adler, Israel. 1966. *La pratique musicale savante dans quelques communautés juives en Europe aux 17 et 18 Siècles.* Paris: Mouton and Co La Haye.

———. 1975. *Hebrew Writings Concerning Music.* RISM, Ser. BIX². München: Henle Verlag.

Algazi, Leon. 1958. *Chants sephardis.* London: World Sephardi Federation.

Amzalag, Abraham. 1984. "The Qasida in Shir Yedidot." *Pe'amim* 19: 88–112 (Hebrew).

Armistead, Samuel G. 1982. "New Perspectives in Judeo-Spanish Ballad Research." In I. Ben-Ami, ed., *The Sephardi and Oriental Jewish Heritage Studies.* Jerusalem: Magnes Press, Hebrew University, pp. 225–36.

Armistead, Samuel G, and Joseph H. Silverman. 1977. *Romances judeo-españoles de Tanger recogidos por Zarita Nahon.* Madrid: Catedra-Seminario Menendez Pidal, Universidad de Madrid.

———. 1978. *El Romancero Judeo-Español en el archivo Menendez Pidal.* 3 vols. Madrid: Catedra-Seminario Menendez Pidal, Universidad de Madrid.

Ashtor, Eliahu. 1960. *The Jews of Moslem Spain.* 2 vols. Jerusalem: Kiryat Sefer (Hebrew). English trans. 1973. Philadelphia: Jewish Publication Society of America.

Attal, Robert. 1973. *Les Juifs d'Afrique du nord: Bibliographie.* Jerusalem: Ben-Zvi Institute.

Attias, Moshe. 1961. *Romancero Sepharadi.* Jerusalem: Ben Zvi Institute (Hebrew).

———. 1972. *Cancionero judeo-español.* Jerusalem: Centro de estudios sobre el judaismo de Salonica (Hebrew).

Avenary, H. 1960. "Etudes sur le cancionero judeo-espagnol du 16 et 17 Siècle." *Sefarad* 20: 377–94.

———. 1964. "The Hasidic Nigun—Ethos and Melos of a Folk Liturgy." *Journal of the International Folk Music Council* 16: 660–63. Reprint in Avenary (1979, pp. 154–58).

———. 1968. "Gentile Songs as a Source of Inspiration for Israel Najjara." *Proceedings of the Fourth World Congress of Jewish Studies,* 2: 383–84. Jerusalem: World Union of Jewish Studies (Hebrew). Reprint in Avenary (1979, pp. 186–190).

———. 1971. "Flutes for a Bride or a Dead Man." *Orbis Musicae* 1, no. 1: 11–24. Reprint in Avenary (1979, pp. 10–22).

———. 1973. "The Science of Music with Jews of the 13th and 14th Centuries." *Proceedings of the Fifth World Congress of Jewish Studies* 4: 53–55, Jerusalem: World Union of Jewish Studies (Hebrew).

———. 1975. "The Earliest Notation of Ashkenazi Bible Chant." *Journal of Jewish Studies* 26: 132–50.

———. 1976. *Melodies of the Pentateuch in the Ashkenazic Tradition from 1500 to 1900*. Tel Aviv: Tel Aviv University (Hebrew).

———. 1979. *Encounters of East and West in Music*. Tel Aviv: Tel Aviv University.

———. 1982. "Contacts between Church and Synagogue Music." In J. Cohen, ed., *Proceedings of the World Congress on Jewish Music, Jerusalem 1978*. Tel Aviv: The Institute for the Translation of Hebrew Literature Ltd., pp. 89–106.

Avishur, Y. 1982. "Iraqi-Jewish Songs of Pilgrimage to the Tombs of Saints in Judeo-Arabic." *Studies on History and Culture of Iraqi Jewry* 2: 151–92. Or Yehuda: Institute for Research on Iraqi Jewry (Hebrew).

———. 1987. *Women's Folk Songs in Judeo-Arabic from Jews in Iraq*. Or Yehuda: Institute for Research in Iraqi Jewry (Hebrew).

Azikeri, A. 1601. *Sefer ha-Ḥaredim*. Venezia.

Baer, Seligman Issac. 1868. *Avodat Yisrael*. Roedelheim (Germany).

Bakhrakh, Ya'ir Ḥayyim. 1896. *Ḥavvat Ya'ir*. Lemberg: Nick.

Bartok, B. 1936. "Why and How We Collect Folk Music" (Hungarian). English version in Benjamin Suchoff ed., *Bela Bartok Essays*. London: Faber & Faber.

Bayer, Bathja. 1963. *The Material Relics of Music in Ancient Palestine and its Environs—An Archaeological Inventory*. Tel Aviv: Israel Music Institute.

———. 1968. "The Biblical Nebel." *Yuval* 1: 89–131.

———. 1978. Unpublished lecture, delivered at an International Seminar on Dance in the Bible, Jerusalem.

Ben-Ami, Issachar. 1975. *Moroccan Jewry: Ethno-Cultural Studies*. Jerusalem: Rubin Mass (Hebrew).

———. 1984. *The Veneration of Saints among Moroccan Jews*. Jerusalem: Magnes Press (Hebrew). French trans. *Culte des saints.*, 1990, Paris: Maisonneuve.

Benichou, Paul. 1968. *Romancero Judeo-espagnol de Marruecos*. Madrid: Castalia.

Benjamin the Second. 1859. *Sefer mas'ei yisrael* (as revised by David Gordon). lyck.

Ben-Moshe, Sh. 1981. "Art and Theatre." *Ba-ma'arakhah* 241: 24 (Hebrew).

Blacking, John. 1978. "Some Problems of Theory and Method in the Study of Musical Change." *Yearbook of the International Folk Music Council* 9: 1–26.

———. 1986. "Identifying Processes of Musical Change." *The World of Music*. 1: 3–15.

Brauer, Erich. 1948. *The Jews of Kurdistan: An Ethnological Study*. Ed. and trans. into Hebrew by Raphael Patai. Jerusalem: The Palestine Institute of Folklore and Ethnology.

Brailoiu, Constantin. 1959. "Folklore musical." *Encyclopédie de la musique*. Fasquelle, Paris.

Claire, Dom Jean. 1982. "Points de contact entre répertoires juif et Chrétiens, 'Vieux-romain et gregorien.' " In J. Cohen, ed., *Proceedings of the World Congress on Jewish Music, Jerusalem, 1978*. Tel Aviv: The Institute for the Translation of Hebrew Literature Ltd., pp. 107–14.

Cohen, Erik, and Amnon Shiloah. 1985. "Major Trends of Change in Jewish Oriental Ethnic Music in Israel." *Popular Music* 5: 199–223.

Cohen, Judith. 1974. "Jubal in the Middle Ages." *Yuval* 3: 83–99.

Cohen, Yardena. 1963. *With Drum and Dance*. Tel Aviv: Sifriyat Po'alim (Hebrew).

Corbin, Solange. 1960. *L'Eglise à la conquête de sa musique*. Paris: Gallimard.

———. 1961. "La cantillation des rituels chrétiens." *Revue de Musicologie* 47: 3–36.

Crystal, David. 1987. *A Dictionary of Linguistics and Phonetics*. 2d ed. Oxford: Basic Blackwell.

Dan, Joseph. 1978. "Mysticism in Jewish History, Religion and Literature." In J. Dan and Frank Talmage, *Studies in Jewish Mysticism*. Cambridge, Mass: Association for Jewish Studies, pp. 1–14.

———. 1980. "Samael, Lilith and the Concept of Evil in Early Kabbalah." *Association of Jewish Studies Review* 5: 17–40.

Daniel, Sh. 1952. *Neginah and Ḥasidism in Beit Kozmir.* Tel-Aviv (Hebrew).

Davis, Ruth Frances. 1984–85. "Songs of the Jews on the Island of Djerba. A Comparison between Two Surveys." *Musica Judaica* 7, no. 1: 23–33.

———. 1986. "Some Relations between Three Piyyuṭim from Djerba and Three Arabic Songs" *The Maghreb Review* vol. 11, no. 5–6, pp. 134–44.

Delacroix, Eugène. 1893. *Journal d'Eugène Delacroix.* Paris: Plon.

Droyanov, A. 1963. *Book of Jokes and Wit.* 3 vols. Tel Aviv: Dvir (Hebrew).

Dumas. Alexandre (Père). 1849. *Le Veloce en Tanger, Alger et Tunis.* Bruxelles.

El Gil Kaʿammim. 1969. Jerusalem (Hebrew).

d'Erlanger, R. trans. 1930–39. *La musique arabe.* 6 vols. Paris: Geuthner.

Farmer, H. G. 1939. *al-Fāzābī's Arabic-Latin Writings on Music.* London: Hinzrichen. second ed. 1960.

———. 1957. "The Music of Islam." *The New Oxford History of Music.* London: Oxford University Press. Reprinted 1960, I, 421–78.

al-Faruqi, L. I. 1975. "Muwashshaḥ: A Vocal Form in Islamic Culture." *Ethnomusicology* 19, no 1: 1–29.

al-Fasi, Rabbi Yitsḥaq. 1884. *Responsa.* Warsaw.

Fellerer, K. G. 1982. "Jewish Elements in Pre-Gregorian Chants." In J. Cohen, ed., *Proceedings of the World Congress on Jewish Music, Jerusalem 1978.* Tel Aviv: The Institute for the Translation of Hebrew Literature Ltd., pp. 115–18.

Fenton, P. 1975. "Les baqqashot d'orient et d'occident." *Revue des Etudes Juives* 134, nos. 1–2: 101–27.

Fleischer, E. 1974. "The Influence of Choral Elements on the Formation and Development of the *Piyyuṭ* Genres." *Yuval* 3: 18–47. Jerusalem: Magnes Press (Hebrew).

———. 1975. *Hebrew Religious Poetry in the Middle Ages.* Jerusalem: Keter (Hebrew).

Flusser, David. 1958. "The Dead Sea Sect and Pre-Pauline Christianity." *Scripta Hierosolymitana* 4: 255–66.

———. 1968. "The Social Message from Qumran." *Journal of World History* 11, nos. 1–2: 107–15.

Frazer, J. G. 1919. *Folklore in the Old Testament.* 3 vols. London: Macmillan.

Friedhaber, Zvi. 1984. *Dance among the Jewish People.* Tel Aviv: The Wingeit Institute (Hebrew).

———. 1988. "Dance in the Jewish Communities of the Duchy of Mantua in the 17th and 18th Centuries." *Peʿamim* 37: 67–77 (Hebrew).

Gaon, M. D. 1930–32. "R. Israel Najjara and his Hymns." *Mizraḥ wu-Maʿarav* 5: 145–63 (Hebrew).

Gerson-Kiwi, Edith. 1964. "On the Musical Sources of the Judeo-Hispanic Romance." *The Musical Quarterly* 50: 31–43; Reprint in Gerson-Kiwi (1980b, pp. 154–66).

———. 1965. "Women's Songs from the Yemen: Their Tonal Structure and Form." *The Commonwealth of Music. In Memoriam Curt Sachs.* New York, pp. 97–103. Reprint in Gerson-Kiwi (1980b, pp. 147–53).

———. 1974a. "Robert Lachmann: His Achievement and His Legacy." *Yuval* 3: 100–108.

———. ed. 1974b. *Robert Lachmann—Posthumous Works I: Die Musik in Volksleben Nordafrikas; Orientalische Musik und Antike.* Jerusalem: The Hebrew University, Yuval Monograph Series, 2.

———. 1975. "Musical Settings of the Andalusian Muwashshah–Poetry in Oral Tradition." *Festschrift Kurt Blaukopf.* Wien, pp. 33–47. Reprint in Gerson-Kiwi (1980b), pp. 167–81.

———. ed. 1978. *Robert Lachmann—Posthumous Works II: Gesange der Juden auf der Insel Djerba.* Jerusalem: The Hebrew University, Yuval Monograph Series, 7.

———. 1980a. "Melodic Patterns in Asiatic Rituals—The Quest of Sound Alienation." *Israel Studies in Musicology* 2: 27–31.

———. 1980b. *Migrations and Mutations of the Music in East and West—Selected Writings.* Tel Aviv: Tel Aviv University.

Ginzberg, Louis. 1968. *The Legends of the Bible.* Philadelphia: The Jewish Publication Society of America. 7 vols.

Goitein, S. D. 1958. "Women as Creators of Types of Literature in the Bible." In Goitein, *Bible Studies.* Tel Aviv: Yavneh, pp. 248–317 (Hebrew).

———. 1962. *Jewish Education in Muslim Countries Based on Records from the Cairo Geniza.* Jerusalem: The Ben-Zvi Institute (Hebrew).

———. 1981. "On the Pilgrim's Way to Ezechiel's Tomb." *Studies on History and Culture of Iraqi Jewry* 1: 13–18 (Hebrew).

Graburn, N.H.H., ed. 1976. *Ethnic and Tourist Arts.* Berkeley: University of California Press.

Gressmann, H. 1927. *Altorientalische Bilder zum Alter Testament.* Berlin: Leipzig.

Hahn-Nordlingen, Joseph. 1722–23. *Yosif Omets.* Frankfurt a. M: Hermon (Hebrew).

Hajdu, André. 1971. "Le Niggun Meron." *Yuval* 2: 73–114.

Halper, G., and H. Abramovitz. 1984. "The Celebration of Seherane in Kurdistan and Israel." In Shlomo Deshen and Moshe Shoked, eds., *Oriental Jews.* Jerusalem.

al-Ḥanafī, Jalāl. 1964. *The Baghdadi Singers and the Iraqi Maqam.* Baghdad (Arabic).

al-Ḥarizi, Yehudah., ed. 1952. *Taḥkemoni.* Tel Aviv: Maḥbarot Le-Sifrut (Hebrew).

Ḥassan, Qasim Sheherazade. 1980. *Les instruments de musique en Iraq.* Paris: Mouton.

Ḥazzan, Moshe. 1886. *Kerekh Romi (Responsa).* Livorno.

Heinemann, Joseph. 1966. *Prayer in the Period of the Tanna'im and the Amora'im.* 2d ed. Jerusalem: Magnes Press (Hebrew).

Hemsi, Alberto. 1932–1938. *Coplas Sefardies (Chansons Judeo-Espagnoles).* Alexandria: Edition Orientale de Musique. 5 fascicles.

———. 1938. *Coplas Sefardies.* op. 33. Alexandria: Edition Orientale de Musique.

———. 1969–73. *Coplas Sefardies* (Chansons Judeo-espagnoles). Paris: Author, 5 fascicules.

Herzog, Avigdor, and André Hajdu. 1967. "A la recherche du *Tonus Peregrinus* dans la tradition musicale juive." *Yuval* 1: 194–203.

Herzog, George. 1950. "Song." In M. Leah, ed., *Funk and Wagnall's Standard Dictionary of Folklore, Mythology and Legend.* New York, pp. 1032–50.

Hirshberg, Jehoash. 1980. "The Emergence of Israeli Art Music." *Aspects of Music in Israel.* Tel Aviv: Israel Composer's League, pp. 3–15.

Idel, Moshe. 1982. "Music and Prophetic Kabbalah." *Yuval* 4: 150–69.

Idelsohn, A. Z. 1908. "The Jews of Yemen and Their Songs." *Luwaḥ Erets Yisrael* 14: 101–54. Offprint, 1908. Jerusalem: A. M. Luntz (Hebrew).

———. 1913a. "Die Maqamen in der hebräischen Poesie der orientalischen Juden." *Monatsschrift für Geschichte und Wissenschaft des Judentums* 57 (N.S. 21): 314–25.

———. 1913b. "Die Maqamen der arabischen Musik." *Sammelbände der Internationale Musikgesellschaft* 15, no. 1: 1–63.

———. 1914–33. *Hebräisch-Orientalischer Melodienschatz.* Vols. 1–10. Hebrew, *Ozar Neginot Yisrael,* vols. 1–5, 1922–28. English *Thesaurus of Hebrew Oriental Melodies,* vols. 1–2, 6–10, 1923–33. All three versions were printed by Breitkopf and Hartel Lecpzig. Reprints, Amsterdam: B. M. Israel, 1965 and New York: Ktav Publishing House, 1983.

———. 1918. "The Jews of Yemen, Their Poetry and Music." *Reshumot* 1: 3–66 (Odessa). Reprint Tel Aviv, 1925 (Hebrew).

———. 1918–19. "The Yemenite Poet R. Shalom b. Joseph Shabazi and his Hebrew Poetry." *Mizraḥ Wu-Ma'arav* 1, no. 1: 8–16; 2, no. 2: 128–37.

———. 1929. *Jewish Music in Its Historical Development.* New York: Henry Holt. Reprint New

York: Tudor Pub. Co., 1944, 1948 and New York: Schocken Books, 1967, 1972, 1975, 1981.

Kadman, Gurit. 1952. "Yemenite Dances and their Influence on the New Israeli Folk Dances." *Journal of the International Folk Music Council* 4: 27–30.

Katz, Israel. 1968. "A Judeo-Spanish Romancero." *Ethnomusicology* 12, no. 1: 72–85.

———. 1973. "The 'Myth' of the Sephardic Musical Legacy from Spain." *Proceedings of the Fifth World Congress of Jewish Studies* 4: 237–43.

———. 1988. "Contrafacta and the Judeo-Spanish Romancero: A Musicological View." *Hispanic Studies in Honor of Joseph H. Silverman*. Newark, Del: Juan de la Cuesta, pp. 169–87.

Kfir, Elkana. 1982. *Shivḥei ha-Ari ha-Shalem*. Safed: E. Kfir (Hebrew).

Kirchhain, Elchanan-Henle. 1727. *Simhath ha-nefesh (The delight of the soul)*. Fürth (Germany). New York: J. Schatzky, 1926.

Lachmann, Robert. 1940. *Jewish Cantillation and Song in the Isle of Djerba*. Jerusalem: Azriel Press, Archives of Oriental Music, The Hebrew University.

Laufer, A. 1973. "Hand and Head Signals used in the Public Reading of the Torah." *Proceedings of the Fifth World Congress of Jewish Studies* 4: 92–105.

Levy, Issac. 1959. *Chants judeo-espagnols*. London: World Sephardi Federation.

Loeb, L. D. 1972. "The Jewish Musician and the Music of Fars." *Asian Music* 4 no. 1: 3–14.

Lord, Albert B. 1965. *The Singer of Tales*. New York: Athenaum.

Manor, G. 1975. *Inbal: Quest for a Movement-Language*. Tel Aviv: Bank Leumi.

Mazar, E. 1983. *Tel-Kasila*. Tel Aviv: Haarez Museum.

Mazor, Yaʿacov. 1978. "The Place of Music in a Ḥasidic Wedding." *Dukhan* 11: 72–75 (Hebrew).

Melamed, E. Z. 1966. "The Renewal of Traditional Singing." *Dukhan* 8:7–22 (Hebrew).

Menaḥem Di Lonzano. 1575. *Pizmonim wu-Baqqashot*. Constantinople.

———. 1618. *Shetei Yadot*. Venezia.

Menendez Pidal, Ramon. 1906–7. "Catalogo del romancero judeo-español." *Culture Española* 4: 1045–77; 5: 161–99. Reprinted with abbreviation of various romances in *El Romancero: teorias e investigaciones*. Madrid, 1928, pp. 101–83. Reprint in *Los romances de America*. Buenos Aires: Mexico D.F., 1948, pp. 121–88.

Merriam, Alan. 1964. *The Anthropology of Music*. Evanston: Northwestern University Press.

Midrash Hag-gadol, ed., 1947. *Mordekhay Margaliot*. Jerusalem: Mosad ha-Rav Kuk.

Muenster, Sebastian. 1524. *Institutes grammaticae in Hebraean Linguam*. Basel.

Nachman of Breslav. 1951. *Rabbi Nachman Writings*. Tel Aviv: A. Steinman (Hebrew).

Najjara, Yisrael. 1587. *Zemirot Yisrael*. Safed.

Ne'eman, Y. L. 1978. "The *Nusaḥ* of the Ashkenazic 'Seven Blessings.' " *Dukhan* 11: 87–98 (Hebrew).

Nettl, Bruno. 1964. *Theory and Method in Ethnomusicology*. New York: Free Press.

———. 1973. *Folk and Traditional Music of the Western Continents*. 2d ed. New Jersey: Prentice-Hall.

———. 1978. "Some Aspects of the History of World Music in the Twentieth Century: Questions, Problems and Concepts." *Ethnomusicology* 22: 423–36.

———. 1983. *The Study of Ethnomusicology*. Urbana: University of Illinois Press.

Nettl, Bruno, and Amnon Shiloah. 1978. "Persian Classical Music in Israel: A Preliminary Report." *Israel Studies in Musicology* 1: 142–58.

Neubauer, Adolph, ed. 1895. *Mediaeval Jewish Chronicles and Chronological Notes*. Oxford: Clarendon.

Noy, Dov, ed. 1964. *Jewish Folktales from Morocco*. Jerusalem: Bitfuzot Hagolah (Hebrew).

Noy, Meir. 1974. "The Cancelled Wedding Motif in Yiddish Folk-Song—A bibliographical Survey." *Folklore Research Center Studies* 4: 53–68 (Hebrew).

Parisot, dom Jean. 1901. *Rapport sur une mission scientifique en Turquie et Syrie*. Paris.

———. 1902. "Notes sur les recitatifs israelites Orientaux." In *Dictionnaire de la Bible de Vigouroux*, vol. 8.

Pirqe Rabbi Eliezer. 1973. Jerusalem: Eshkol. English annotated trans. by Gerald Friedlander. 1965. New York: Hermon Press.

Raphael, F. 1974. "Le mariage Juif dans la Campagne alsacienne dans la deuxième moitié du 19 Siècle." *Folklore Research Center Studies* 4: 181.

Ratzabi, Yehudah. 1966. "Alien Melodies in Hebrew Music." *Tazlil* 6: 8–13 (Hebrew).

———. 1968. "Form and Melody in the Jewish Song of Yemen." *Tazlil* 8: 15–22 (Hebrew).

Ravina, M. 1927. "Judaism in Music." *The Daily Davar.* June 3, 1927 (Hebrew).

Redfield, R. and M. Singer. 1969. "The Cultural Role of Cities." In R. Senett, ed., *Classical Essays in the Culture of Cities.* New York: Appleton-Century-Crofts, pp. 206–33.

Reuchlin, Johannes. 1518. *De Accentibus et Orthographia linguae Hebraicae.* Hagenau.

Royce, Anya Peterson. 1977. *The Anthropology of Dance.* Bloomington: Indiana University Press.

Sachs, Curt. 1963. *World History of the Dance.* New York: Norton.

———. 1943. *The Rise of Music in the Ancient World. East and West.* New York: Norton.

Schirmann, H., ed. 1969. *Romanelli's Selected Writings.* Jerusalem: Mosad Bialik (Hebrew).

Schirmann, H. 1979. *History of Hebrew Drama and Poetry.* 2 vols. Jerusalem: Mosad Bialik (Hebrew).

Schleifer, Eliahu. 1986. "Idelsohn's Scholarly and Literary Publications: An Annotated Bibliography." *Yuval* 5: 53–180. Jerusalem: Magnes Press.

Scholem, Gershom. 1967. *Major Trends in Jewish Mysticism.* New York: Schocken.

———. 1971. "Kabbalah." *Encyclopaedia Judaica.* Vol. 10, pp. 490–653.

———. 1975. *The Beginning of the Kabbalah and the Bahir Book.* Jerusalem: Akademon (Hebrew).

Sharvit, Uri and Ya'acov Ephrayim. 1984. "The Hallelot of the Jews of al-Hujariah and of Central Yemen." *Pe'amim* 19: 130–62 (Hebrew).

Shetrit, Joseph. 1982. "Songs on Historical Events in Jewish Moroccan Poetry." In I. Ben-Ami, ed., *The Sephardi and Oriental Jweish Heritage.* Jerusalem: Magnes Press, pp. 315–38 (Hebrew).

Shiloah, Amnon. 1962. "Reflexions sur la danse artistique musulmane au moyen age." *Cahiers de Civilisation medievale* 4: 461–474.

———. 1964 and 1966. "L'epître sur la musique des Ikhwān al-Ṣafā." *Revue des Etudes Islamiques* (1) 1964: 125–162; (2) 1966: 159–193.

———. 1966. "Melody and Meter in the Kuzari." *Tazlil* 6: 5–8 (Hebrew).

———. 1970. "The Aliyah Songs in the Traditional Folk Literature in Israel." *Folklore Research Center Studies* 1: 349–68 (Hebrew).

———. 1972. "On the Musical Activities of Qehal qadosh ḥadash Synagogue (Yanina) at the Beginning of the twentieth Century." *Folklore Research Studies* 3: 209–22 (Hebrew).

———. 1974. "Le Poète-musician et la Création Poético-musicale." *Yearbook of the International Folk Music Council* 6: 52–63.

———. 1977. *Music Subjects in the Zohar, Texts and Indices.* Jerusalem: Magnes Press, Yuval Monograph Series, 5.

———. 1978a. "The Chapter on Music in Ibn Falaquera's Book of the Seeker." *Proceedings of the Fourth World Congress of Jewish Studies* 2: 373–77.

———. 1978b. *The Epistle on Music of the Ikhwān al-Ṣafa.* Tel Aviv: Tel Aviv University.

———. 1979a. *The Theory of Music in Arabic Writings.* RISM, Ser. B, vol. 10. München: Henle Verlag.

———. 1979b. "The *'ūd* and the Origin of Music." *Studia Orientalia Memoriae D. H. Baneth Dedicata.* Jerusalem: Magnes Press, pp. 395–407.

———. 1981. "The Arabic Concept of Mode." *Journal of the American Musicological Society.* 34, no. 1: 19–42.

———. 1983. *The Musical Tradition of Iraqi Jews.* Or Yehuda: Iraqi Jew's Traditional Culture Center.

———. 1986. "The Traditional Artist in the Limelight of the Modern City." *The World of Music* 1: 87–99.

Shiloah, Amnon, and Erik Cohen. 1982. "The Dynamics of Change in Jewish Oriental Ethnic Music in Israel." *Peʿamim* 12: 3–25 (Hebrew).

———. 1983. "The Dynamics of Change in Jewish Oriental Ethnic Music in Israel." *Ethnomusicology* 27, no. 2: 227–52. Reprint in Alexander Weingrod, ed., *Studies in Israeli Ethnicity.* New York: Gordon and Breach, 1985, pp. 317–40.

Shmueli, Herzel, ed. and trans 1953. *Higgajon bechinnor: Betrachtungen zum Leirspiel des Jehudah Moscato.* Tel Aviv: Dissertation, Zurich University.

Shokeid, Moshe, and Shlomo Deshen. 1977. *The Generation of Transition: Continuity and Change among North African Immigrants in Israel.* Jerusalem: Ben-Zvi Institute (Hebrew).

Simonson, Shlomo. 1962. *The Jews in the Duchy of Mantova.* 2 vols. Jerusalem: The University of Tel-Aviv and Ben-Zvi Institute (Hebrew). Reprint in English. Jerusalem: Kizalh Sefer, 1977.

Slobin, Mark. 1984. "Klezmer Music: An American Ethnic Genre." *Yearbook for Traditional Music* 16: 34–41.

Sol, Hachuel (the righteous). 1954. *The Results of the 1952 Literary Contest on the Theme "Sol the Righteous."* Casablanca (Hebrew and French).

Spector, Johanna. 1960. "Bridal Songs and Ceremonies from Sanʿa." In Raphael Patai, ed., *Studies in Biblical and Jewish Folklore,* pp. 225–54.

Stillman, Yedida. 1980. "The Art of Women Singing in Morocco." In M. Avitbol, ed., *African Jewry in the Nineteenth and Twentieth Centuries.* Jerusalem: Ben-Zvi Institute, pp. 163–71.

Stuchevsky, Yehoachin. 1959. *The Klezmers: Their Life, Manners, and Works.* Jerusalem: Mosad Bialik (Hebrew).

Tharaud, Jerome. 1923. *Rabat: ou, Les heures marocaines.* Paris: Plon.

Tishbi, Isaiah. 1957. *The Doctrine of the Zohar.* Jerusalem: Mosad Bialik. 2 vols. (Hebrew).

Tovi, Yosef. 1978. "Jewish-Yemenite Wedding Songs." *Dukhan* 11: 15–24 (Hebrew).

Tovi, Yosef, and Shalom Seri, eds. 1988. *Amallel Shir (Anthology of Yemenite Poems).* Ramat-Gan: Eʿeleh Betamar.

Valensis, Johannes. 1545. *Opus de Prosodia Hebreaorum.* Paris.

Villoteau, G. D. 1823. *Des instruments de musique des Orientaux—Description de l'Egypte.* Vol. 13. Paris: Imprimerie de C.L.F. Pancoucke.

———. 1826. *L'Etat actuel de l'art musical en Egypte—Description de l'Egypte.* Vol. 14. Paris: Imprimerie de C.L.F. Pankoucke.

Warkov, E. 1987. *The Urban Arabic Repertoire of Jewish Professional Musicians in Iraq and Israel: Instrumental Improvisation and Culture Change.* The Hebrew University of Jerusalem: Ph.D. thesis.

Weich-Shahaq, Suzana. 1979. "The Wedding Songs of the Bulgarian-Sephardi Jews." *Orbis Musicae* 7: 81–107.

———. 1982. "Structural Phenomena in the Wedding Songs of Bulgarian Sephardic Jews." In Ben-Ami, ed., *The Sephardi and Oriental Jewish Heritage.* Jerusalem: Magnes Press, pp. 413–20.

Werner, Eric. 1959. *The Second Bridge.* New York: Columbia Press.

———. 1968. "Scope and Aims of Jewish Music Research (Isolation or Integration)." *Fourth World Congress on Jewish Studies.* Jerusalem: Magnes Press. Vol. 2, pp. 157–61.

———. 1976. *The Voice Still Heard.* PA: Pennsylvania University Press.

———. 1982. "Identity and Character of Jewish Music." In J. Cohen, ed., *Proceedings of the Congress on Jewish Music Jerusalem, 1978.* Tel Aviv: The Institute for the Translation of Hebrew Literature Ltd., pp. 1–14.

———. 1984. *The Sacred Bridge.* Vol. 2. New York: Ktav.

Yaʿari, Abraham, ed. 1942. *The Travels of Safed's Envoy in Oriental Countries.* Jerusalem: Tarshish (Hebrew).

Yadin, Yigael. 1962. *The Scroll of the War of the Sons of Light Against the Sons of Darkness.* Mass.: Oxford University Press.

Yahalom, Yosef. 1982. "Rabbi Israel Najjara and the Renewal of Hebrew Poetry in the Orient after the Expulsion from Spain." *Pe'amim* 13: 96–124 (Hebrew).

Yehudah he-Ḥasid. 1924. *Sefer Ḥasidim.* Ed. J. Wistinetzki Freimann. Frankfurt a. M.: Wahrmann.

Yosef, Obadia. 1976. *Yabbiya 'Omer (Responsa).* 6 vols. Jerusalem.

Yuval, V. 1986. *The Abraham Zvi Idelsohn Memorial Volume.* Jerusalem: Magnes Press.

Zephira, Bracha. 1978. *Many Voices.* Jerusalem: Massada (Hebrew).

Index